He teaches Dhamma that is good
in the beginning, good in the middle
and good in the end, with the right
meaning and expression.

UNCOMMON WISDOM

UNCOMMON
WISDOM
LIFE AND TEACHINGS *of* AJAAN PAÑÑĀVAḌḌHO

Written & Compiled by
AJAAN DICK SĪLARATANO

A Forest Dhamma Publication
Virginia – USA

UNCOMMON WISDOM
LIFE AND TEACHINGS *of* AJAAN PAÑÑĀVAḌḌHO

Published by:
Forest Dhamma Publications
Forest Dhamma Monastery
255 Snakefoot Lane
Lexington, VA 24450
USA

This book is available for free download at
www.forestdhamma.org

ISBN 978-1-4951-1519-6

Original Cover Photo (B&W) by David Salim Halim.
Cover and Interior Design by Mae Chee Melita Halim.
Set in Warnock Pro and Novecento sans wide.

First edition, 20,000 copies.
Printed in Malaysia by Bolden Trade, 2014

Venerable Ajaan Paññāvaḍḍho
(1925 - 2004)

CONTENTS

GOOD IN THE END

Forest Dhamma would like to
acknowledge the generous support
of the many people who aided in
the preparation of this book, with
special thanks to the Kataññutā
Group of Malaysia, Singapore
and Australia for bringing it into
production.

PREFACE

It is important that Venerable Paññāvaḍḍho's biography is being written and published due to the efforts of Tan Ajaan Dick who has been close to this most venerable and reclusive monk. Ajaan Paññāvaḍḍho spent most of his monastic life at Wat Pa Baan Taad, a remote forest monastery in Udon Thani, North-East Thailand. He trained and practiced under the guidance and support of one of Thailand's most respected bhikkhus, Tan Ajaan Mahā Boowa—now generally best known in Thailand as "Luang Dtaa Mahā Boowa."

I arrived in Thailand at the New Year of 1966 after serving in the American Peace Corps in Sabah, Malaysia, for two years. At that time there were very few western men taking ordination in Thailand. I came to Thailand with the deliberate intention of ordaining and to receive teaching and instruction in Buddhist meditation. I lived my first six months in Bangkok, investigating the possibilities for ordination and beginning my initial efforts in meditation at a Buddhist temple in Bangkok. At this time, I met Tan Ajaan Mahā Boowa at Wat Bovornives and was told about his disciple, Ajaan Paññāvaḍḍho. However, I did not have the opportunity to meet him until three years later, when Luang Por Chah took me on a tour in order to meet some of the respected "Krooba Ajahns" in North-East Thailand. We came to Wat Pa Baan

Taad to meet Tan Ajaan Mahā Boowa. During this time, I had the opportunity to meet Ajaan Paññāvaḍḍho for the first time.

I went to see Ajaan Paññāvaḍḍho several times during the following years. Then, in 1976, my parents who lived in California requested me to visit them. I was given an air ticket on the Thai International Airline for returning to Thailand from London, since Thai Inter had not established air routes in the United States as yet. So, in the summer of 1976, I spent several days in London waiting to take the return flight to Bangkok. Ajaan Paññāvaḍḍho had given me the name and telephone number of George Sharp who was the acting Chairman of the English Sangha Trust in London.

Ajaan Paññāvaḍḍho was closely associated with the E.S.T. Before going to Thailand, he had lived in the premises of the E.S.T. in London. He had been active in teaching Dhamma in England. Those were the early years when there was a growing interest in Buddhism in the Western world and especially in England. He had many friends and students of Buddhism who assumed that one day he would return to the U.K. to share his acquired knowledge with them. He was very much respected by many. However, he did not have the intention to return. And I eventually went to England to establish a forest monastery for the teaching and training of bhikkhus. Ajaan Paññāvaḍḍho encouraged me to do this. He spent the rest of his life at Wat Pa Baan Taad with his teacher Luang Dtaa Boowa. He became very well-known and respected by many in Thailand. He passed away in 2004.

The generation of Buddhists in England that remember him is now very old or dead. I spent thirty-four years in England and established several monasteries there—the main one being Amaravati Buddhist Monastery in Hertfordshire. I personally feel so much gratitude to Ajaan Paññāvaḍḍho who was a source of inspiration and one of the early pioneer teachers in the West. He is now better known in Thailand than in the U.K.

I feel that it is important to acknowledge this fine teacher and monk. Therefore, I am having a portrait painted to be placed in the Uposatha hall at Amaravati. This event comes together with this biography that Ajaan Dick has written.

Theravāda is a very ancient tradition. And, "tradition" means that we acknowledge the predecessors—from the Buddha who established the tradition 2557 years ago in India, to the present day. Tan Ajaan Paññāvaḍḍho is regarded as one of our predecessors in the lineage of Tan Ajaan Mun, Tan Ajaan Mahā Boowa, and Tan Ajahn Chah. This is generally referred to as "The Thai Forest Tradition."

Those of us who have had the wonderful opportunity to live, train and practice within this tradition realize that the universal wisdom that the Buddha pointed to, through the original teaching of the Four Noble Truths, has now been discovered and appreciated by the Western world. Tan Ajaan Paññāvaḍḍho is one of those who discovered and realized the profundity and efficacy of this way. He is a contemporary Westerner who actually developed the practice of meditation through this ancient tradition. Through his example, we can increase our faith and determination to do the same.

Ajahn Sumedho
May 2014

INTRODUCTION

The life and teachings of Venerable Ajaan Paññāvaḍḍho are the inspiration behind this book. His biography recounts an exceptional life, and it teaches many lessons. But this biography is more than just a historical account of the events that comprise a life. In fact, some people leave their mark on the world in such an elusive way that a biographical account fails to capture its deeper significance. Because Ajaan Paññāvaḍḍho's lifelong quest was ultimately a journey of the mind, it possessed a quality that transcends any mundane account of its comings and goings. For that reason, the biographical sketch presented here is intended to render not so much the facts of a life, but rather a more essential type of truth about the essence of a person.

Biographies are usually chronological in nature, although it is also possible to probe certain dimensions of a person's character, thus chronicling his evolution over the span of a lifetime. This account of Ajaan Paññāvaḍḍho's life attempts to interlace the thread of events with the thread of character, so that narrative strands intersect at intervals with thematic ones to portray the rich tapestry of Dhamma that was his life. Through this twofold presentation, I hope to provide a satisfying view of the range and depth of Ajaan Paññāvaḍḍho's spiritual life, to serve as a guideline for the path to Nibbāna.

Due to the ephemeral nature of human memory, a life is always to some extent imagined, whether we are recounting the life of another person or our own life. This account of Ajaan Paññāvaḍḍho's life unfolds in that creative area between the factual and the fictional. It attempts to present an accurate representation of his life, placing special priority on the lessons to be learnt.

The main purpose of this book is to provide an introduction to the Dhamma teachings of Ajaan Paññāvaḍḍho, teachings whose breadth and richness tend to defy comparison. Toward that end, I will present the biography of a teaching at least as much as the story of an individual. I will focus on the historical context that shaped his teachings and the charismatic character that defined him as a teacher. To understand the foundation from which his teaching grew, we must look into Ajaan Paññāvaḍḍho's life and practice up to the time he became a mature teacher.

In his formative years, Ajaan Paññāvaḍḍho constantly sought refuge in his mind's ability to think logically and arrive at reasoned conclusions. He found in rationality a safe haven for the mind, but an uncertain footing for the heart. Motivated to resolve that tension, he probed deeply into Buddhist practice using cause-and-effect methods until he discovered the limits of conditioned reasoning. It was in this border area between the conditioned and the intuitive that he reconciled the two. His teachings were often an attempt to take cause-and-effect reasoning methods to their ultimate limits, and then to go beyond them entirely.

The chapters in this book are compiled from a series of talks given by Ajaan Paññāvaḍḍho to his disciples: monks, nuns and lay people. Since they are put together mainly from the questions of Ajaan Paññāvaḍḍho's disciples and his responses to them, these are not Dhamma talks in the formal sense. Rather, they are the informal teachings of Ajaan Paññāvaḍḍho as he responded to the questions of his students in an attempt to clear up their doubts. Sometimes his response was short, direct and spontaneous. At other times he seemed to use the question as a springboard to expand upon crucial aspects of the Buddha's teaching. Through those exchanges, he always managed to bring his students back to the essence of Dhamma.

Ajaan Paññāvaḍḍho was a unique Dhamma teacher of uncommon wisdom. He had the ability to connect all the diverse aspects of Dhamma to a central theme, making the complexity of Buddhist teachings comprehensible to monks and lay people alike. His life and his teachings have therefore assumed a patriarchal significance in the annals of the Western Sangha.

It is hoped that through this presentation of his life and his teachings, Ajaan Paññāvaḍḍho's presence can be invoked and remembered as an inspirational guide, friend, and teacher of the Buddhist path.

Ajaan Dick Sīlaratano
May 2014

BIOGRAPHY
OF A TEACHING

It's impossible to equate worldly intelligence with the wisdom of Dhamma. If intelligent people would turn away from their mundane concerns and instead turn their attention to the practice of Buddhist meditation, they could greatly benefit the world we live in.

———————————

LIFE

On the barren terrain of India's Deccan Plateau, several days journey south of the Ganges Plain where the Lord Buddha walked the earth and awakened mankind, rich veins of gold run deep through the land. Antiquity records the mining of gold in the folds of these windswept plains. Over the millennia, kingdoms flourished and kingdoms perished in rhythm with the fortunes of those seeking this precious metal. Half a millennium ago the last of these kingdoms fell into ruin and vanished. Its name was Kolar.

With the fall of the kingdom, Kolar became a barren and thorny plateau where gusty winds blew unchecked, and the land remained rocky, arid, and uninhabited. Then, in 1873, an adventurous British soldier leased the land from the Maharaja of Mysore and began digging. The earth refused to relinquish its treasure so easily. For several years, he dug in vain, until the famous John Taylor and Company from Great Britain was brought in to supervise the project. The enterprise finally struck gold in 1880 at an outpost called Oorgaum.

By 1883, four mine shafts were operating fulltime, and the Kolar landscape changed rapidly. Colonial bungalows with colorful gardens, club-houses, hospitals, schools and long rows of huts for the laborers mushroomed up from the plains. Mine shafts began to dot the landscape as more and more veins were struck.

It was there, forty years later, in the gold fields of India's Mysore state that the life of Peter John Morgan began. He was born at 7:45 am on October 19, 1925 at Oorgaum, Kolar Gold Fields, the site of the first mine shaft excavated by British engineers. The time and place of his birth would be significant to the trajectory of his life.

His father, John Morgan, was the son of an Anglican vicar who grew up in Llanelli, Wales, and began working in the local mines just as World War I erupted. Fortunately, John Morgan was sent to Mesopotamia and the Suez Canal Zone, avoiding the fate of most young officers who ended up in the trenches of Europe. In Mesopotamia, he helped to build a railway along the Suez Canal and was awarded the Military Cross Medal for his service.

When John Morgan returned to England after the war, the local mining industry was going through hard times. He decided to apply for a mining job with John Taylor and Company, which operated the mines at the Kolar Gold Fields in India. Fortunately, due to a connection with the Taylor family, he succeeded immediately in securing a job at the Kolar Gold Fields.

In 1924, John, accompanied by his wife Violet, traveled by steamer from England to India. There, John assumed the position of assistant manager in the mines. India at that time was still part of the British Empire. The couple took up residence in the British mining community at Kolar Gold Fields, which was well known for its colonial ambience, where rows of well-appointed, majestic bungalows were flanked by manicured lawns and big shady trees.

Electricity was still a novelty in India in those days, but Kolar Gold Fields was one of the first places in the country to enjoy its benefits. A hydroelectric dam, built by the British, provided electricity for the mining, milling and stamping operations of the gold fields. With electricity for the bungalows as well, British employees enjoyed luxuries such as ceiling fans and electric lights. Before long, a large flourishing town sprang up in a once desolate wasteland, complete with most of the conveniences and institutions of European life. As a result, Kolar Gold Fields became known to the British as "Little England."

Peter grew up in the mining community's multicultural milieu—a mingling of Europeans, Anglo-Indians and indigenous laborers drawn from the neighboring Tamil and Telugu regions. Every family of means employed a retinue of domestic helpers. It was a small town, and everyone knew everyone else. The different classes all mingled freely. His mother, a simple good-natured woman, took pleasure in kindness and generosity. Nannies, housemaids, gardeners, sweepers and tea-boys were all treated as part of the family.

Peter's earliest memories were of the repetitive sounds and movements of the mining operations: the siren whose whistle regimented the lives of the laborers; the giant hoists with thick black cables that lowered men into the belly of the earth, and lifted out cages filled with ore; the echo of ore-laden trolleys rattling along cavernous underground passages crisscrossing between the shafts; the rumble of rock bursting deep underground that rattled windows and cracked walls; and miners streaming out of the shafts at day's end, dark and sooty with the underground dust, talking in loud voices about mundane everyday matters.

Occasionally, Peter accompanied his father to the mine shaft and watched as the electric motor unwound gigantic reels of cable that lowered the elevator car into the mine shaft. He watched with awe and alarm as his father's head slowly disappeared below ground. He gazed at the cable, unwinding long after his father was out of sight, and waited until the elevator car reappeared.

Peter's father had a knack for crafting things with his hands, and he often improvised playthings for his son. He began with simple toys like spinning tops, wind-blown kites and rolling wheels, and eventually went on to devise complex mechanical toys with moving parts, such as a fire truck or a steam engine. Occasionally, he also bought Peter cast-iron mechanical toys. It soon came to be that if it moved, Peter was fascinated.

He enjoyed watching his father while he made the toys and soon learned how they were put together. His father explained what he was doing in simple language, and Peter began to understand the principles behind their mobility. Before long, he was able to repair a broken toy by himself, turning to his father for help only as a last resort.

Of all the toys, a little red racing car that his Aunt Nana brought from England most fully captured his imagination. It was a toy unlike any he had seen before: it was sleek, handsomely built, and sped across the floor, seemingly of its own accord. A key wound up the mechanism that powered the front wheels. True to its name, the car raced across the floor when fully wound.

Clockwork toys had become popular in England in the mid-1920s. A simple one like Peter's car offered an excellent tutorial in miniaturized mechanical engineering. But because the mechanism in the little red race car was fully encased under the bonnet, Peter did not understand at first how it worked. He was far too captivated by its fast acceleration and careening trajectory to pay much attention to the mechanics. However, after the racer had ricocheted into the wall once too often, damaging the delicate wind-up mechanism, the time came for him to look under the hood.

Peter's gaze followed intently while his father disassembled the toy, re-coiled the mainspring, and patiently explained how the mechanism worked to create movement. Peter learned how the winding of the key added energy to the system, tightening the metal spring, storing the energy until it was released by a set of gears to power the wheels across the floor. He learned that it is hard to squeeze sturdy metal into such a small space, and that was why the spring stored energy so effectively. The harder one worked to compress the spring, the more energy it held. But Peter needed no reminder of that power's limitations: if he got more than a minute's entertainment for thirty seconds of winding he was doing well.

Peter's enjoyment of these mechanical toys, and his fascination with how they functioned, unleashed a natural disposition for logic and the power of rational thinking. This ability to think logically and to arrive at reasoned conclusions became a refuge for young Peter as he struggled to cope with the changing circumstances and allegiances of life. After a somewhat sheltered and uneventful existence at the Kolar Gold Fields, he was unexpectedly yanked out of British India and the enclave of "Little England" to be deposited on the other side of the world in England proper.

IN 1932, AFTER MUCH DELIBERATION, PETER'S PARENTS decided to send him to England to receive a "full and proper" education. Seven-year-old Peter filled a small trunk with his personal belongings and traveled by train to Bombay where he and his family boarded a large mail steamer. The steamer sailed straight across the Arabian Sea and into the Red Sea by way of the Gulf of Aden.

Peter had never sailed on a steam ship before, and the journey became an indelible part of his childhood memories. He was captivated by the ship's movement, the bow plowing through the swelling waves and the stern churning out its wake. He wanted to learn its secret—and also allay the tedium of gazing out onto an endless expanse of sea in every direction. He tried to work out the answers, but when he had little success, he turned to his father for inspiration.

With his customary calm and patience, his father explained the basics of how the steam engine worked. Using boiling water as a starting point, he showed how mechanical motion was produced by the steam it created. He explained the workings of the two basic components of a steam engine: the boiler to generate steam, and the motor to drive the crankshaft that propelled the ship. Although his father would have expounded on about cylinders and piston strokes, Peter was content with rudimentary knowledge for the time being. Without a mechanical model to view, he found it impossible to imagine the whole process. But he was not discouraged: he thought he might even build a steam ship of his own one day!

Before long his fascination with the ship's movements ceded to the wonders of the sights around him. In the Red Sea, flanked by the coastlines of Africa on one side and of Asia on the other, the ship bore north, revealing vistas of the landmasses that awed and delighted him. He was never to forget the vast arid landscapes bordering the Red Sea; nor the strong winds and blinding dust storms that forced them to retreat below deck several times during the passage. Proceeding through the Suez Canal, his father pointed out, with lingering pride, the railway that he helped build during the war.

When the Egyptian coast receded from view and the ship emerged from the Suez Canal, they entered the calm blue waters of the Mediterranean. Peter thrilled with a child's excitement at seeing the island of Malta as they slipped by. They then pushed through the Straits of Gibraltar, skirted north around the southern coast of Portugal and finally steamed out into the swollen grey seas of the Atlantic. Three weeks after setting sail from Bombay, the ship finally arrived in England, and Peter and his family docked at the port of Southampton.

An overland journey now lay ahead for the Morgan family. Their first destination was the Welsh city of Swansea, 150 miles to the northwest. Peter's paternal grandfather was an Anglican clergyman, the Dean of St. David's Cathedral. This parish church, located in the upper Swansea valley, was to be their first stop.

Reverend David Watcyn Morgan, Clerk, Bachelor of Arts and Dean of St. David's, had been appointed perpetual curate of the neighboring parish at Llangyfelach when he was twenty-six. Llangyfelach was a large and ancient parish that ministered to many neighboring towns in the Swansea valley. Reverend Morgan's vision was to build a new place of worship in the neighboring township. In 1886, funds were raised from local magnates, a suitable site was purchased and after a decade of construction, the new "Chapel of Ease" was formally consecrated as St. David's by the local bishop. At seventy-two, with a long and distinguished service to his name, he was duly appointed dean of the cathedral that he had envisioned in his youth.

Peter and his family moved into the vicarage house adjoining the church. St. David's Cathedral was a massive stone edifice, and Peter was awed by its size and appearance. Built in the early English style with a towering belfry, the cathedral featured a nave that could accommodate 600 worshippers, an exterior wall of grey pennant stone, a green slate roof and a broad stone porch, opening onto the arched entrance to the main chapel. Inside, a soaring arch, twenty-six feet high, divided the nave from the chancel. The barrel-shaped roof of the chancel was supported by timbers of pitch pine, with carved designs in the intersecting beams. The sweet-timbred pipe organ was the pride of the congregation. Sunday lessons were held in a spacious "schoolroom," known as the crypt, on the floor beneath the nave. Grandfather Morgan was fond of reminding his congregation that the church should be seen as a school, not as a sewing circle!

To his bewilderment, Peter soon discovered that Grandfather Morgan was his grandfather only in name. He learned that his father was born John Davies—not John Morgan; that he was the son of John Davies and Elizabeth Morgan, sister of Grandfather Morgan; and that his birthplace was Australia, not Wales! Elizabeth Morgan had emigrated to Australia in the early 1890s, married John Davies, and settled in northern Queensland where they raised a large family. At the time of a long visit to the Davies, Reverend Morgan and his wife were childless—a matter that gave them some concern. Quite magnanimously, John Davies offered them two of his own children, saying that he had too many as it was, and could spare a few. Thus it came to be that Peter's father, John, who was then four years old and his sister, Meuna, aged two, left for England with the Reverend and his wife, and never saw their real parents again. At the vicarage in Wales, their surnames were changed to Morgan.

Not long after their arrival at Grandfather Morgan's, Peter and his family were on the move again. The plan was to leave Peter at his mother's home with his maternal grandparents, who were to assume responsibility for his education. William John Rees, Peter's maternal grandfather, brought them to the Rees family estate at Bryn, a large farm known as Gelly House, in the Carmarthenshire countryside east of Llanelli. Although the Rees family holdings had once straddled three Welsh counties, the family farm still remained large and spacious, with rock breaks and thickly wooded areas dissecting the landscape.

Gelly House became Peter's new home. His parents returned to India, and he began attending Park House Boarding School in Swansea on weekdays, returning to Gelly House for weekends. Gelly was a fairly large Victorian-style house made of brick with a slate roof, with a large porch and garden in the front, and a large walled garden in the back. The main traffic in and out of the house took place through the side door, the front entrance being used only by visitors and on special occasions. Peter was given a room to himself on the upstairs floor.

Peter found the change both exciting and frightening. Everything was new and challenging, with so many unknowns. He also felt removed, being so far from home and somewhat confused by the rush of events—so many novel sensations in such a short time. His parents' departure had left him with a sinking feeling of abandonment. He understood their reasons for dropping him off in Wales, but the disadvantages felt immense and the apparent benefits appeared hollow. His life had suddenly been turned upside down. His world was no longer familiar to him. With little to anchor him, Peter took refuge in his mind's ability to think logically and to form reasoned conclusions. In the end, he accepted his lot and learned to live with the pain, making the best of his new circumstances.

Grandfather Rees considered himself a master in the laws of reason and rational discourse. Remarkably intelligent and with diverse talents, he could do anything he set his mind to, and do it well. In this, he took considerable pride. Something of a prodigy, he left school in 1882, at age seventeen, to manage his father's collieries at Maesarddafen, which were located just north of the farm and were part of the Gelly Estate. An engineer by temperament and profession, he had designed and built the Rees farmhouse himself. He also ran the Glanmor Foundry, where pig iron was cast into various implements, or passed on to the rolling mill for conversion into wrought iron. He was also an excellent painter and writer, and a successful barrister who skillfully represented clients in court.

Due to his rational inclination, Grandfather Rees took a hard-eyed look at almost everything, and found it difficult to summon much sympathy towards unscientific attitudes. He expected the same rationality in his grandson. He scrutinized Peter's education and recreation in the cold light of objective purpose. He regarded idleness as waste and expected good results to issue from a reasoned application of the mind.

After years of managing his companies, Grandfather Rees was stolidly set in a business-like manner. He always gave Peter the impression of being a very busy man engaged in something of great importance. He appeared to perform his actions with a sense of his own worth, and had a tendency to demand of others what he himself could not live up to.

Peter settled uneasily at first into his new life and the routine of boarding school on weekdays and the farmhouse on weekends. He was unaccustomed to strict discipline, and shied away from it. But after an initial period of close supervision, he was mostly left to his own devices. Being in their late sixties and unused to having children about, his grandparents were not forthcoming with their time and affection. His grandfather was always busy and his grandmother was often away, or preoccupied with her own affairs. Neither showed much sense of humor.

Grandfather Rees also proved to have limited patience. He had constructed a beautiful workshop next to the farmhouse, which naturally caught Peter's fancy. It was stocked with an array of instruments and tools. Although he wasn't a mischievous boy, he could not resist having a go at them. He always found an excuse to enter and poke around. When Grandfather Rees discovered his whereabouts, he barked out his displeasure with mild anger, scolding Peter for messing up the place, then chasing him out the door.

Peter found his grandmother to be a bit eccentric. He rarely saw her as she usually appeared only at tea time. She made a hobby of being ill. She was either off in London convalescing at a nursing home or being nursed at the farmhouse by a staff of servants. With a shy manner and a gentle voice, she was a kind person, but she knew nothing about children.

Peter often played with the servants, finding them congenial and down-to-earth companions. He felt more comfortable in the kitchen than in the dining room, and often took his toys there to play when the weather did not permit playing in the garden. His grandmother did not object: she realized that boys were bound to be untidy and she preferred a mess in the kitchen to disorder elsewhere in the house. Her attempts at affection were awkward. Feeling shy, Peter often received her demonstrations with a solemn face.

Grandfather Rees dutifully sent Peter off to the boarding school every Monday morning; nevertheless, he was skeptical of the education Peter received. Suspicious of rote learning and believing firmly in "learning by doing," he was determined to provide Peter with a technical and mechanical education at an early age. As part of this strategy— and as a means of keeping him constructively engaged—he bought Peter a Meccano set.

Meccano was the brand of a popular model construction set designed on the principles of mechanical engineering. More than a mere plaything, it was designed to teach children how to build mechanical models and animate them with basic levers and gears. With his Meccano set, Peter could now design and build his own machinery and mechanical devices. The Meccano set came with instructions for building a variety of models: a sports car, a cargo ship, a double-decker bus, a dump truck and a motorcycle. It gave him the components and the technology: perforated metal strips, plates and girders, tiny nuts and bolts, and wheels, pulleys, gears and axles to make the models move. The only tools he needed were a tiny screwdriver and a few small wrenches. And the only limits to the models he could create were limits imposed by his imagination and ingenuity.

As Britain entered the age of aviation and Peter's imagination soared with the idea of flying, he became preoccupied with model airplanes. He sensed, with a child's intuition, that steamers would soon give way to air travel. At first, Peter took the model airplanes apart and reassembled them to see how all the parts fit together. To learn the basics of powered flight, he started experimenting with ready-made lightweight models that used a wound up rubber band as their means of locomotion. Eventually, he began to build his own models from special kits, which included a clockwork mechanism to rotate the propeller in flight.

Meccano also made a series of specialty kits that included components for airplane construction, with interchangeable parts for making realistic models of various types of aircraft. These kits included an instruction manual for building the airplane, and detailed instructions involving the mechanical principles required for maintaining an aircraft in flight. Working with these kits, Peter was able to fit the fuselage of each model with a clockwork motor, which rotated the propeller and drove the landing wheels at the same time. His collection of model airplanes steadily grew, many of them being quite sophisticated. With practice and fine-tuning, he achieved smooth, powerful long-distance flights.

IN 1938, AT THE AGE OF TWELVE, Peter discovered the radio. Encouraged by his grandfather, he acquired an old crystal radio set, which he promptly disassembled to ferret out its working principles. In the process of learning how the radio worked, he discovered the fundamentals of electrical circuits. Once he understood the principles and the parts he was ready to make his first radio.

He started by building a simple crystal radio receiver, collecting inexpensive parts here and there—a length of wire, solder, a wooden breadboard—for his model. He was resourceful: he fastened a lump of crystal to the breadboard for the circuit, sharpening one end of a thin brass wire to a point and pressing this "cat's whisker" into the crystal. Together, these parts formed the detector element, which picked out the sound wave from the radio wave. He learned to drill holes, mount components, thread wires, assemble parts, and wind just the right amount of wire to form the coil that would capture the right radio frequency. Then, he experimented and fine-tuned his work until he got the volume and sound quality he wanted.

Radios and other simple electronics became a passion that consumed most of his leisure time. He threw himself into radio technology with the same abandon he had previously shown for model airplanes and Meccano sets. A quiet and reserved young boy, his weekends at Gelly House were passed in self-imposed solitude. But it was a solitude that hummed with creativity: making Meccano motors, model airplanes, radios, and anything else that inspired his imagination. His adolescent hands were constantly molding materials to express a specific form and function.

While the days passed in relative harmony at Gelly House, storm clouds were already brewing on the horizon of his cloistered life. Peter would soon find himself in the vortex of events that would upend his sheltered existence and keep him on the move for years to come.

It began when his mother came from India for a visit in 1938. With her were his sister Patricia and his brother David, who were to be "dropped off" at his grandfather's house just as he had been five years earlier. Before sailing back to India and out of his life again, his mother enrolled him at Tonbridge, a boarding school in Kent on the eastern coast of England, 100 miles from his home at Gelly House. It was one of the leading boys' boarding schools in the country. It offered the kind of academic curricula that his mother, Violet Morgan, believed her son deserved. Peter entered Tonbridge School as a boarder in the autumn of 1938. But his education was soon to be disrupted.

It was early 1939 and war with Germany seemed imminent. The country was on the alert with the threat of air attacks on British cities, especially those in the south, and expectations of a land invasion along the southern coast. In the town of Tonbridge, tank traps and rolls of barbed wire soon appeared on the streets. Tonbridge students wore gas masks as a precaution during all school periods. As the situation deteriorated, air-raid sirens began sounding almost nightly, prompting the boarders to hurry into underground shelters where they passed the night until the all-clear signal sounded at dawn. Before long, the atmosphere at Tonbridge was no longer very conducive to academic study.

Meanwhile, Peter's parents in India were becoming increasingly alarmed by reports from home. The south of England had become too dangerous. They transferred Peter to Wood Norton Hall, a boarding school to the northwest of London, and—they hoped—out of harm's way. It was a slightly down-at-the-heel preparatory school, set in the rolling Worcestershire countryside and having at its hub a rather pretentious baronial estate that once belonged to France's Duke of Orleans. The main building was heavily decorated with the French regal emblem, the *fleur-de-lis*, most notably on the dark oak paneling.

But Peter barely had a chance to settle in before he was moved again. When France fell on July 16, 1940, Peter's parents withdrew him from Wood Norton and moved him back to Wales to be near his grandparents. They enrolled him in St. Michael's School, not far from his grandfather's house, which was considered to be one of Wales' leading independent preparatory schools. However, it did not offer the quality of education that Peter's parents wanted for him.

In 1941, Peter's mother sailed back once more from India to put her son's life in order. Braving German U-boats, she arrived on the shores of England in December, and promptly enrolled Peter as a boarder at Cheltenham College in the relatively safe surroundings of the English Midlands. Built in the fifteenth century, Cheltenham College was a leading independent preparatory school, known for its classical, military and sporting traditions.

Several months after his arrival at Cheltenham, Peter fell sick. He had a fever and night sweats; then later, leg pain and loss of appetite. A medical examination revealed that he had bovine tuberculosis, a disease which he probably contracted by drinking raw milk from infected cows. A small group of tuberculosis bacilli was already in the bones and joints of his right foot; and because of a breakdown of the body's resistance, the germs were free to multiply and spread.

Tuberculosis in the bones and joints was common in the 1930s and early 1940s, before the pasteurization of milk and the virtual elimination of tuberculosis from cows. The most common route of infection was from drinking unpasteurized milk or eating dairy products made from raw milk. Because of its relatively slow rate of growth, bovine tuberculosis was a chronic disease that typically took many months to develop.

After infecting Peter's ankle, the disease spread, inflaming the lining of the joint. As fluid collected there, bone deterioration increased. Peter suffered pain, swelling and stiffness, which forced him to walk with a limp. As the disease worsened, abscesses appeared in the infected tissue.

In 1941 there was no cure for tuberculosis. Instead, a regimen of rest and good nutrition was prescribed as offering the best chance for the patient's immune system to recover and "wall off" the disease. Sanatoriums were recommended as the preferred places for treatment, especially in the beginning stages of the disease. Continual rest, a balanced diet and abstaining from excesses of any kind were prescribed. Consequently, patients were exposed to plentiful amounts of fresh air and good food.

Peter was admitted to a countryside sanatorium. As part of the treatment, his hospital bed was placed on the open-air verandah where he lived for months in all kinds of weather—including snowstorms! When his condition failed to improve after several months of therapy, the doctors decided to operate.

The surgeon found that Peter's right ankle bone had a chronic tubercular infection. To save the foot from further damage, he cut away the offending portion of the ankle bone, cleaned the tissue, and fused the ankle bone to the adjoining bones. For the rest of his life Peter would live with an ankle that was frozen in place, with none of its normal mobility. Though he was eventually able to walk, always with a slight limp, he never regained full use of his right leg. He would later claim that although this disability had definite disadvantages, it ultimately saved him from the unfortunate destiny of serving in the military during the war. Given his passion for airplanes, he would probably have served as a bomber pilot, and would have incurred grave karmic consequences for his actions.

His right foot was encased in a stout plaster cast for nine months to prevent any movement in his ankle joint while the fused bones healed. He got around by using wooden underarm crutches. It was difficult at first because it required considerable upper-body strength to manage the crutches. With constant practice and unyielding determination, however, his shoulders and hands developed a size and strength that would become prominent features of his physical appearance for the rest of his life.

Peter spent the following summer at his grandfather's house in Wales. Still believing firmly that fresh air was the best cure for tuberculosis, his mother arranged a summer house in the garden where he spent the whole summer while she nursed him back to health. He was often seen sitting in a chair on the verandah with his mother at his side. To enhance the fresh air therapy, his chair was mounted on a turntable mechanism so he could maneuver it to face the direction of the sun. He busied himself by building increasingly more sophisticated radio receivers.

In late summer the cast was removed and the operation declared a success. He could walk again, but tubercular arthritis lingered on. His foot was still swollen and tender when he returned to Cheltenham in the autumn to continue his studies. His mother signed on as an assistant matron and moved to the school to be with him. There she helped the housemaster's wife and looked after her son at the same time.

Peter resumed his studies with good-natured acceptance and without a trace of self-pity or bitterness about his swollen foot. It seemed that his foot problem did not really change his life in any significant way. He was never discouraged by it; nor did he blame it as having ruined his life. He was, by nature, not very outgoing or social anyway; so, he remained his rather taciturn and reserved self. He also never had much time or inclination for sports and competitive games. He disliked cricket and he had no interest in playing rugby—a fact that saddened his father, who loved sports and had been a very good rugby player in his youth.

In his spare time, Peter continued to experiment with the radio, taking sets apart, modifying their components and putting them back together. His room at Cheltenham was strewn with radio parts. By that time, radio technology had become more functional with the invention of the vacuum tube, making it possible not only to receive weak signals but to amplify them as well. Peter found it easy and natural to apply his knowledge of building crystal sets to building vacuum tube sets. Once he had collected all the necessary components, he set to work and assembled this new and more powerful radio receiver. As always, he experimented with his design until he was able to improve the quality and functionality of the device. He tried out different speaker designs until he achieved the best possible sound characteristics, which enhanced the quality of his listening experience.

DURING THE WAR, FOOD SHORTAGES, CLOTHING SHORTAGES and the lack of other basic necessities became a fact of life. Strict rationing was imposed, and remained in effect throughout the three years Peter attended Cheltenham College. Fruits, vegetables, butter, flour, milk, sugar, meat and fish were usually in short supply and the amount allowed for each child was carefully monitored. In fact, a scarcity of fresh milk may have inadvertently resulted in Peter drinking the infected milk that caused his bout with tuberculosis.

Due to this ongoing health issue, the school authorities felt it important that Peter's school dinners include sufficient fruits and vegetables and a full meat ration. Being situated in the countryside, Cheltenham managed to supplement its students' diets with fresh game, caught in the surrounding countryside. The school plowed up sports pitches to grow vegetables. Still, to Peter the food was rather boring, with rabbit stew and tripe and onions frequently appearing on the menu.

Because of textile shortages, Peter had to make do with clothes that were still serviceable while his mother mended the splits and tears in others. In the classrooms, a shortage of basic equipment meant that students could not perform experiments of their own; rather, the instructor had to perform the experiments for the whole class. However, the hardships had a positive benefit as well: they instilled in Peter an appreciation for ingenuity, moderation, and resourcefulness that would remain with him for the rest of his life.

In contrast to his interest in the analytical methods and careful reasoning of the practical sciences, Peter showed little enthusiasm for organized religion even though his paternal grandfather was an Anglican minister and Cheltenham's curriculum had an Anglican bias. Relying on his intellect, Peter excelled in his studies, and graduated from Cheltenham College on schedule.

After graduation, Peter moved to London. In April of 1944, he entered Faraday House Electrical Engineering College, located on Southampton Row, to pursue a degree in electrical engineering. Faraday House was a specialist college that provided a university level education in electrical engineering. It was recognized by the profession as being a pioneer in the use of "sandwich" courses, combining theoretical study with practical field experience.

Peter lived in Hampstead with his sister, Patricia, who was studying architecture. They arrived in London in the midst of nightly German bombing raids that were soon replaced by V-1 flying bomb attacks across the city. Although the old borough of Hampstead was not as badly affected as were some parts of London, powerful explosions occasionally sounded in Peter's neighborhood. Always curious, he would walk to the site later in daylight to inspect the large craters.

His period of study at Faraday House saw Peter's development into a mature young man. He was fundamentally motivated to learn, to acquire knowledge; he took the initiative himself without needing any outside encouragement. Nor did he need strict discipline to keep focused. It was instinctive, arising naturally from his person. During classes, he was likely to ask incisive questions of his professors; and even though he may have anticipated the answers, he nevertheless listened attentively to the logic of their answers.

Peter's thirst for knowledge was not confined solely to electrical engineering. Mathematics, physics and chemistry were other parts of the Faraday House curriculum in which he excelled. Metallurgy and hydraulics attracted his attention because he could see a need for them in the overall picture of his studies. Stemming from the intellectual maturation that those studies gave him, he soon branched out into other theoretical areas that were indirectly related to electrical engineering. His larger goal became a comprehensive understanding that was not merely an ingestion of other people's concepts and ideas, but a deeper, more personal grasp of the fundamental principles in the sciences.

Peter fulfilled the necessary conditions for the institutional portion of his study at Faraday House in 1946, the year after the war ended. He qualified with high marks in such subjects as mathematics, physics, chemistry and the theory and design of electrical machinery. He now needed practical field experience to complete his degree. To obtain this, Peter traveled to India to undertake the fieldwork.

The doctors agreed to the idea, reasoning that the good food and the mild climate in India would help with his lingering tubercular condition. Food rationing in England immediately after the war was even more limiting than that during the war. Even bread and potatoes were being rationed. Peter boarded a ship and traveled to India in June 1946 to take up a position in the electrical department of his father's gold mine. The trip took sixteen days, from England to Bombay—a relatively quick passage for those days.

Peter arrived in India at a time of increasing turmoil. The independence movement had reached a climax; Mahatma Gandhi was leading a civil disobedience campaign, and the country was racked by communal violence that occurred regularly. By contrast, the mining community at Kolar Gold Fields functioned normally, insulated from the social unrest and impervious to external influences. The little town was virtually untouched by the struggle for independence that consumed the rest of India. When the nation celebrated its independence on August 15, 1947, the mood was relatively subdued at the Kolar Gold Fields.

The local landscape had changed in the fourteen years since Peter had departed for England. A sprawling British township was now in place at Kolar Gold Fields, sporting ever more elegant bungalows replete with huge gardens and green lawns. Many clubs had sprung up, with tennis and badminton courts, golf courses, dance halls and swimming baths. "Little England" had come to resemble a typical English township. Each mine had its own bungalows and houses for the staff and separate quarters for the laborers, each house being supplied with free electricity and drinking water. A sprawling market town flourished nearby where miners shopped for all their needs.

Peter's responsibility was to oversee the operation of all the electric generators and other equipment needed to operate the mine. Reaching a depth of nearly 9000 feet, it was one of the deepest underground mines in the world. The sheer depth placed enormous stress on the electric motors operating the hoists that lowered and raised the giant cages in the subterranean mine shafts. The lives of the miners were dependent on those machines, as was the extraction of gold ore. As Peter had a very good grasp of the theory and design of electrical machinery, he was able to repair, and in some cases rebuild, the outdated components of the mine's vital machinery.

Peter occupied a spacious room in his father's colonial bungalow, which included a wide verandah. Radio equipment invariably cluttered much of his living space. Several sets had travelled with him from England, and fiddling with them occupied much of his free time. With some testing and fine-tuning he was able to pick up BBC and All India Radio English-language broadcasts.

However, the news his radio equipment enabled him to receive frequently troubled him. Reports of marches, riots and freedom speeches arrived daily. News of Mahatama Gandhi's non-violent campaign was drowned out by the uproar of communal riots in Calcutta and elsewhere. He could sense the tension, the anger and the fear growing among the Hindu and Muslim communities, and the continuing violence appalled him. Then three months before his return to England, he received the saddest news of all: Gandhi's assassination.

The constant intrusion of a violent world on his consciousness dimmed Peter's infatuation with the radio as a herald of good tidings and a source of inspiration, until gradually his enthusiasm died altogether, never to be rekindled.

IN MAY 1948, HAVING FINISHED HIS TWO-YEAR stint in India, Peter returned to London to receive his diploma from Faraday House. Seeking employment, he moved to Stafford in the West Midlands. He quickly found a job as an "application engineer," in which he utilized his experience from the Kolar Gold Fields to design mine hoists for an engineering company.

Several months later, his father returned to England on leave from his job in India. On holiday during this time, Peter drove with his parents to Switzerland where his youngest sister was attending school at Les Avants. Upon reaching Switzerland, his father suffered a massive heart attack. He and Peter had been fiddling with the car, sharing a pastime they both enjoyed. Peter had just enough time to call his mother. His father died in her arms with Peter at her side.

As he watched her arms cradle his father's lifeless body—a body that was once so strong and vital—he felt a cold shiver pass through his heart, piercing him with a chilling reminder of his own mortality. He was aware, like everyone else, that all people must die. At the same time, death's sudden manifestation, and the realization that the same fate awaited him, affected him deeply.

As he thought about his father's death, and then about his own death, he began to feel a profound sense of acceptance emerging through the sadness. He held no firm religious beliefs at the time, but kneeling over his father's dead body he experienced a profound insight that anyone can die at any moment. He felt a sense of life's impermanence looming in his heart, and saw that when death came, there was nothing to do but accept it. A seed of realization—that he should dedicate his life to spiritual practice—began to take root in his heart.

After his father's death, Peter began to hear the faint sounds of his own footsteps on the spiritual path. Had he known then about the life of the Buddha, he would have known that a similar perception of death's universality had caused the Buddha to forsake his home and step out on the path in search of knowledge that would free him from the pain of the cycle of repeated birth and death.

Initially, Peter set out on that path unaware that he was embarking on a search; nor did he have any clue as to what he might be looking for. He knew only that there was a hollow at the bottom of his heart that needed to be filled. Perhaps the search began with a restlessness. He sensed that the path leading to the root cause of that deep restlessness was also the path that would lead him to freedom from pain and sorrow. The path, however, would be overgrown with thorns of desire, anger and fear, and thickets of ideas and prejudices.

His father's death shattered Peter's complacency. It initially ignited in him an interest in organized religion that he had not shown before. His family belonged to the Anglican Church, but they had never participated very actively. There was a saying in England that you go to church three times in your life: when you are baptized, when you get married and when you die. So his experience with the Anglican Church did not go very deep. Although he was brought up in the Church, he couldn't see much substance in the Anglican religion. He felt Anglicans to be good moral people, but morality on its own was not enough. He felt it was necessary to go much deeper than simply accepting the rules and the beliefs of the doctrine. The Anglican Church Peter knew gave him little reason to be interested in religion while he was growing up.

Peter began searching for a religious experience better suited to his character. When the American evangelist Billy Graham toured England, giving sermons and saving souls, Peter attended one of his sermons out of curiosity. He came away from the large London gathering, feeling disappointed and with a sense of unfulfilled promises. When he returned to his job in Stafford, he began taking the sacraments from a Catholic priest, and inquired into the principles of the Catholic doctrine.

He even considered converting to Catholicism. But, he was stumped by a problem that resisted resolution: the problem of cause and effect. For reasons he could not explain at the time, he always found himself getting stuck on that issue. Emotionally, Catholicism gave a positive impression; but intellectually, he found the explanations lacking clarity.

When reading stories about the saints, Peter learned that one of the big hurdles they encountered was doubt. Doubt arose from meditative experiences which could not be reconciled with the doctrine espoused in the Bible and other Christian texts. These saints had a clear sense of their own personal religious experiences, but those experiences simply did not fit with the beliefs of the Church. That inconsistency did not necessarily render Christian beliefs invalid, but it exposed contradiction within the Christian doctrine. In the end, Peter became dissatisfied with traditional Christian thought.

After his experiments with Catholicism, Peter decided to think things through for himself. Determined not to be influenced by preconceived notions, he swept away the established laws of good and evil from his Christian background with the intention of discovering for himself the precepts of life. Were such precepts necessary at all? That was one of the things he wanted to find out. Clearly, much of conventional truth appeared valid only because it had been handed down as gospel.

As part of his daily routine, Peter rode his bike through the streets of Stafford to work each day. On the return leg at the end of the day, he walked his bike back. This walk was his time for inner reflection. One of the questions he contemplated was about causation and agency: "Here I am and here is the world about me in a particular state of being. Looking back, a lot of factors must have come together to create this present state; otherwise, this state could not exist." It seemed to him that everything in the world operated in a certain manner at a certain moment because of a chain of previous events and states that all led up to that moment. And he wondered: "What is the determining factor there?"

He began to glean some insight into this when he read Dasgupta's five-volume series "A History of Indian Philosophy." Although he never finished the series, in it he discovered the philosophical idea that all sensations are internal; that the majority of people believe only in what their senses perceive, and they accept anything that their senses convey as unquestionably real. They fail to understand that their senses, at best, are imperfect instruments, and that the mind constantly interprets what the senses are reporting. This was immediately a revelation for Peter, and it struck home right away. He thought: "Oh, that's true, why didn't I see it before?" The notion that the senses and their objects are essentially an internal, mental experience would become a constant source of inspiration for him when he later began contemplating the nature of body and mind, the relationship between the external world and internal phenomena.

After this discovery, Peter stopped reading Dasgupta's history of Indian philosophy. Having absorbed a fair amount of Indian philosophy already, he began to suspect that much of it actually derived from Buddhist thought. So the obvious next step was to go straight to the source, to Buddhism, and study it directly.

Peter had come across many references to the Buddha and his teachings in his readings during that time, but he did not know much about either. Then a friend lent him a book on Buddhism. It laid out the very basics of the Buddha's teaching—the Four Noble Truths, the Noble Eightfold Path and the Three Characteristics of Existence. It was a remarkable revelation to him that a path to the truth had already been laid out, one which embraced many of the principles he already believed in. He was astonished that a religion existed that actually taught this approach.

Peter read eagerly, expecting to find specific guidelines by which he could train his mind. He discovered that mental training was at the heart of the Buddha's teaching. So he acquired more books on Buddhism and learned as much as he could about the Buddhist path. Reading the Buddha's words, he felt the excitement of a traveler in a strange and exotic new country. His heart leapt when he came across noble words that expressed what he himself vaguely felt but could not capture in words.

He also read related subjects, like Western philosophy, which he did not find nearly as fulfilling for his quest. His mind operated concretely—with things that were tangible, specific and practical—and he found it difficult to deal with the theoretical ideas and symbolic representations of abstract philosophy. No philosopher offered him what he was seeking. Philosophy was rich in theory and lofty ideas. Among his acquaintances, Peter found many people who were mesmerized by the subtlety and sophistication of scientific and philosophic ideas. Yet these same individuals exhibited moral behavior that was coarse and undeveloped.

Peter began to notice these shortcomings more and more in the workplace. He noticed how inefficient the company was, because people were thinking of themselves far more than their jobs. The top priority of many employees was to get ahead, to climb continually up the ladder of success. The ones most intent on climbing were usually the ones who didn't really know very much. They were clever enough at climbing, but not clever at their work, and were usually rather ineffective. In the company, the work you did mattered less than your position within the workforce and the people you knew. That attitude not only led to an unhealthy competition at work; it also degraded the relationship among the workers. Employees saw themselves, individually, as being more important than their co-workers. To protect that status, they felt compelled to get their share of success and to get it before the others could. In sum, co-workers faced off against one another on a continuing basis, perceiving each other as competitors.

Dismayed by the senseless rivalry, Peter thought: "I don't want to be like that. I don't want to end up caught in that situation." Their attitude was fundamentally wrong. They achieved nothing meaningful, just a higher rank or social standing, which in the end were hollow and empty worldly accomplishments. The external world was not what truly mattered. What truly mattered was a person's inner worth. People should really be focusing inward, looking at the quality of their intentions and the quality of their work. Their attitude toward work—how they view it, how they approach it—should be their most important consideration.

There were also other aspects of their attitude that led Peter to feel that this way of thinking was the biggest problem affecting his fellow workers. On the job, they appeared easy-going and disengaged, like bystanders. Because they lacked a meaningful relationship with their work, they were not motivated to think too much about the job they were doing. They were involved out of necessity but they did not really care about the results. Caring about what they were doing was considered unimportant or unnecessary. Sometimes Peter wanted to ask them: Did you ever ask yourself where your desires come from? What do you really expect to achieve in life? Why are you so sensitive to others' criticism? Why is it that, when you achieve what you have worked so hard for, you are never really satisfied?

Peter's daily contemplations on living in an imperfect world awakened his mind to the inadequacies of worldly life. It brought the challenges of human existence into clearer focus, and along with it, an acute awareness of what constituted a foundation for lasting happiness, for him and for all human beings. As his thoughts steadily gravitated toward Buddhist teachings, he was amazed to find how tiresome a place the world really was.

SEARCHING FOR A DEEPER COMMITMENT to a life of Buddhist practice, Peter decided to move to London in 1953. He had been working in Stafford for nearly five years while mulling over his religious options. Buddhism had given birth to a great tradition of virtue and wisdom, and he wanted to be a part of that tradition. He knew he must proceed with great determination if he was to succeed. He wanted to throw his energies into living in a way that would allow the seeds of Buddhism, which had sprouted in his heart, to grow and bear fruit. Once he had set his heart's compass firmly on its course, he felt an urgent need to meet like-minded companions and seek out the tradition's true source. Stafford at that time lacked a community of dedicated Buddhists. Peter had heard encouraging reports about a venerable institution of Buddhist learning in London. It was there, at the Buddhist Society, that he intended to make earnest inquiries.

Peter's move to London in 1953 heralded important changes in his life. His mother moved to London at the same time and bought a house in Richmond, allowing him to live with her in relative comfort. Nonetheless, he was nearly twenty-eight years old and his mother expected him to make his own way in the world. He soon found employment in London, working for the Canadian Standards Association as an electrical engineer responsible for testing electrical appliances to certify that they met recognized standards for safety and performance.

Shortly after he arrived in London, Peter began his quest to explore Buddhism in greater depth. He visited the Buddhist Society, then located at 16 Gordon Square, across from the central gardens, and signed up to become a member. The Buddhist Society was a lay organization that offered talks and classes on the teachings of all the major Buddhist schools and traditions, as well as a structured program of courses on Buddhism in general. It was run by Christmas Humphreys, who liked to describe the institute as the oldest, largest and most influential Buddhist organization in the West. Thousands of books filled the shelves along all the walls of the Buddhist Society's extensive library, books representing all schools and traditions. It was rare at that time to find so many books on Buddhism, including the Pāli Canon. The prospect of reading them added to Peter's enthusiasm and excitement.

From its inception, the Buddhist Society had been open, in principle, to all Buddhist traditions and their respective schools. In practice, most of Christmas Humphreys's public lectures were focused on the Zen school of Buddhism. Peter attended those lectures whenever he had the chance, and was intrigued by what he heard.

On the suggestion of Christmas Humphreys, Peter started reading the literature on Zen. Intellectually, he found Zen very attractive, energetic and inspiring. But when he turned his attention to practicing those teachings, the attraction faded. To him, the way of Zen, as described in the books, lacked structure. It was not well set out in a graduated manner, beginning with the preliminary practices and graduating to the more advanced ones. The teachings of Zen established themselves somewhere at the high end of the path and focused toward the summit. He felt that such a lofty approach to practice could easily lead to damaging doubt and confusion.

Peter studied the social and religious backgrounds from which Zen had developed. First in China, then in Japan, Zen had really sprouted and taken root in environments where religion was deeply ingrained in people's character. People already held strong beliefs in the supernatural, in the power of the nonphysical world around them; and Zen helped them to put this into perspective and make sense of it.

In the Western world, the mythic language of those earlier traditions had been abandoned in favor of a language based on sensory experience and scientific concepts. Because of that, students in England approached Zen with a mind full of modern ideas that did not resonate well with the original teachings. The tendency in modern Zen circles was to embrace the teachings with a wayward spirit, and to practice them for the wrong aims. Because a step by step teaching was not available to guide the Zen students, Peter sensed that very few had really gained reliable results from their practice.

His skepticism of Zen as a practical training led Peter to delve more deeply into the Theravādin literature at the Buddhist Society; especially the Pāli texts. He soon realized that the original teachings of the Buddha, preserved in the Pāli language by Theravādin texts, came as close as one could get to the actual words of the Buddha. The Buddha often expounded the practice as a gradual training that unfolded in stages from the first step on the path to the final goal. The Buddha's message was said to be good in the beginning, good in the middle and good in the end; that is to say: good at the stage of moral discipline, good at the stage of meditative concentration and good at the stage of penetrative wisdom.

The way of Theravāda was, therefore, more structured than Zen because the practice started with the basics and slowly worked up along a gradual progression. That approach appealed to Peter's sense of methodology, causing him to experience a strong and immediate connection as he read through the suttas one by one. He had found a path of practice that addressed both cause and effect: a proper foundation leading to proper results. Firstly, undertake the rules of discipline to bring one's behavior into harmony with the world at large and establish an inner environment that is conducive to meditative concentration. Secondly, remove the main obstacles to meditative concentration so that the mind becomes collected, unified and deeply calm. Finally, with concentration as the basis, investigate to develop insight leading to wisdom and attainment of the final goal. Peter had found a teaching that was good in theory, good in practice and good in realization.

Peter believed he should make an effort to apply the principles of the Buddha's teaching to his everyday life. To accomplish this, Peter devoted himself wholeheartedly to every task he was required to perform. In his job at Canadian Standards, Peter felt that his duty as a Buddhist was to serve the task rather than the employer; that, for a Buddhist, the doing should matter more than the reward, that openness, humility and freedom came from serving in a selfless way.

Even while he was employed at Canadian Standards, Peter knew that he would not be working as an electrical engineer all his life. That was his chosen profession, but he had a keen awareness that he was doing it only temporarily. He did not know what he would be doing later on, but he knew it would not be that.

Though not particularly discontented in London, he had a nagging feeling that he did not yet understand his role in the larger picture of his life. When he was younger, Peter had dreamt about finding an ideal place to live. As he looked around now, he realized that there was no such place to be found. Everywhere he looked he saw the disadvantages, and an uncertain future.

Even people who worked hard and took pride in their work were bound to be stopped short in their tracks by the onslaught of old age, sickness and death. And there loomed the dread of losing a once sharp intellect as the mind began to falter with age. A person becomes frightened, seeing his physical and mental energy slip away. No matter how much effort he has funneled into a successful career, once the time comes, the slate of his worldly accomplishments is cleared. With such prospects, how can he expect to live out his final years with peace of mind—even though he has made every effort to live an exemplary life?

For Peter, Buddhism was not merely a passing interest that made sense only under certain conditions; its teachings should always hold true, regardless of one's age or circumstances. The truth, as Buddhism conveyed, was that all things which appear in the world constantly change. Something is born; it remains briefly and then dies away— birth, ageing and death. No amount of effort can avoid the process of growing old. No strategy can evade death. Whatever was built would be destroyed; all that was accumulated would be lost; whatever came into existence would die. What was the sense in pursuing worldly goals when death and decay would wipe the whole slate clean; when everything that one worked so hard for and clung to as important would be torn from one's grasp?

The futility of worldly existence reminded Peter of the story of Sisyphus in Greek mythology. Sisyphus was condemned to an eternity of rolling a great boulder to the top of a steep hill. Every time Sisyphus attained the summit by the greatest of exertion and toil, the boulder slipped his grasp and rolled back down again. People, Peter saw, are wandering through repeated rounds of birth and death, suffering from the same futility and indignity. They are born and they work hard to establish a solid position in the world only to have death snatch it from their grasp. Facing rebirth, they repeat the process all over again without any end in sight.

BORN WITH AN ACTIVE AND LOGICAL MIND, Peter instinctively questioned everything in the light of Buddhist principles. In his leisure time, he persistently grappled with the problem of reconciling Buddhist principles of causation with the principles of scientific inquiry, Buddhist notions of truth with those of science methodology.

Peter reasoned that concepts such as matter, energy, and so forth were science's attempt to explain how things work. But those explanations were merely mental constructs formulated by the scientist. They were not scientific truth, merely suppositions whose validity could be tested and proved. In other words, a scientist forms a concept of why this gave rise to that, and then tests it to prove the correlation correct.

Based on that link, he proposes a theory about how matter and energy interact.

Later discoveries negate the theory in certain situations, so the theory is modified to fit the new circumstances. More probing reveals that the theory does not cover other circumstances; so it is modified again. Eventually, enough inconsistencies are discovered to discredit the entire theory, forcing the scientist to scrap the original theory and construct a new one. That is the way science works: it functions with relative, provisional truths. Science is an evolving method which tries to fathom the physical world by harnessing the power of the human mind.

The paradox that encumbers science is that of the mind. Mind has no physical properties, yet scientists cannot escape its predominance over everything they do. Logic and the principles of reason exist only in the mind. But scientists never attempt to fathom the nature of the mind itself, the very key they use to unlock the mysteries of the world's shifting landscape.

To search for the truth of the mind is to search for unconditioned truth, the one unchanging truth. Science, on the other hand, with its plethora of facts, theories and suppositions, diverts the search away from the path of absolute, unchanging truth and into a maze of ambiguous relative truths. This line of reasoning led Peter to question the efficacy of cause and effect, that ability of the mind to think logically and arrive at reasoned conclusions which he had always held so dear.

The Buddha taught the law of kamma—that our present experiences are conditioned by causes: our own past thoughts, words and deeds. In daily life, people find themselves in undesirable circumstances all the time, even when it seems that they have done nothing to create them. They agonize, trying to find a reason why these things are happening to them. In doing so, they analyze conditions to find causes. In spending so much time and energy analyzing the conditions, they never get to the cause, the real source of the problem. They might get a provisional answer as to how the condition materialized; but as long as the original cause remains undiscovered, they will never be able to prevent it from happening again. In Buddhist practice, analyzing the present conditions is seen as merely an effort to alleviate current suffering, rather than to eliminate suffering altogether. A deeper investigation must search for the original cause of suffering, the original cause of being reborn, growing old, getting sick, and dying in life after life.

The Buddha discovered the fundamental source of suffering, the real hindrance that prevents true freedom. He taught that mental defilements and their resultant negative emotions, such as greed, anger and delusion, keep us trapped in the cycle of birth and death; that they are the root causes of this unending struggle. Negative emotions lead to negative actions, and negative actions lead to negative kamma, and negative kamma results in karmic consequences.

ALTHOUGH PETER STILL COULD NOT FIT ALL THE PIECES together, the truth to be found at the heart of the Buddha's teaching gradually began to take shape in his mind. He knew that the missing pieces did not lie in the realm of science; if anything, the scientific outlook was part of the problem, one of the reasons that the answers remained a mystery. Looking around him, Peter could see the hand of rational scientific thought at work in the ongoing social and spiritual confusion affecting post-war Britain. Instead of allaying people's doubt and perplexity surrounding their beliefs and values, the scientific approach to life helped to perpetuate social disquiet.

Post-war Britain was entering a period of increasing affluence and freedom, where many of the old social and cultural structures were being challenged, and slowly eroded away. The commercialization of society coincided with a steady increase in material wealth. Consumption had become less connected with utilitarian needs, and more with status and comfort. For many people, their lifestyle choices and consumption patterns began to underpin their personal identity. The car, the outings, the shopping sprees, the visits to the local pub several times a week, the annual holiday to the same hotel in the south—those were the pleasures they lived for, that defined them.

Peter remembered society being much more restrained when he was young. People back then had a much better sense of morality, of the difference between right and wrong; for instance, they regarded telling lies as being sinful. He felt that now people had only a vague idea of what morality meant, and that fewer and fewer of them cared about moral issues—a clear indication to Peter that British society was heading in the wrong direction.

Although a general feeling of optimism prevailed in post-war British society, it masked a foreboding sense of uncertainty. New liberties had been gained at the cost of greater social fragmentation and weakened religious underpinnings. Consequently, a thick vein of anxiety ran deep beneath the surface of post-war British society. To Peter, British society became an illustration of all the values that led people away from the truth, made it hard to aspire and live for the truth, and in fact, discouraged people from even believing that the truth existed.

As a result, Peter felt set apart from the ordinary society around him in his search for truth. He felt that he was confronted with a problem which others knew nothing about. He began to believe that the only meaningful life was a life that strove for individual realization of the truth. Nothing in the world around him supported that choice, and the entire society in which he lived seemed to negate every idea of sacredness or deeper meaning. He realized that in order to truly embark on a search for the truth, he would have to leave behind all worldly involvement and the social and cultural ties that entangled him.

An aching gap opened in Peter's heart between his mundane predicament and the truth he aspired to attain. He thought that he could not continue to delay a decision on his future indefinitely; otherwise, his life would pass by and he would have lost the opportunity to do something about it. He now had the opportunity, and he had the strength to do it. And above all, he had the Buddha's teaching to guide him.

Sitting in the quiet of the Buddhist Society's library evening after evening, Peter read a great deal of the Pāli Canon, and even some of the commentaries. But sometimes his choice of reading material was more random, less organized. The books filling the library shelves covered a diverse range of Buddhist literature, and he tended to read whatever struck his fancy. Although the aim of the teachings was the same, the paths recommended to reach that goal varied. In the end, he began to feel a sense of incoherency about what he had imbibed in his readings; he began to feel unsettled inside. He was still stuck with the same predicament: how to decide on the correct path of practice. The mental confusion he suffered begged for a good teacher to straighten it out.

By early 1955, Peter had settled on a course of action. He prepared to devote his whole life to the practice. He was not in a hurry. There was still a great deal to learn, and he could not expect to accomplish that quickly. Success was not simply a matter of spending time and energy; he had to spend his life. Not many people were willing to go that far. Knowing that he needed to find a qualified teacher to show him the path of practice, he believed that if he was earnest and ready to learn, then either he would find the right teacher or that teacher would find him.

Working in London as an electrical engineer, his mind was always divided. By day, he performed mechanical applications of routine engineering tasks, but his thoughts constantly gravitated toward the Dhamma. Peter had always been a quiet and socially reserved young man, and now he preferred to pass his leisure time perusing Buddhist texts in his room or at the library. He felt that he must practice before he could understand. The main thing was to subdue his desires and quiet his mind. He felt that the true significance of finding refuge in the Triple Gem could only be realized when the seeker was totally committed to persevering. He had to be committed not so much to formal acts of devotion as to striving relentlessly toward the realization, within his own heart, of the singular qualities represented by the Buddha, the Dhamma and the Sangha.

Since his arrival in London, a monastic vocation had been a vague possibility hovering on life's horizon. At times, he sensed the hand of karmic destiny orchestrating his future, as though ordination was somehow preordained—the natural outcome of his quest for the truth. Peter had always viewed ordination as a turning point, the line one crossed when one wanted to dedicate body and mind to Buddhism. As time passed, he realized he could no longer be complacent in his current situation. The time had arrived for him to step across that time-honored threshold and undertake the monastic life of a bhikkhu in the Theravāda tradition.

On his frequent visits to the Buddhist Society at Gordon Square, Peter had become acquainted with an Englishman named William Purfurst. Since they first met, William had traveled to Thailand to ordain as a Theravādin monk, and taken on the monastic name Kapilavaḍḍho. Bhikkhu Kapilavaḍḍho returned from Thailand in November 1954 and joined two Sinhalese monks residing in the London Buddhist Vihāra at Ovington Gardens, Knightsbridge, which had opened in May of that year. Quite fortuitously, Bhikkhu Kapilavaḍḍho's arrival coincided with Peter's decision to seek the path to monkhood.

The arrival of Bhikkhu Kapilavaḍḍho offered Peter the opening he needed: here was someone who knew how to go about it. Bhikkhu Kapilavaḍḍho, whose own ordination had been the culmination of a long-standing movement by English Buddhists to establish a viable Sangha in England, welcomed Peter at the London Buddhist Vihāra and encouraged his ambition to ordain. He would facilitate in whatever way he could. Peter was to learn—from this mentor's own practical experience—the life and the discipline practiced by Buddhist monks ordained in the oldest lineage of Buddhist monasticism.

Two more aspiring candidates for bhikkhu ordination, Robert Albison and George Blake, joined Peter at the London Buddhist Vihāra. Together, the trio took guidance from Bhikkhu Kapilavaḍḍho and occasionally accompanied him when he traveled to give lectures, first at the newly-initiated meditation week in Oxford and later at the Buddhist Society's summer school.

First Robert Albison, and then George Blake, ordained as novice monks at the London Buddhist Vihāra and were given the monastic names Saddhāvaḍḍho and Vijjāvaḍḍho respectively. Peter had a difficult time convincing his mother to support his vocation. But finally, on his thirtieth birthday she conceded that he was sufficiently mature to choose his life's direction, and though she was deeply skeptical, she would not stand in his way. Twelve days later, on October 31, 1955, Peter ordained as a novice monk or sāmaṇera at the London Buddhist Vihāra. He was given the name Paññāvaḍḍho, "Cultivator of Wisdom."

Many years later, Paññāvaḍḍho would explain his motivation to ordain: "British society resembled a huge tangled cocoon in which all its members could see only other parts of the cocoon, while the whole thing whirled about without any purpose or direction, and nobody in it could differentiate right from wrong. People formed opinions and theories about almost everything, clinging to them tightly. Before long everyone started arguing and quarreling, which eventually led to strikes and student riots and wars. The only sane choice was to tiptoe quietly out of that mess while everyone else was too busy quarreling and fighting to notice."

The three new novices took up residence at the London Buddhist Vihāra. As junior-most members of the community, they were expected to strictly observe the ten precepts, to learn the Dhamma and the monastic code of conduct from their elders, to attend upon the senior

monks, and to prepare themselves to become eligible for higher ordination as bhikkhus.

With the completion of all three novice ordinations, planning
accelerated for a trip to Thailand. Their bhikkhu ordinations were to
be held at Pak Naam Monastery, which belonged to the Mahānikāya
sect, the oldest and largest in Thailand's monastic order. Bhikkhu
Kapilavaḍḍho and his three charges boarded a plane in London on
December 14, 1955 and flew to Bangkok. They were met at the Bangkok
airport by a lay supporter who drove them to Pak Naam Monastery,
which was located at the mouth of the Chao Phraya River. The abbot, Chao Khun Mongkol-Thepmuni, met their arrival. Chao Khun
Mongkol-Thepmuni, known affectionately by his supporters as Luang
Por Sot, began making preparations to confer higher ordination on the
three sāmaṇeras.

Pre-ordination celebrations were held at Pak Naam Monastery on
the evening of January 26, 1956. The ceremony was held in an open-air
courtyard where tiered gold-leaf and lacquered tables were piled high
with flowers, monks' robes and ceremonial fans. Kapilavaḍḍho and the
three sāmaṇeras sat in the middle space surrounded by a vast crowd of
Thai well-wishers, who offered token gifts to the monks and novices.

The following day the three sāmaṇeras were ordained together as
bhikkhus in a ceremony reported to be one of the largest of its kind
in Thailand. Thousands of people crowded the monastery grounds to
witness what they felt to be a historic event.

The ordination ceremony began on the afternoon of January 27,
1956 with a long procession that escorted the monks and novices three
times around the Uposatha Hall before entering the sanctified building. The procession started with the emergence of the English novices
from the library building where they had resided since their arrival.
The ensuing parade was led in traditional Thai fashion by a serpentine
figure, the mythical nāga, in the form of a man draped by an enormous
and colorful dragon's head which spewed real flames from its gap-

ing mouth as it bobbed and weaved through the crowd of onlookers. Scores of white-robed lay devotees, carrying folded bundles of white cloth, walked two abreast behind the nāga figure. The three candidates for ordination came next, walking slowly with deliberation and carrying lotus flowers, candles and incense in their raised palms.

Moving slowly with bare feet on warm tiles, the entire procession made three sweeping passes around the Uposatha Hall, then entered in a single file, through a stone gateway, into the consecrated space. A flight of stone steps led up from a small courtyard to the Uposatha Hall, which by then was crowded with monks and lay devotees. The hall's oblong interior featured rows of pillars, forming an inner space with broad aisles at the sides. On stepping into the hall, one's eyes were immediately drawn to the great Buddha statue, elevated on its seat at the far end; and then, an instant later, to the abbot, seated amid the mass of offerings and array of multicolored flowers decorating the Buddha. The abbot, Luang Por Sot, sat calmly, facing the assembly. On either side sat elders of the order, each according to seniority. Junior monks, draped in yellow robes of various hues, sat in rows, down along the two sides of the long hall. In the middle of the hall stood the three young candidates for ordination, and behind the candidates, the space at the entrance to the hall and in the aisles to the sides overflowed with lay devotees.

An impressive sense of order and solemnity pervaded the inner sanctum as the proceedings began, precisely following procedures as they had been laid down nearly two thousand five hundred years before. The three candidates were first ordained again as sāmaṇeras. The bhikkhu higher ordination followed, with Luang Por Sot officiating as the preceptor. The kammavācariya instructor was Chao Khun Dhammatiloka and the anusāsanācariya instructor was Bhikkhu Kapilavaḍḍho. After being presented with their monk's robes and bowls, the candidates approached the waiting Sangha together. The candidates received brief instructions about the ceremony before being given their official monastic names. The two instructors took the candidates aside to question them on their suitability for the monkhood. Being deemed suitable, the candidates each formally requested bhikkhu ordination from the assembled Sangha. For each candidate, a proposal was put forward and accepted with silence. In that solemn, time-honored way, the Sangha formally consented to receive Paññāvaḍḍho and his companions as fully-ordained members of the order.

Following his ordination, Bhikkhu Paññāvaḍḍho remained in Pak Naam Monastery trying to master Luang Por Sot's unique meditation method, which was referred to as sammā arahaṁ. It involved seeing light nimittas in varying degrees of form and subtlety. While silently repeating "sammā arahaṁ" and remaining attentive to this internal repetition, the meditator mindfully focused on the following: first the right nostril, then the corner of the eye, then to the center of the head, down to the throat, down below the navel and then up to the solar plexus. After a time, the meditator should begin to see images of light. That, at any rate, was Bhikkhu Paññāvaḍḍho's understanding of the method.

It was said that the first image to appear would be a sphere of light. From that translucent sphere an image of the gross human body would first emerge and become visible, followed by an image of the subtle human body. The next images would then arise in their proper order: sīla, samādhi, paññā, vimutti, vimuttiñāṇadassana. After these five images appeared and vanished, other bodies would emerge in turn: the gross and subtle deva bodies, followed by the gross and subtle brahma bodies and then the Sotāpanna body progressing all the way up to the Arahant body.

Initially, Bhikkhu Paññāvaḍḍho found the practice helpful in that it led to a measure of mental calm and concentration. Beyond that, he was unable to make much sense of it. Because he could not figure out the reason behind the appearance of light images, he failed to understand what was meant to be happening. He did not know whether he should use his imagination to create the various images, or whether they were images inherent to the mind that arose spontaneously. Due to that uncertainty, he lacked confidence in the method.

Two months after their ordinations, Bhikkhu Kapilavaḍḍho moved the three new monks to Wat Thaat Tong on the eastern outskirts of Bangkok and returned alone to England to resume his work of spreading the Dhamma. Bhikkhu Saddhāvaḍḍho soon became discontented and a month later flew back to England as well. Bhikkhus Paññāvaḍḍho and Vijjāvaḍḍho then proceeded to Wat Vivekaram, a small forest monastery south of Bangkok in Chonburi province.

By that time, Bhikkhu Paññāvaḍḍho had dropped Luang Por Sot's meditation method. He concluded that to practice a method that inspired little confidence was unlikely to bring satisfactory results. Realizing that he needed a reliable meditation technique to draw his mind away from its distractions and its impurities to achieve a more unified and refined state of mind, he turned to the meditation practice that the Buddha recommended: ānāpānasati or mindfulness of breathing. All the texts he had read stated that mindfulness of the breath was especially useful for countering a scattered and distracted mind—a problem that had plagued him from the beginning—and was thus a suitable basic practice for most beginners. At the same time, it restored his confidence to recall that the Buddha himself had expressly used mindfulness of breathing as his primary meditation subject for the attainment of Nibbāna.

Seated comfortably, Bhikkhu Paññāvaḍḍho began by placing his full attention on the normal cycle of the breath—each inhalation followed by each exhalation. Breathing was a fixed and ongoing natural activity. He needed simply to relax and focus his attention on the tip of the nose, being aware of each breath as it passed in and out through the nostrils. He made no attempt to control the breath. He wanted to focus on the natural and spontaneous rhythm of breathing and allow the resulting concentration to draw his mind inward.

He had just begun to develop his skill at this when his stay at Wat Vivekaram was abruptly cut short. His companion, Bhikkhu Vijjāvaḍḍho, became very ill and needed urgent medical attention. Much to Bhikkhu Paññāvaḍḍho's disappointment, circumstances obliged him to hastily escort his friend back to Bangkok. Before departing, the abbot, Ajaan Lun, gave the monks a small meditation guide he had written. Several years later, Bhikkhu Paññāvaḍḍho would translate the guide into English as "Handbook for the Practice of Dhamma."

In Bangkok, Bhikkhu Vijjāvaḍḍho was taken first to the British Embassy. Following consultations with the staff, he entered an infirmary. His symptoms showed little sign of improvement; but nevertheless, Bhikkhu Paññāvaḍḍho stayed at the infirmary to help attend to his needs. When Bhikkhu Kapilavaḍḍho, then in England, heard of his worsening condition, he quickly flew back to Thailand, took one look at the situation and decided to take both Vijjāvaḍḍho and Paññāvaḍḍho back to England immediately.

THE THREE MONKS RETURNED TO LONDON in June 1956. Bhikkhu Vijjā-vaḍḍho, still suffering the debilitating symptoms of a chronic illness, soon disrobed and returned to lay life. Bhikkhu Paññāvaḍḍho suddenly found himself engaged in the relative hustle and bustle of big city life. Swept up in his teacher's busy schedule, he dutifully followed Bhikkhu Kapilavaḍḍho to his appointments to meet lay supporters, give lectures and raise funds for Sangha activities.

One of the Buddhist projects closest to Bhikkhu Kapilavaḍḍho's heart was the Manchester Buddhist Society, which he had helped found in 1951. Aside from London, Manchester had the largest and strongest group of Buddhists in Britain. Bhikkhu Kapilavaḍḍho traveled there often to teach the Dhamma to supporters who gathered regularly at a rented house in a quiet suburban neighborhood. Manchester lacked a permanent Sangha presence, and he decided to remedy that by sending Bhikkhu Paññāvaḍḍho to take over the day-to-day operations of the Manchester Buddhist Society. In September 1956, Bhikkhu Paññāvaḍḍho obediently made the long journey north to take up residence in the Society's rented house at Grovenor Square in Sale, Cheshire.

A clipping from the Manchester Evening News dated September 21, 1956 read: "In the front room on a quiet, leafy Sale, Cheshire, road sits a young man of history. For he is the first resident minister in the English provinces of a world religion born about 2,400 years ago. Peter Morgan was the Christening name given to Bhikkhu (monk) Paññāvaḍḍho, aged 30 who once worked as an electrical engineer. He spent most of his life in Llanelly, Carmarthenshire. Then he picked up a booklet on Buddhism. It interested him...and in January this year he was ordained as a Bhikkhu in Thailand. Now Paññāvaḍḍho (Pāli for "He who spreads and increases wisdom") has only eight worldly possessions—and exactly 227 rules of life. He owns: Three robes, a begging bowl, razor, water strainer, needle and cotton. He is maintained by the small but growing Manchester Buddhist community. His rules forbid him to possess or handle money."

In May of that year, while Bhikkhu Paññāvaḍḍho was still residing in Thailand, the English Sangha Trust had been set up in London. Its aim was to promote the teachings of the Buddha in the United Kingdom by establishing an English branch of the Bhikkhu Sangha, and by providing and maintaining residences for the Sangha's welfare. By December 1956, sufficient funds had been raised by the Trust to lease a house in London for a Sangha residence. Bhikkhu Kapilavaḍḍho moved into the house at 50 Alexandra Road, Swiss Cottage shortly thereafter. The address at Swiss Cottage soon became known as Sangha House.

Bhikkhu Kapilavaḍḍho's weekly teaching schedule often saw him in Manchester on weekends, presenting classes, talks and interviews in connection with the Manchester Buddhist Society's agenda. That timetable afforded Bhikkhu Paññāvaḍḍho an opportunity to consult with his teacher on a regular basis. The weekly teaching circuit also included trips to Leeds, Oxford, Cambridge and Brighton before returning to London. As the months passed, Bhikkhu Paññāvaḍḍho became increasingly concerned about his teacher's exhausting schedule and the effect it had on his health.

In February 1957, after having resided only five months at the Manchester Buddhist Society, Bhikkhu Paññāvaḍḍho was summoned back to London. His help was needed because the burden of so many engagements had taken a serious toll on Bhikkhu Kapilavaḍḍho's health. As his health deteriorated further over the next several months, Bhikkhu Kapilavaḍḍho was forced to retire from the Order and return to lay life. Bhikkhu Paññāvaḍḍho, his dutiful student, was asked to officiate at the disrobing ceremony in June 1957.

That turn of fate placed the responsibility for the English Sangha Trust in the hands of Bhikkhu Paññāvaḍḍho, a monk of only one year. Though somewhat overwhelmed by the added duties and responsibilities, he assumed his new position with a calm and a sincerity that belied his junior status. Sangha House was now his to manage. Living with him were two German sāmaṇeras, Saññāvaḍḍho and Sativaḍḍho, who had come to stay in London with Bhikkhu Kapilavaḍḍho after meeting him on a lecture tour in Germany. The elderly Russian nun Jhānānanda also lived at Sangha House to help look after them. Bhikkhu Paññāvaḍḍho had suddenly become the teacher, tasked with training the other Sangha members and teaching the small group of lay people who came regularly to see him. His practice suddenly became the practice of teaching others.

His main challenge at the beginning was focusing clearly on his own meditation practice. Time after time, when he sat down to meditate, his mind became distracted, and he was forced to constantly rein it in and refocus on the breath. His precipitous return to England, so soon after his ordination in Thailand, turned out to be a bigger challenge than he had expected. The main reason was that the monks he had ordained with had all given up the robe, and he was left, alone, holding "the baby." That baby was the English Sangha Trust, which was a burdensome responsibility.

During that period, Bhikkhu Paññāvaḍḍho's mother lived at her parents' house in Wales. At one point, she and his sister came for a visit at Sangha House in London. Upon arriving, they were ushered into a waiting room. They had not seen him for many years, and when Bhikkhu Paññāvaḍḍho entered the room, his mother was so overjoyed that she jumped up to hug her son! When she was told that the monastic code of discipline forbade him to have physical contact with her, she was deeply dismayed. She had not known about the rules. She refused to accept his new circumstances and never went to see her son again.

In 1958 Bhikkhu Paññāvaḍḍho taught at the Buddhist Society Summer School for the first time. The Buddhist Society Summer School attempted to create the conditions necessary for students to engage in skillful conduct and to learn and discuss the practice of meditation, with the aim of developing a basic level of tranquility and insight. Every year the Buddhist Society invited speakers to their summer school sessions, many of whom stayed and gave meditation courses. The Buddhist Society Summer School convened for one week every year on a large rural property where as many as fifty people regularly attended. Each person received a private room in a large country house. The atmosphere was relaxed and informal, lacking the strictness and formality of a retreat. Most of those present were adherents of either Zen or Theravāda Buddhism and they tended to form groups along those interests. Talking and socializing were tolerated at Summer School and the groups mingled freely at certain hours of the day.

Bhikkhu Paññāvaḍḍho was tasked with giving instruction from the Theravāda Buddhist perspective. Christmas Humphreys presented discourses on Zen Buddhism. Bhikkhu Paññāvaḍḍho gave two Dhamma talks a day, one of which was intended to be a good introduction for people who had a limited knowledge of Buddhism. The main thrust of his meditation course was mindfulness of breathing leading to calm and concentration. When the opportunity arose, he also gave insightful explanations of such difficult topics as dependent origination. He was self-sacrificing and generous with his time, talking individually with each meditator about their experiences at least once a day.

Bhikkhu Paññāvaḍḍho also accepted invitations to lead the meditation week at Oxford, which differed significantly in tone and intensity from the Buddhist Society Summer School. Following in Kapilavaḍḍho's footsteps, he taught a strict Mahāsi Sayadaw method of meditation, stressing the importance of mindfulness and clear comprehension. At the beginning of the week, he gave an instructional talk outlining the meditation procedure. Meditators were to anchor their attention on the rising and falling sensations of the abdomen during breathing, observing carefully any other feelings or thoughts that might arise. They were encouraged to sharpen their focus by making sure that the mind was attentive to the entirety of each process.

Every bodily movement was to be done deliberately and with conscious attention to detail: walking with exaggerated slowness at all times; eating the meals in slow motion. At the same time, thoughts were carefully considered, and breaks in concentration noted. He stressed that such diligence should be carried out continuously throughout the day, the objective being a deep, clear, precise awareness of the mind and body.

Oxford Meditation Week did not take place at Oxford University but rather in a villa in the town of Oxford which overlooked a wooded park. Meditators bunked in separate rooms, mingling only at mealtimes. All participants observed the eight precepts, which included not eating after mid-day. No talking, reading or entertainment was allowed. The whole day was devoted to a strict regimen of meditation practice under Bhikkhu Paññāvaḍḍho's instruction and guidance.

Bhikkhu Paññāvaḍḍho also explained the fundamentals of Buddhist practice at various venues in London and in religious forums at Jesus College, Oxford. He believed fully and without reservation that the truth taught by the Buddha was a very important matter for human beings to understand. Many people were willing to practice methods that helped them live their lives in relative comfort. But in his teaching engagements, he rarely met people who were willing to reach beyond superficial techniques to the real fundamentals of Buddhist practice.

In 1958 Bhikkhu Paññāvaḍḍho arranged for the higher ordinations of the two German sāmaṇeras who had been training under his guidance. In preparation, he tutored them thoroughly in the ordination procedure and in the Buddhist monastic rules. Then, at the culmination of a historic ceremony at the Thai Embassy on July 2, 1958 Bhikkhus Dhammiko and Vimalo became the first Buddhist monks to be ordained on British soil.

In September 1959, Bhikkhu Paññāvaḍḍho was invited to give a Dhamma talk in Victoria, near Buckingham Palace. A member of the audience was so impressed by what he heard that, at the conclusion of the talk, he donated the sizeable sum of £24,000 to the English Sangha Trust. In June 1960, a longtime supporter who was instrumental in the formation of the English Sangha Trust bequeathed a donation of £15,000 to the Trust. As manager of the Trust, Bhikkhu Paññāvaḍḍho maintained the integrity of those two donations, which several years later made it possible for the English Sangha Trust to purchase three properties for the Sangha's use. The house at 131 Haverstock Hill was purchased in September 1962 and the one next door at 129 Haverstock Hill in January 1963. Shortly thereafter, the country estate Biddulph Old Hall was purchased as a meditation centre.

Even though Bhikkhu Paññāvaḍḍho approached Buddhist practice with a single-minded devotion and taught that practice with such tireless energy that his audience expanded continually as the years went by, still he did not feel comfortable in his position. The talks he gave on Buddhism were based primarily on theory rather than practice. Lacking sufficient practical experience to guide his discourse, he consistently referred to the Pāli texts for his descriptions of the practice. He felt like a doctor who possessed expert medical knowledge but did not have the talent to practice and cure an actual disease. How could he possibly help others to rid themselves of their defilements as long as he still could not vanquish them from himself? Deep within his heart, he knew that, as soon as an opportunity presented itself, he must search for a teacher whom he could depend on for guidance.

At some point, he discussed his desire with a Thai graduate student living in London, who agreed to locate the most renowned Thai meditation masters when he returned home. The graduate student's work as a mining engineer required him to travel to the Mekong River area searching for mineral deposits. When traveling in the area, he liked to spend the night at a nearby monastery. He said he would be glad to ask people about the famous teachers residing in the area.

Bhikkhu Paññāvaḍḍho's sojourn in Thailand had been brief and unsatisfying, his return to England lengthy and unfulfilling. Yet he sensed from the beginning that the answer to satisfaction and fulfillment lay in the faraway country of his ordination lineage. His stay in Thailand was so short that he had no time to learn the language, much less the customs. If he were to return one day, language would be important, he was sure of that. There being so few Thai people in London at that time, he found no chance to learn spoken Thai. He decided to teach himself by making an English translation of the meditation book that Ajaan Lun, the abbot of Wat Vivekaram, had given him before he left.

With the aid of a Thai-English dictionary and his own extensive knowledge of the Pāli Canon, he extracted the meaning, word by word, sentence by sentence, from the Thai original. Though slow and painstaking at the start, the process gained pace and fluency as he became more familiar with the Thai alphabet and the gist of the Thai text, which was largely a summary of canonical works such as the Visuddhimagga and the Abhidhammattha Sangaha.

By 1961 Bhikkhu Paññāvaḍḍho had completed his 100-page translation of "Handbook for the Practice of Dhamma," which was eventually printed for free distribution by the Buddhist Association of Thailand. Excerpts of the translation were printed in *Sangha*, a journal published by members of the English Sangha Trust.

Bhikkhu Paññāvaḍḍho made known his wish to return to Thailand for further training, and eventually a bhikkhu to replace him was arranged. On November 9, 1961, Bhikkhu Ānanda Bodhi, a Canadian-born monk, arrived at Sangha House to take over responsibility for the English Sangha Trust from Bhikkhu Paññāvaḍḍho. Free at last to pursue his goal, Bhikkhu Paññāvaḍḍho bid his supporters farewell and on November 21st boarded a plane bound for Bangkok.

The Buddhist Society later published this tribute to him in The Middle Way: "On November 21st Bhikkhu Paññāvaḍḍho left by air for Thailand, where he will continue his training in an atmosphere more conducive to progress than that of London. Peter Morgan was ordained in Thailand and returned to Britain after only a few months. Not long after his return he found himself in charge of the English Sangha, and for the next five years was responsible for training new bhikkhus and sāmaṇeras and teaching the laity. This involved fortnightly visits throughout the year to Manchester and Leeds, and a host of other responsibilities which he never shirked, though they were not of his seeking. He has now decided that the time has come to get on with his own development. On 2nd November he conducted Mrs. Robins' meditation class and was presented with a book, and on 9th November, Council, at an informal reception, presented him with further books and wished him every success in Thailand. He will be missed by many whom he has helped, but all such must remember that, as it has been said, "The laity don't own bhikkhus, even when privileged to support them." A fine photograph of him now hangs in the entrance hall of the Society's premises, and we would also draw attention to the tape recording of three short talks made by him shortly before he left, and available on our usual terms.

"The Association is most deeply indebted to Bhikkhu Paññāvaḍḍho. Under his guidance the small, young movement grew and gained stability. This led to an increase in the number of members, and a widening of its relationship with the general public. Two magnificent donations given while he was Bhikkhu in charge at Sangha House have made possible, among other things, the new Vihāra at 131 Haverstock Hill and the meditation centre at Biddulph; and have enabled the Sangha Trust to send the sāmaṇeras he trained to the East for further study. When he returned to Thailand, he left a movement as firmly established, as is possible in this anicca world. We owe, and will continue to owe a debt of gratitude for his instruction in Dhamma."

ARRIVING AT BANGKOK ON NOVEMBER 22, Bhikkhu Paññāvaḍḍho proceeded to Cholapratan Monastery in the Rungsit district on the outskirts of Bangkok, settling into a new beginning under the guidance of the abbot, Ajaan Paññānanda, who had an excellent reputation as a scholar and teacher. Though near the capital, Cholapratan Monastery provided a quiet and secluded environment for his meditation practice while he searched for a way forward.

In April of the following year, at the height of the hot season, the tubercular arthritis in his right foot flared up, leaving it painfully swollen and inflamed, and unable to support his full weight. With the kind assistance of Ajaan Paññānanda, he was admitted to a hospital in Bangkok for treatment. By that time, an effective treatment for tuberculosis was readily available.

Streptomycin, following its 1943 discovery, became the first reliable cure for tuberculosis. The drug, which had been widely used in Thailand for many years, was administered in measured daily doses

taken continuously over a period of several months. To stabilize
Bhikkhu Paññāvaḍḍho's arthritic foot while the streptomycin took effect, his foot and calf were encased in a thick plaster cast, which was to
remain in place for the next seven months. Once again, he was given
a pair of underarm crutches to increase his mobility and help him remain active.

In June 1962, on a subsequent trip to Bangkok for a checkup, he
met the Thai mining engineer he had known in England, who told him
he had found many excellent Thai ajaans who could give him good
guidance. He described the story of Ajaan Mun Bhūridatto, who had
led a life of ascetic wandering and meditation practice in the vast wil-
dernesses that had once blanketed the northeast region of Thailand.
Ajaan Mun became a great teacher and exemplar of high standards of
conduct. Almost all of the accomplished and revered meditation masters of twentieth century Thailand were his direct disciples. Their lineage was known as the Thai Forest tradition.

The Thai Forest tradition was the branch of Theravāda Buddhism
that most faithfully held to the original monastic code laid down by
the Buddha. The Forest tradition also emphasized meditative practice
and striving for the realization of Nibbāna as the focus of monastic
life. Forest monasteries were primarily oriented toward practicing the
Buddha's path of contemplative insight, including living a life of renunciation, strict discipline and meditation in order to fully attain the
inner truth taught by the Buddha.

One particular teacher in that tradition had impressed the engineer very much. His name was Ajaan Mahā Boowa Ñāṇasampanno,
the abbot of Baan Taad Forest Monastery. At that time, Ajaan Mahā
Boowa's upajjhāya, the elderly monk who had officiated at his ordination, was lying deathly ill in a Bangkok hospital. Due to gratitude
and respect for his dying preceptor, he traveled often to Bangkok to
visit him. On those occasions, Ajaan Mahā Boowa preferred to stay
at Bovornives Monastery in central Bangkok. The engineer knew that

to be the case and kindly arranged to take Bhikkhu Paññāvaḍḍho to Bovornives Monastery to meet Ajaan Mahā Boowa.

The young English monk's first impression of Ajaan Mahā Boowa was striking. He saw an intense, wiry man with a dignified face who displayed the quick decisive movements of a boxer. He sat erect with a wide impassive expression that made him appear extremely grounded and stable. Having paid heartfelt respects, the engineer explained that his companion had come all the way from England seeking a teacher who could show him the true way. When Ajaan Mahā Boowa replied, his manner was gracious but somewhat aloof.

Ajaan Mahā Boowa spoke at length about the hardships of life as a forest monk and, perhaps because he saw Bhikkhu Paññāvaḍḍho's leg encased in plaster, voiced some skepticism that he would be able to put up with the rigors of forest life. The accommodations were rustic and the food was rough; there were the grueling extremes of heat, cold and damp; there was the daily grind of scrubbing, cleaning and hauling water; the barefoot walk to the village every day to collect alms food was a sacred duty that could not be neglected; and there were long draining hours of sitting and walking meditation to endure.

Bhikkhu Paññāvaḍḍho sat attentively and listened with respect, though he understood precious little of what was spoken. This was no obstacle, however: he liked Ajaan Mahā Boowa. He appreciated his demeanor and his straightforward approach to teaching. The force of his personality was magnetic. Suddenly, he felt a strong surge of reverence for the monk sitting calmly before him: he had a completeness about him that did not hanker after students. Bhikkhu Paññāvaḍḍho thought to himself, "You'll have to beg him to take you. Bow down and ask him to accept you."

Asking the engineer to translate, Ajaan Mahā Boowa advised him to use ānāpānasati to concentrate his mind and consolidate its strength. At times when he was not engaged in formal practice, he should strive to always keep his awareness within the confines of the body, thus preventing it from flowing out to external things. Practicing in that way safeguarded the mind and preserved its energy. Exactly what method was used to keep the mind within the body was not so important: it could be done by visualization or by feeling sensations or by allowing the mind to wander at will within the body. All of them were valid as long as they prevented the mind from escaping into external distractions. Lastly, he stressed the importance of maintaining mindfulness in every activity at all times.

Bhikkhu Paññāvaḍḍho left Bovornives Monastery invigorated by the Dhamma teaching and determined to pour that renewed energy back into his meditation practice. When he heard that Ajaan Mahā Boowa's preceptor had passed away in July, he was concerned that he might never see that remarkable teacher again.

The cast was finally removed from his leg in November. His inquiries about Ajaan Mahā Boowa led him to Bovornives Monastery once again, where he discovered that his esteemed teacher still occasionally traveled to Bangkok. Bhikkhu Paññāvaḍḍho subsequently paid his respects to Ajaan Mahā Boowa at Bovornives Monastery several more times. Each time, he asked permission to be accepted as a student at Baan Taad Forest Monastery. Concern about his recent health issues had made Ajaan Mahā Boowa reluctant to accept him at first. At their third meeting, Bhikkhu Paññāvaḍḍho decided to allay those concerns by requesting permission to visit Baan Taad Forest Monastery for a temporary stay. Ajaan Mahā Boowa granted that request. Many years later, Ajaan Mahā Boowa would say, with a chuckle, that Bhikkhu Paññāvaḍḍho asked to come for a temporary stay and he's been living here temporarily, for the last forty-one years!

ON THE EVENING OF FEBRUARY 15, 1963, Bhikkhu Paññāvaḍḍho boarded an overnight train bound for the Northeastern provincial city of Udon Thani. It was a journey of over 300 miles, lasting nearly ten hours. He was met at the Udon Thani train station by a lay supporter of Ajaan Mahā Boowa, who came in a dated and beat-up Land Rover to cheerfully drive him the remaining thirteen miles to his destination. At a certain point along the main highway, the Land Rover veered from the road and jostled down an earthen ramp, then bounced across dry and dusty rice fields. That was as close to the monastery as the provincial roads extended; the rest of the journey was across the flat, straw-stubbled paddy fields that stretched to the horizon. In the dry winter season, that makeshift road proved passable enough; but at the height of the monsoon season, when the rice fields flooded their embankments, that stretch of the journey required a dugout canoe with stout paddles.

Baan Taad Forest Monastery stood out against the skyline as they approached—a leafy island of green against the expansive background of parched fallow earth. Bhikkhu Paññāvaḍḍho was entering a secluded and quiet forest monastery in the lineage of Venerable Ajaan Mun Bhūridatto—a community of monastics who had left the life of ordinary society to live in the forest so as to be close to the natural environment that was the setting for the Buddha's own search for the Dhamma and provided inspiration for his Awakening.

Since the Buddha's time, monks have retreated into the depths of the forests and mountains, seeking physical seclusion to aid them in the development of meditation and realization of the sublime truth that the Buddha taught. Those monks lived lives of simplicity, austerity and diligence.

The Buddha himself was born in the forest and reached Awakening in the forest. He frequently dwelt in woodland regions, both during his noble quest and after his Awakening. He taught in the wooded surroundings and passed away in a Sal grove between giant twin trees. In the Pāli discourses, the Buddha often instructed his disciples to seek out the seclusion of forest dwellings as the places most conducive to purifying the mind of all defilement.

Bhikkhu Paññāvaḍḍho was escorted to just such a dwelling: a small wooden hut, or kuti, nestled in a wooded spot behind the main assembly hall. Firmly built and simple in design, the kuti blended naturally into the forest setting. The structure stood about three feet above the ground and was surrounded by a smooth, well-swept area of sandy soil. A path for walking meditation extended east to west along the rear.

Although the design of the kuti was well suited to the sub-tropical climate, it produced countless cracks and crevices, nooks and crannies, which were inhabited by a host of sentient beings. No screens covered the shuttered windows. When they were open—which was most of the time—an astonishing array of insects intruded. Bats flitted overhead and small lizards scurried across the walls and ceiling, catching mosquitoes and other flying insects.

The monastery's appearance differed from Bhikkhu Paññā-vaḍḍho's expectations. He had imagined a virgin forest, harboring wild animals, like tigers and elephants. But the forest he found was somewhat tame and hospitable. Dozens of small wooden huts stood on scattered clearings throughout its sixty-three acres. The only wild animals he met were tree squirrels, snakes and lizards. The pristine wilderness that once blanketed the countryside had long since disappeared as the land was cleared for cultivation. The forest that remained within the monastery's domain was only a remnant of that primary wilderness. The big cats, too, were only a memory, although tigers and leopards had occasionally wandered among the monks' huts when the monastery was first built.

Despite these changes, Baan Taad was an exemplary forest monastery, rich in the ancient traditions of Buddhist practice, and untouched by modern conveniences, such as electricity and running water. The monks lived with nature in simple solitude. Candlelight illuminated their hours of darkness. Water was drawn by hand and carried from the well to all the dwellings in pairs of water buckets, suspended from a long bamboo pole that was balanced on the carrier's shoulder. The water was used for bathing and laundering. During the monsoon months, rainwater was collected for drinking and stored in tanks and barrels. In the dry seasons, well water had to suffice.

The simple lifestyle encouraged contentment in living with little. Inside the kuti, Bhikkhu Paññāvaḍḍho's possessions were spare: a klot—the large forest umbrella that could be fitted with a mosquito net—a grass mat, a blanket, an alms bowl, lower, inner and outer robes and a few other small necessities. Practicing contentment with little meant forgoing many of the comforts and conveniences normally associated with pleasant living.

Confining oneself to the barest of material needs is at the heart of the Buddha's teachings. Conditions in life constantly change; they are ultimately unreliable and disappointing as a basis of happiness. Lasting happiness can be found only in a heart that has overcome the mental defilements of greed, hatred and delusion. These corrosive influences create strong attachment to comfort and convenience—conditional states that fluctuate and change, and in turn, bring on dissatisfaction and suffering. To stem the flow of misplaced desires, forest monks shunned unnecessary conveniences. Set on penetrating the heart of the Dhamma taught by the Lord Buddha, monks confined their requisites to the minimum.

Early each morning, the monks walked a two-mile route to the village and back for their morning alms round. As the pace was likely to be too quick for Bhikkhu Paññāvaḍḍho, a separate alms round had been arranged for him inside the monastery's perimeter. To relieve the strain on his ailing foot, he was required to walk only two hundred yards to the kitchen area where the resident nuns faithfully placed small packets of cooked food in his alms bowl.

The monks ate very simple foods: mostly sticky rice, supplemented with fish, vegetables and fruits. Bhikkhu Paññāvaḍḍho had expected the local food to be mostly unpalatable. But, apart from sometimes being too spicy or consisting too much of fish, he was surprised to find it generally plentiful and nutritious. In terms of food value, it was probably better than what he had been offered in Bangkok. And the spicy fare added character to the lumps of sticky rice!

Bhikkhu Paññāvaḍḍho still struggled with fluent communication in spoken Thai. During his sojourn in London, he taught himself to read and write Thai; but after a year of living in Thailand, he still lacked proficiency in distinguishing the tonal sounds and their meanings. That shortcoming made dialogue with Ajaan Mahā Boowa and the other monks challenging. Ajaan Mahā Boowa remedied the problem by writing out his instructions in Thai script for his student to translate into English. It was a somewhat time-consuming process, and not entirely satisfactory; but it created a close rapport between teacher and student which would develop with time into a strong bond, grounded in trust. Bhikkhu Paññāvaḍḍho resolved from the start to believe wholeheartedly in his teacher. He never found reason to regret that trust.

Bhikkhu Paññāvaḍḍho carefully saved those initial hand-written instructions from his teacher and reread them whenever he sought inspiration. One of them read:

"Baan Taad Forest Monastery is a meditation community. We are meditation monks. Since its beginning, this monastery has been dedicated solely to mind development. No other type of work is allowed to disturb the peaceful environment here. If other work must be done, I've made a rule that it take up no more time than is absolutely necessary.

"Your primary work as a meditation monk was given to you on the day of your ordination. In that ceremony, you were told to contemplate five things: kesā—hair of the head; loma—hair of the body; nakhā—nails; danta—teeth; and taco—the skin that encases the body. These five parts of the body taught during the ordination ceremony should become your meditation subjects. It's up to you to contemplate them and develop them in your meditation to the best of your ability. This is the true work for those monks who practice according to the principles of Dhamma that were taught by the Lord Buddha."

In another, he spoke of monastic harmony:

"It is wrong to watch other monks with an aim to find fault. This attitude will do nothing to help your practice. It is not your job to criticize other monks, even when they behave improperly. Observe the annoyance that arises in your own heart instead. Wisdom does not arise from blaming others for their faults. It arises from seeing your own faults. The monastic discipline is training in restraint of body, speech and mind that is designed to complement the meditation practice. Treat it with respect by constantly being mindful of your own behavior."

Bhikkhu Paññāvaḍḍho resolved that his first task was to adopt an appropriate monastic attitude; the second was to deport himself with proper monastic demeanor; the third was to speak purposefully, not frivolously, just chatting away about meaningless things.

Thai people had a penchant for brevity, especially with names and colloquial expressions. Most monks in the greater Thai Sangha were referred to by their given names rather than their formal Pāli names. Given names were usually reduced to simple nicknames of one or two syllables. The rather long and formal name Bhikkhu Paññāvaḍḍho proved a mouthful for monks used to more casual forms of address. Ajaan Mahā Boowa soon remedied that by shortening his name from Paññāvaḍḍho to just Paññā or Wisdom, a strong name and one very much in character. He preceded it with the honorific Tan, a common

Thai expression of respect. From that time on, Bhikkhu Paññāvaḍḍho was known as simply Tan Paññā, meaning Venerable Wisdom.

It soon became obvious to Tan Paññā that Ajaan Mahā Boowa was very demanding of his disciples. He was on their case constantly with strictness severe enough to provoke fear and dread. He lived up to his reputation as being an uncompromisingly fierce teacher. Tan Paññā, who fully believed in his teacher, knew instinctively that he would never instruct his disciples with harmful intent. He reasoned that when Ajaan Mahā Boowa used harsh or abusive language with his students, the words were spoken with a deeper purpose. They may cut his students to the bone, but as a consequence, the words would arouse them to alertness and force a sharp inward focus. He was prying their hearts open so the Dhamma could penetrate deeply.

Ajaan Mahā Boowa always had his eye on the potential of his disciples. When he saw that a monk possessed strong virtuous roots, he made a constant effort to prepare a fertile environment for his growth in the Dhamma. Tan Paññā realized that Ajaan Mahā Boowa believed in what he could become in the future, despite the fact that his Buddhist practice had not yet matured. Ajaan Mahā Boowa worked compassionately with his new pupil, day in and day out, to raise the level of his meditation to a higher, more stable plane.

Supported by his unflagging belief in Ajaan Mahā Boowa, Tan Paññā resolved to work things out for himself, diligently and without complaint. He felt he must strive to solve his own problems before seeking advice. Only in that way could he test the boundaries of his own wisdom. If he faltered, he knew his teacher would be there to help him expand those boundaries. Ultimately, having faith in Ajaan Mahā Boowa and in the Forest tradition was to believe in the unbounded wisdom of the Buddha, Dhamma and Sangha.

Capable of solving nearly all problems by himself, Tan Paññā approached Ajaan Mahā Boowa only occasionally with questions about his practice. He also gained a deeper understanding of meditation by

listening to Ajaan Mahā Boowa's spoken expositions on Dhamma practice, and by reading printed copies of his formal discourses. Drawing
from his experience, Ajaan Mahā Boowa tended to address the problems of his students while he spoke, giving them an answer even before they asked their question. Often, there was very little need to ask
explicitly.

In the seclusion of his kuti at Baan Taad Forest Monastery, Tan
Paññā continued to work with ānāpānasati to deepen his samādhi
meditation. He sensed that his calm and concentration still lacked sufficient depth. His mind inclined naturally toward thinking and reasoning, signaling a predisposition toward wisdom. His teacher encouraged
him to think of samādhi as a tool that one forged to prepare the ground
for investigating various aspects of Dhamma. He must avoid placing
too much emphasis on forging the tool, thereby neglecting the work.
Once the tool was ready, he must quickly learn its most effective use.
Eventually, Tan Paññā resolved to exploit his existing resources of calm
and concentration to probe the Dhamma for deeper insights—a strategy which achieved satisfying results.

In the tropical forests of northeastern Thailand, things grew quickly and decayed quickly. The forest paths, when left untended, soon
disappeared from sight under a profusion of weeds and bushes. Even
simple bamboo dwellings did not last long. Looking out his window
into the jungle-like forest, the verdant flora appeared entwined with
broadleaved creepers that grew up to six inches a day in the humid
heat. The wild vegetation had to be continually hacked back, or it could
swallow up the monks' residences within six months. Even with vigor-
ous hacking, Tan Paññā thought that somehow wild nature would win.

The secluded environment of Baan Taad monastery soothed the
heart and gave peace of mind. Tan Paññā had no access to newspapers
or radio, and so remained blissfully unaware of events happening in the
world, supposing them to be the same as before—strikes, riots, wars.
Those events no longer impinged on his awareness. However, when a

snake found its way into his hut, which seemed to happen quite often, his awareness lit on an event of vital importance. Although the atmosphere in the monastery was tranquil, with few worldly concerns, it was not an easygoing atmosphere. The self-awareness required by the monastic discipline and the constant reminder of Ajaan Mahā Boowa's presence and instructions, brought intensity and the immediacy of the Dhamma into almost every situation.

One day, quite spontaneously, the sounds of spoken Thai fell into place with the written language that Tan Paññā had mastered in his translation work in England. Because of his ear's unfamiliarity with the strange tones and vowels of Thai, he had been unable to connect articulate sounds with their intended meanings. Suddenly, after living in Thailand for over a year, a gear appeared to click in his mind, allowing an effortless connection between sound and meaning. It was like discerning a language after living among only its sounds. Hearing Ajaan Mahā Boowa speak, the meaning of his words emerged along with the voice. From that moment on, his Thai verbal language skills developed in conjunction with the spoken word, giving him the latitude he needed to converse clearly with his teacher and his fellow monks.

At that time, the instructions of the Thai Forest masters remained largely an oral tradition of spontaneous discourses and impromptu teachings. They were generally not written down or recorded. Ajaan Mahā Boowa, for instance, delivered spontaneous Dhamma talks to his disciples on a regular basis. His discourses usually took place in the cool of the evening, in an open-air pavilion with candles illuminating the shrine as darkness descended on the assembled monks. The silence was broken only by the incessant sounds of cicadas droning in the surrounding jungle.

Ajaan Mahā Boowa observed a few moments of stillness as he gathered the Dhamma and then let it flow naturally from his heart. As the theme of his talk unfolded with unrehearsed spontaneity, the pace of his voice quickened and took on increased intensity, leaving his listeners transported by the strength and depth of his teaching. Ajaan Mahā Boowa spoke of the realization of Dhamma in terms so graphic and electric that his listeners felt they were catching a glimpse of the splendor of Awakening. His teachings resonated with the listener right there in the present moment. The talks were later remembered as much for their immediate emotional impact as for their clear and comprehensive specifics.

A desire grew among Ajaan Mahā Boowa's disciples to preserve his oral teachings for the benefit of other practitioners, now and in the future. Listening to his teachings would have a positive impact on their practice and on that of future generations. A lay supporter had offered the monastery a large Grundig TK reel-to-reel magnetic tape recorder, which none of the monks could operate with the required skill. Tan Paññā, with his practical knowledge of electrical engineering, volunteered to take on the responsibility of recording his teacher's spoken discourses. Thus began one of the most prolific bodies of Dhamma recordings ever compiled by one teacher. From open reels to cassette tapes to digital recorders, Tan Paññā utilized the latest sound recording techniques to capture thousands of hours of the most precious Dhamma discourses over a period spanning four decades. Thanks to the tireless efforts of an Englishman who gave up a career in electrical engineering to become a simple Buddhist monk, the extensive range of Ajaan Mahā Boowa's discourses on the Buddha's teaching has been expertly preserved for future generations.

Tan Paññā always made a special effort to listen with open and serious attention to Ajaan Mahā Boowa's spoken discourses, seeking to absorb at least something of the diverse levels of meaning they contained. He discovered that listening to Ajaan Mahā Boowa expound on the Dhamma was a far more difficult practice than he had imagined. To listen truly, so that the act of listening itself becomes a meditation practice, meant emptying his mind completely of the thoughts and ideas that pervaded his mental and intellectual being. It required letting go of all the knowledge, all the views, all the concepts and prejudices filling his head. When he emptied his mind and really listened to the teaching with an open and receptive heart, he found that the power of his teacher's Dhamma penetrated slowly and steadily, clearing away the mental barriers preventing his progress. The mysterious potency of the spoken word was a revelation to him.

Of course, he needed far more than the spoken truth to dissolve all his doubts. Wisdom, of the sort that can pierce through all falsehood to penetrate the mind and heart, would take time and perseverance to develop. Along with steadfast concentration, he had to bring this development to bear on a comprehensive investigation of the entire teaching until he could experience the deep coherence and harmony underlying all the diverse aspects of the Buddha's Dhamma.

At the time of Tan Paññā's first retreat during the rainy season— or rains retreat—Ajaan Mahā Boowa hinted that he would warmly welcome other Western practitioners who came to learn meditation. On one occasion, he also casually hinted that he might one day travel to England. Tan Paññā was somewhat taken aback, thinking he was either being polite, or perhaps joking. But then Ajaan Mahā Boowa started coming to him for daily English lessons. He made a habit of spending half an hour each day learning English at Tan Paññā's kuti, memorizing the short English sentences which his student read out for him. Tan Paññā began to sense that, in dropping these hints, his teacher was foreseeing what could take place in the future.

Watching Ajaan Mahā Boowa's dynamic interaction with his disciples—many of whom were senior monks—Tan Paññā began to discern the kind of image they had of their teacher. They harbored an unspoken yet unequivocal belief that he was an arahant, a fully enlightened being. They respected his impeccable wisdom and his brilliant expository skills so highly that they gave the impression that it was beyond their power to equal him.

Tan Paññā approached the view that his teacher was an arahant with characteristic caution. He knew it was unreasonable to assume that the ordinary person could distinguish the difference between the stages of higher attainment. That considered, he also felt that they could be right in their assessment since he saw nothing in his teacher's demeanor to disprove the idea of his being an arahant. He saw in Ajaan Mahā Boowa a man who displayed no conceit, always appearing either cheerful and happy, or neutral and detached. He exhibited tireless energy, and his countenance was always bright and without blemish.

At the conclusion of one of their daily English lessons, Tan Paññā took the opportunity to broach the topic of his uncertainty about his teacher's reputation as an arahant. In his reply, Ajaan Mahā Boowa did not comment on his own attainment; instead, he turned the subject into a Dhamma lesson for his young pupil:

> "As Buddhists we have no valid reason to doubt our own potential for attaining magga, phala and Nibbāna in this lifetime. In fact, we would not be true Buddhists if we did not believe in the potential for enlightenment. The Buddha himself stated that as long as human beings practice correctly in line with the Noble Eightfold Path, arahants will continue to emerge in the world. In the suttas, the Buddha speaks often of the rewards to be gained by those who follow the path to Nibbāna. He tells of the happiness that comes from practicing generosity; the happiness that comes from living according to principles of virtue; the happiness that comes from developing loving kindness; the happiness that comes from practicing meditation and discovering the sublime tranquility of samādhi; the happiness that comes from overcoming the kilesas and abandoning suffering.
>
> "Those levels of happiness can be accomplished by anyone through the correct practice of Dhamma. Personally verify-

ing the Buddha's fundamental teachings in that way makes it easier to accept the possibility that the highest of his teachings is equally true—including his teaching that the supreme happiness of Nibbāna is accessible to everyone who practices the Noble Eightfold Path with unwavering diligence and insightful wisdom.

"Nowhere in the Pāli Canon does it state that the Buddha took the path to Nibbāna with him when he departed this world. On the contrary, the Buddha clearly proclaimed that the Dhamma and Vinaya he left behind were to be our guides along the Noble Eightfold Path. The Dhamma and Vinaya that we inherited from the Buddha are in no way deficient. They are just as complete and valid today as they were when he taught them 2,500 years ago. If Dhamma and Vinaya are faithfully put into practice with utmost sincerity and determination, nothing in the realm of saṁsāra is capable of preventing the result of ultimate happiness from arising in the mind.

"Today, many people are born with enough good kamma to come into contact with Buddhism and to study the Buddha's teachings as they were handed down in their entirety. There is no reason why people with enough merit and intelligence cannot put what the Buddha taught into practice for their own benefit and the benefit of living beings everywhere. It is only the defilements in our hearts and minds that prevent us from undertaking that task. Removing those defilements is the purpose of the Buddha's path of practice.

"When the defilements are strong, the path is weak, which causes us to have faith in the ways of the world more than the ways of Dhamma. The worldly outlook says that practicing the Buddha's teaching for the sake of attaining Nibbāna is too difficult; and because we want to avoid suffering and hardship in our lives, we claim that it is no longer possible. By taking that attitude, we avoid feeling guilty about not making the effort. And because of that, when we hear that someone else has aroused great effort and attained arahantship we don't want to believe it's true.

"But the suffering we experience in our lives goes to the heart of the Buddha's first noble truth, a truth that we must strive to examine and understand. Instead, people feel uncomfortable when they are told about the noble truth of suffering, and shy away from its profound implications. This attitude simply shows that people do not have enough knowledge of Buddhism to understand its true aims. The Buddha's teaching on suffering is completely in line with the way things really are. This is why it is called a "noble truth." Suffering is a basic principle of Buddhism because it is true.

"The Buddha was a person who truly knew the reason for suffering, which is why he taught people not to simply avoid pain and suffering—which are effects—but to get rid of the causes, the defilements that bring them about. Those defilements make up the Buddha's second noble truth, the origin of suffering. When the causes are eliminated, the effects cease of their own accord. The Buddha starts out with suffering in order to point out the evidence that establishes the truth, so that we can search out the causes and correct them in the proper way.

"The third noble truth, the cessation of suffering, is the ending of pain and suffering within the heart through the power of our practice of the path, which is the fourth noble truth. The path of practice refers to the methods used to cut away the causes of suffering, step by step, until all have been eliminated.

"All of the noble truths that the Buddha taught were meant to free living beings from suffering. Not a single noble truth directs us to remain mired in a world of suffering. The Buddha taught the noble truths so that people would become wise enough to entirely rid themselves of suffering and attain Nibbāna. He did not restrict his message to any age, race, gender or time period. Nor did he deny the attainment of the fruits of this path to anyone of any generation. Instead, he said that the Dhamma is timeless, existing beyond time and space. It is, therefore, just as relevant in this day and age as it ever was.

"When magga, phala and Nibbāna are viewed as being beyond the reach of modern man, it is we who are at fault for neglecting our duty as Buddhists to strive for the highest goal. When it comes to Dhamma, we too easily settle for mere philosophical inquiry over practical action. We become opinionated bookworms vainly chewing at pages of the Tipiṭika while we insist on holding tenaciously to the Dhamma we have learned by rote. This happens because we cannot be bothered to make an effort to investigate the supreme noble truths that are an integral part of our very own being. Instead, we mistakenly appropriate the great wealth of the Lord Buddha's words as our own personal property. Simply because we have memorized his Dhamma teachings, we believe we are wise enough already, even though the defilements filling our hearts are piled as high as a mountain and have not diminished in the least.

"Many of us find justification for our views in the very Pāli scriptures that were used to proclaim the Buddha's timeless message. Students of the Pāli scriptures tend to believe that the written texts comprise the sum total of all aspects of Dhamma. They self-righteously assert that scriptural doctrine and convention are the only legitimate criteria for authenticating all of the countless experiences known to Buddhist practitioners over the ages. But the true Dhamma arises in the hearts and minds of those who put the living teaching into practice here and now in the present. Consider the Lord Buddha and his arahant disciples, for instance. They knew and thoroughly understood Dhamma long before the Pāli texts appeared. Clearly, they achieved their exalted status at a time when no scriptures existed to define the parameters of Dhamma for them.

"The true Dhamma is always the Dhamma of the present moment. Time and place are merely mundane conventional concepts that are incapable of affecting the Dhamma of the Lord Buddha in any way. For that reason, those who practice the Buddha's teaching correctly are entitled to know for themselves all those aspects of Dhamma that fall within the range of their own natural abilities, regardless of what age or century they live in."

The more Tan Paññā observed his teacher, the more convinced he was that he could not have chosen a more competent master. Ajaan Mahā Boowa exhibited no flaws in his approach to Dhamma. He seemed to intuit the mistakes in a student's practice with great facility and correct those faults more through the charismatic force of his presence than through conversation.

Tan Paññā now understood why the Forest tradition placed such a sacred emphasis on the relationship between teacher and disciple: that relationship was essential to the living transmission of Dhamma, from mind to mind, from heart to heart. He realized that without Ajaan Mahā Boowa's guidance, the possibility of him realizing the truth of the teachings would have been severely limited.

The more he reflected on faith and its overall place in the teachings, the more deeply Tan Paññā realized that faith is essentially a skillful means of making one more receptive to the truth expressed in the teacher's words. Viewing his teacher as a living master enabled him to listen unreservedly to the teaching and put it into practice with the greatest possible commitment. Tan Paññā's conviction in Ajaan Mahā Boowa translated into total respect for the Dhamma embodied in his teacher and conveyed through him. The greater his faith, the more open to the teachings he became; the more open he was to the teachings, the greater the opportunity for them to penetrate deeply into his heart.

He now felt strongly that these same teachings could greatly benefit the people in England whom he had spent so much time teaching and whom he had now left behind. His attempts at teaching them had lacked a firm compass bearing in the direction of the highest good, the supreme happiness, Nibbāna. It was for this reason, no doubt, that his teaching had achieved such limited results. He now saw that practitioners needed to perceive how each step on the path interlocks to form the pattern of the whole teaching. Otherwise, they will meander on an eclectic journey, missing all the important way stations along the path. They need a clear-cut and unambiguous formula for advancement. He felt that Ajaan Mahā Boowa laid out the progressive steps so persuasively as to convince even the most skeptical practitioners of their validity.

Concerned with the spiritual welfare of English Buddhists, Tan Paññā resolved to translate Ajaan Mahā Boowa's basic teachings on meditation practice into English. He chose to start with a concise exposition written by Ajaan Mahā Boowa entitled "Wisdom Develops Samādhi." The text explains how to subdue and discipline an unruly mind by first cultivating moral virtue, then focusing and strengthening the mental faculties, using various concentration techniques, before investigating with wisdom to search out the reasons for the mind's misguided cravings. Thus, the meditator must make use of his own ingenuity in finding a means to train the rebellious mind until it sees in line with the truth as proclaimed by the Lord Buddha.

Tan Paññā hoped to have the translation published serially by the Buddhist Publication Society in Kandy, Sri Lanka as part of their Wheel series. But when the first draft was sent, the editor objected to what he deemed unorthodox passages in the text and insisted that those passages be corrected to reflect scriptural orthodoxy. He specifically objected to the unconventional view summarized in the exposition's title. In the discourse, Ajaan Mahā Boowa states that if the mind cannot be stilled in the traditional way, by concentrating it on a meditation-word, then wisdom must be used to search out the reasons for the mind's unruliness. If the unruly mind can be stilled by investigating with wisdom, then wisdom should be used for the development of concentration. Even more objectionable to the editor was a unique, perhaps, but essential aspect of Ajaan Mahā Boowa's teaching: the uncommon view that the knowing mind existed separately from the mental aggregates that comprised all transient states of mind.

Tan Paññā was familiar with canonical orthodoxy and might himself have objected to those apparent "heresies" at one time. But through direct insight, he had come to accept their validity. With all due respect to the Buddhist Publication Society, he felt he could not possibly alter a single word of the text he had translated. To do so would be to negate the very truth that he had traveled so far and worked so hard to realize. He would simply have to find another means to publish the manuscript. Eventually, in 1967, his supporters in England printed "Wisdom Develops Samādhi" as a booklet, and distributed copies as free gifts of the Dhamma.

BAAN TAAD FOREST MONASTERY BELONGED to the Dhammayut sect of the Thai monastic order. Dhammayut had its beginnings in 1833, as a reform movement that placed greater emphasis on the monastic discipline and the meditation practices found in the original Pāli texts. It held monks to a strict interpretation of their monastic obligations, intending to restore proper orthodox practices in the Thai Sangha. In its push to institute strict compliance with the rules, the Dhammayut movement was eventually recognized as a separate sect or *nikāya*. The original Thai monastic order, from which Dhammayut separated, became known as the Mahānikāya. This was the sect under which Tan Paññā had originally ordained, and to which he still belonged.

Ajaan Mahā Boowa was gladly willing to teach Mahānikāya monks like Tan Paññā, but insisted that they fully observe the Vinaya while studying with him. He also strictly observed the Dhammayut directive not to include Mahānikāya monks in the Pāṭimokkha recitation, which was a formal monastic meeting and thus was limited to the members of the same denomination. That restriction applied to Tan Paññā, who was prohibited from taking part in the formal recitation of the monastic rules.

Once it became apparent that Tan Paññā's "temporary" residence would, in fact, be a long-term one, Ajaan Mahā Boowa preferred to see him become a full member of his monastic community. Upon his teacher's request, Tan Paññā decided to formally ask for a second ordination in the Dhammayut sect. Although he was not obliged to part with his monastic robes to achieve that status, he was required to relinquish the nine years of seniority that he had accrued as a Mahānikāya monk. As a newly-ordained Dhammayut monk, he would start afresh at the most junior level.

Tan Paññā traveled to Bangkok together with his teacher and re-ordained in the Dhammayut Nikāya on April 22, 1965 at Bovornives Monastery, the very same temple where he had first met Ajaan Mahā Boowa three years earlier. Somdet Phra Ñāṇasaṁvara, abbot of Bovornives Monastery, presided over his ordination ceremony as upajjhāya. His kammavācariya instructor was Phra Thep Ñāṇakavi and his anusāsanācariya instructor was Ajaan Mahā Boowa. Ordained with him in the same ceremony was a young Canadian who had lived as a novice at Baan Taad Forest Monastery for the past year.

Tan Paññā returned from Bangkok a monk of junior rank, but now a full member of his monastic community. Because he had been a member in good standing of the community for so long, his monastic routine changed little. Normally, junior monks were expected to undertake the most basic duties and perform them with energy and humility. But, because of his age—at thirty-nine, Tan Paññā was a decade or two older than most of the other junior monks—and his educational background, his responsibilities evolved over time to include more sophisticated tasks dealing with the practical application of engineering principles. He soon found himself drawn into a lengthy and arduous undertaking.

In recent years, the local villagers had been clear-cutting the forest closer and closer to the edges of the monastery's property. As there was no established boundary line, Ajaan Mahā Boowa was concerned that they might inadvertently encroach upon monastery land. In order to safeguard against unwelcome intrusions, Ajaan Mahā Boowa determined that the exact location of the boundary line should be fixed and a perimeter fence erected along its full length. He enlisted Tan Paññā's help to supervise the project.

Although Tan Paññā understood the principles involved in land surveying and knew the types of instruments required, he himself had never performed that type of work before. Living in the forest without access to standard technology, he would have to improvise. First, he took a few monks with him to walk the perimeter of the monastery, at least three quarters of which was densely overgrown. With machete-wielding villagers leading the way, four hours were needed to trek around the mile-and-a-half-long perimeter. Tan Paññā remarked drily that he felt like Stanley plunging through the impenetrable African jungles.

Although his foot ached from the strain and he felt frustrated at times with the inconvenience of the workload, he exhibited a calm acceptance of everything that came his way. From a source of inner quiet, he understood that faith in his teacher meant that he must accept without objections; that he must agree to undertake the project, no matter how difficult it might seem. Should he be told to do something he had never before attempted, he must never, under any circumstances, refuse to accept the challenge. Instead, all of his concentrated effort must be dedicated to the task, no matter how much time it took. With a firm belief in the teacher and the training, he carefully worked up a plan and executed it himself, without complacency or complaint. Many people shunned activities that aroused adversity, but Tan Paññā refused to regard such work as a hardship.

To properly ascertain the shape of the monastery and record those features on a map for future reference, he painstakingly constructed, from his limited stock of materials, a conventional surveying instrument with a rotating telescope that measured horizontal and vertical angles. Once the device was assembled to his exacting specifications, he proceeded to survey the boundary. It was a laborious undertaking that took many weeks in the dense forest and tangled vegetation. With the survey map as a guide, post holes were dug at intervals and a sturdy fence was erected around the monastery's perimeter.

With the boundary fence completed, an additional project came his way. The nuns who lived in the monastery's kitchen compound were in urgent need of a new pavilion. He was feeling exhausted and his foot swelled menacingly from too much standing; but he patiently resolved to accept the added burden with a smile. In sincere and hearty appreciation for his teacher's liberating wisdom, he would carry every assignment through without complaint.

The original pavilion in the nuns' quarters had been constructed by splitting sections of bamboo lengthwise, spreading them out flat, and securing them to a bamboo frame suspended from tall posts and covered with a thatched roof. The thatch was now so moldy from dampness and the bamboo so weak from termite damage that it was ready to fall down under its own weight. Tan Paññā employed his draftsman's skills to draw up plans for a new structure to take its place. Unlike its predecessor, the new pavilion was large and massively strong: a broad hardwood floor supported by twenty-nine great hardwood posts mounted atop concrete blocks. The corrugated tin roof covering the entire structure looked out of place in that sylvan environment, but it would cut down mightily on future repair work.

Most of the monks in the monastery also lived in simple quarters of bamboo platforms with thatched roofs. Cloth curtains hung between the posts to serve as "walls." One such platform was constructed for each monk, and each platform was spaced far enough apart from the others to afford adequate privacy. The thick foliage between each platform acted as a natural screen. Local villagers helped to clear a walking meditation track alongside each platform. There, the monks practiced walking meditation, often for many hours each day. Standing erect and alert with hands joined just below the waist, they would pace from one end of the path to the other in quiet contemplation.

A series of foot trails connected the monks' simple dwellings to one another and to the main meeting hall or *sala*. The sala was a plain building, an open-walled post-and-beam structure that served as the main center for group activities. It was the setting for a variety of monastic functions: every morning the monks gathered under its roof to eat their one daily meal; the monks congregated in that space to listen to the teacher's instructions; and monks and lay devotees used the room for special religious ceremonies. Built of hardwood, the sala was a rectangular building, raised above the ground on wooden posts to a height of five feet. The floor—also made of hardwood and highly polished—was constructed in three levels. The Buddha image illuminated the hall from a broad, raised platform at the back of the building. The area immediately surrounding the sala was swept immaculately clean each afternoon, and kept clear of vegetation.

The most anticipated gatherings in the sala were Ajaan Mahā Boowa's evening Dhamma talks, delivered spontaneously to a full assembly of monks and novices. These monastic gatherings were unscheduled and unannounced beforehand. On these occasions, Ajaan Mahā Boowa strode from his kuti to the sala at dusk and informed the duty monk that a Sangha meeting would convene before dark. What ensued then was a race against time, as the duty monk dashed through the forest, spreading the word to every corner of the monastery. All of the resident monks were expected to be formally robed and seated before their teacher ascended the sala steps at the appointed time and took his place at the head of the assembly.

By 1968 the audience included a number of Westerners who had joined the Sangha at Baan Taad Forest Monastery since Tan Paññā's arrival. Because their Thai language skills were limited, Ajaan Mahā Boowa requested that Tan Paññā translate his talks into English for the group. He presented the gist of a discourse from memory immediately after his teacher finished speaking. Since the discourses often lasted well over an hour, he was usually only able to remember the highlights. Though not entirely satisfactory, he tried his best to convey the most important aspects of the night's teachings. By that time, he had been offered a new-model cassette tape recorder, which was lightweight and easy to carry. With that small device in hand, he religiously recorded every Dhamma exposition received by the monks in those evening sessions, recordings which could later be reviewed for a more thorough rendering.

Monks and lay people intent on the practice have always been inspired to study the words of the great teachers. Tan Paññā's recordings of Ajaan Mahā Boowa's discourses would come to be an invaluable resource. Tan Paññā took on the task of making formal English translations of many of those talks, with the hope that Ajaan Mahā Boowa's

Western students could benefit from their teacher's skillful guidance, and uncover the true nature of their own minds. He worked tirelessly, turning transcriptions of his teacher's talks into clear English, bringing Ajaan Mahā Boowa's Dhamma talks to his fellow monks, as well as to a wider Western readership.

Ajaan Mahā Boowa had never been a dogmatic teacher. He always stressed that one had to discover the truth for oneself, rather than merely relying on a learned explanation. He used words, ultimately, to direct people inward toward their own minds. When listening to the Dhamma, he often emphasized, one's primary focus should be on one's own mind, and not on the teacher's words. If you wish to truly experience a place you do not just read about it; you must step onto the path and travel there. In the same way, the practice of Dhamma is all about walking the noble path.

UPON COMPLETION OF THE NUNS' PAVILION and with the hot season fast approaching, Tan Paññā sought to advance another step along that noble path. He paid his respects to Ajaan Mahā Boowa and asked permission to move to another monastery for several months in order to deepen his commitment to the practice. Permission kindly granted, he set out one April morning for Khao Chin Lae Monastery, to the south in Lopburi province. He rode the slow day train to the end of the line, reaching the monastery just as dusk descended.

Limestone caves dotted the hills surrounding Khao Chin Lae Monastery. The caves were silent and comfortably cool in the extreme sub-tropical heat. For the first six weeks, Tan Paññā spent much of his time underground, until the start of the monsoon season, when the downpours rendered the underground grottoes uncomfortably damp. Most of the caves were so dark during the daylight hours that he needed candles and torches to move about. These large, dark caverns possessed a strange and eerie quality that elicited feelings of vastness, emptiness and deep silence. Timelessness occupied Tan Paññā's mind as he contemplated amidst the ancient stones. Many of the rocks still held fossils from the epoch when that plateau lay beneath the sea—a humbling thought, conducive to introspection. Reminded again that life is short and the time of death uncertain, he diligently applied himself to his meditation.

The silent stillness of the caves lifted Tan Paññā's whole being to a natural and dynamic state of rest, calm and concentration, freeing his mind to pose probing questions and search within for fresh discoveries. He kept probing: "What forces come into play at the heart of the human condition?"

Simply by being born on earth, people assume they are knowledgeable about the world around them. Human beings inhabit physical bodies composed of the same sort of stuff as rock and mud, wood and water. They share a belief that those material substances are ultimately real, that the physical realm is the world's sum total of what exists.

Reflecting on common materialistic views, he reasoned that such notions are programmed into human beings by the circumstances of their upbringing. Because our earliest experiences in life consist of material things in our immediate environment, it is hardly surprising that those objects should be considered "real."

The Buddha called such firmly-held beliefs *sammuti* or supposition—everyone supposes that their view of the world is true. They assume that the information their senses convey about the world around them represents a true picture of reality. They suppose all that, but they do not know it. Their confidence in these suppositions is largely based on the fact that everyone else supposes the same worldview, giving them no reason to seriously question that view's validity.

Reflecting that knowledge of the world comes through the five senses, Tan Paññā probed deeply into how the senses function. What occurred when he saw, heard, smelled, tasted or touched something? What did sights, sounds, odors, flavors and touches tell him about the

objects that he perceived? If everything he knew about the external
world came to him through his senses, did the world out there exist
apart from those sensations?

Incoming sensations were recognized and interpreted by the
mind, meaning that the perception of external objects actually arose in
the mind. The incoming sense data reflected the object, but the sense
data were not the same as the object. The sense organs picked up light
and color, waves and chemicals, heat and pressure—not the objects
themselves. Color and shape were filtered through memory to seek
images from the mind's database of previous experience in order to
recognize and interpret incoming sense impressions and thus place
them in context.

He reached the conclusion that he had no means of directly knowing an object in the world as distinguished from the colors and shapes
that arose in his field of vision. Because of that, he did not really know
the outside world at all. What he knew was the world inside his mind.
In other words, the mind knew only the effects caused by incoming
sense impressions, and the perceptions based on that knowledge composed the entire world of his experience. Tan Paññā was convinced
that memory was the linchpin in the cog that maintained coherence
in the process of perception. He saw that memory is a key component
of thinking and imagination, and by extension, of a person's perceived
place in the world. Visual and audible objects reveal their identity
only when compared to impressions stored in memory. The names
and shapes and forms given to things depend on the stored images
accumulated in memory, which constantly bring up analogies to previous experience. Without that recognition and process of association,
thought, speech and action would be incoherent.

Sense contact triggers pleasant and unpleasant feelings, but memory defines the distinctive quality of those feelings. Feelings arise based
on contact with forms, sounds, odors, flavors or tactile sensations.
Memory then tests the effects against past experience, resulting in a

reaction. When they compare favorably, the feeling is embraced as pleasant; when they compare unfavorably, it is rejected as unpleasant. The sense object evokes a desirable or an undesirable emotion accordingly. Liking and disliking are the two sides of craving, and craving causes the suffering that keeps living beings bound to the great cycle of repeated birth and death.

Tan Paññā concluded that the interplay between the senses, memory and feeling is an important dynamic playing out at the heart of the human condition, one that needs unraveling to reach the end of suffering. Everything in the world is seen as it is because living beings have repeatedly solidified their experience of inner and outer reality in the same way, lifetime after lifetime. That continuity of experience leads to the mistaken assumption that what they perceive is objectively real. As Tan Paññā progressed further along the Buddha's path, he learned how to work directly with such habitual perceptions. As his old concepts of the world gradually dissolved, a wholly new realm of perception started to open up.

The role memory played in perception was crucial—that appeared obvious to him. He was puzzled why English translations of the Pāli texts never mentioned memory. When he read Thai language translations of the same Pāli texts, the mental aggregate *saññā* was clearly referred to as memory. In English translations, the same word was invariably rendered as "perception." Although he saw the general reasoning behind that interpretation, he believed it overlooked the specific function of memory in the overall picture of perception. The true meaning of *saññākkhandha* would be much better served by the translation "aggregate of memory."

In general, Tan Paññā viewed many of the widely accepted translations of Pāli terms as artifacts handed down from early twentieth century scholars who pioneered the translation of Pāli texts into Western languages. Those early interpretations of the original Pāli had gone largely unchallenged. They were supposed to be correct because they came from a venerable and authoritative source. Certainly, in some cases, a revision was in order. He did not hold scholastic orthodoxy to be sacrosanct; traditional interpretations should always be examined in the light of direct experience.

TAN PAÑÑĀ RETURNED TO BAAN TAAD FOREST MONASTERY, refreshed and reinvigorated, just in time for the rainy season retreat. He resumed his duties, helping the Western monks and lay people who came to train there. The number of Western monks had grown to six: three English, two Americans and a Canadian. Tan Paññā continue to translate Ajaan Mahā Boowa's spoken discourses for them, at the same time working on written translations of some of his teacher's more salient Dhamma talks.

When the 1972 rains retreat ended, Ajaan Mahā Boowa requested Tan Paññā's assistance on another project. He asked him to design and oversee the construction of a new monk's residence. He envisioned a hardwood structure of spacious proportions containing a single room with an L-shaped veranda that connected to a bathroom. Stout posts supported the entire building four feet above the ground. Tan Paññā drafted the design and set to work, aided by several of his fellow monks and a few carpenters from the village. As the plans were his, he had to be present the whole time to make sure everything was done properly, which meant that he had virtually no spare time.

The project was already half completed when he heard a rumor that the kuti—being built with such attention to detail—was actually intended for him. Ajaan Mahā Boowa had yet to mention it publicly, but Tan Paññā was pleased by the prospect, because he felt that the site was one of the best locations in the monastery. The surrounding clumps of tangled bamboo effectively screened off the kuti from the rest of the monastery, giving the occupant a satisfying sense of seclusion. As was rumored, upon completion of the kuti, Ajaan Mahā

Boowa gave the word for Tan Paññā to move in. He would reside in that kuti for the rest of his life.

By the early seventies, an increasing number of Westerners—both monks and lay people—were drawn to the Thai Forest tradition, and many of them found their way to Baan Taad Forest Monastery. Through association with Tan Paññā, Ajaan Mahā Boowa was gaining notability among English Buddhists in particular. Some intrepid practitioners even journeyed all the way from England to do retreats at the monastery. Tan Paññā felt a special responsibility to introduce them to the practices of the Thai Forest tradition, which had reintroduced the ancient standards of Buddhist practice into contemporary monastic life. Accordingly, Tan Paññā familiarized them with the fundamentals of forest living, moral discipline and meditation as supporting principles in their search on the Buddha's path to enlightenment.

Since the Buddha's time, monks have retreated into the depths of forests and mountains, seeking physical isolation to help them develop their meditation practices so as to realize the truth to which the Buddha's teachings point. They lived a life of simplicity, austerity and dedication. The forests and mountains became the practitioner's equivalent of academies of higher learning, where monks, thoroughly trained in the Dhamma, dedicated themselves to becoming a living expression of the Buddha's teachings, thus making those teachings their own. Because that period of independent study was carried out in the solitude of the forest, the Dhamma they realized in their hearts and shared with their disciples came to be known as Forest Dhamma.

That ancient pathway was pristinely exemplified by forest teachers such as Ajaan Mahā Boowa, whose mode of practice emphasized the union of discipline and wisdom to forge a powerful medium for achieving the goals of Buddhist practice. While pointing to the ineffable mysteries of the mind's pure essence, his teachings also gave his disciples down-to-earth, practical methods that guided them at every stage of the path, up to the highest goals of Buddhist meditation. To capture the unique forest spirit of Ajaan Mahā Boowa's Dhamma and spread it throughout the English-speaking world, Tan Paññā spent several years translating his teacher's recorded discourses.

He put together a collection consisting of a select number of talks. When Tan Paññā finished translating a talk to be included in the collection, he would send the manuscript to England where his supporters at the Hampshire Buddhist Society published it for free distribution. At first the talks were published serially, as individual booklets. In 1972, all five talks, plus his earlier translation of "Wisdom Develops Samādhi," were published in a single volume, entitled "Forest Dhamma."

Tan Paññā received much encouragement and many invitations from Buddhists in England. Individuals and Buddhist organizations asked him on several occasions to return to England to establish a proper Sangha community. In attempts to persuade him, they offered all manner of huts, cabins and rural farm retreats for his use. He received many interesting offers, and he weighed each of them with measured caution. Although he was always willing to discuss the possibilities, he was never quite satisfied with the long-term prospects of these generous proposals.

He had not made a firm commitment to spending the rest of his life in Thailand. Yet, he felt a deep reluctance to abandon the security of his teacher for uncertain prospects back in his home country. Surely the cool climate of the English countryside was more favorable, and the living conditions more to his liking, but those were not valid reasons to forsake such favorable conditions for his training and return home. He saw no purpose in returning to England without having first completed the training and gained a rock-solid footing in the Dhamma. He saw that those who ordained in the East, training with a teacher only briefly before returning to the West, were invariably overwhelmed by the situation, and came to naught as teachers. Perhaps one day his mental fortitude would be firm enough to return. Until then, he would not take the risk.

Tan Paññā's potential sponsors were content to have him return to England alone to spread the Dhamma; but he was not confident enough in the fruits of his practice to seriously consider taking on that responsibility. He did, however, have a strong desire to bring the true Dhamma to those back in his home country. He hoped, therefore, to accompany Ajaan Mahā Boowa to England so that the Buddhist community could benefit from the rare opportunity to meet and listen to a monk of such exalted attainment. His teacher's persistence in studying English fortified Tan Paññā's belief in his teacher's willingness to make the long trip westward.

By 1972, the Dhammapadīpa Vihāra at Haverstock Hill (also known as Hampstead Vihāra), which operated under the auspices of the English Sangha Trust, was experiencing a shortage of resident monks. Since the charter of the English Sangha Trust expressly acknowledged its mission as being to support the Bhikkhu Sangha, a concerted effort began to find an English monk capable of fulfilling that role. Having had limited success at home, the directors of the English Sangha Trust decided in early 1974 to invite Ajaan Mahā Boowa to England for a visit, along with the monk they still remembered as Bhikkhu Paññāvaḍḍho. The directors of the Trust maintained the hope that Ajaan Mahā Boowa would allow his English disciple to remain in England as the new incumbent at the Dhammapadīpa Vihāra.

On June 8, 1974, Ajaan Mahā Boowa stepped off the plane in London, accompanied by Tan Paññā and Bhikkhu Abhiceto, the Canadian monk who had ordained with him nine years earlier. All three accepted accommodations at Dhammapadīpa Vihāra. As was the custom at their monastery in Thailand, the monks ate one meal a day early each morning, during which time public attendance was always welcome. Having received generous offerings of food and eaten the meal simply and without ceremony, Ajaan Mahā Boowa gave a brief talk on Dhamma practice, which was often followed by a lengthy question-and-answer session. Tan Paññā acted as his teacher's official translator for the entire visit.

Each evening, Ajaan Mahā Boowa delivered a discourse, followed by another question-and-answer session with those in attendance. Prominent members of the Buddhist scene in England, such as Christmas Humphreys and Maurice Walshe, came to pay their respects to this renowned teacher from the Thai Forest tradition, as did scores of Buddhist lay followers. The talks they heard were thought-provoking and inspiring. In deference to his teacher, Tan Paññā refrained from giving formal Dhamma talks, but he did make himself available to answer questions on practice.

For the most part, the visiting monks kept to that same schedule throughout the two weeks of their stay at the Dhammapadīpa Vihāra. As their departure for Thailand drew near, the directors of the English Sangha Trust approached Ajaan Mahā Boowa and requested him to allow Bhikkhu Paññāvaḍḍho to remain in England as a teacher, for the purpose of establishing an English Sangha in the United Kingdom.

Ajaan Mahā Boowa replied that in order to teach others, one must first clearly know the Dhamma for oneself. For the most part, he considered that those who had yet to see the true nature of Dhamma were unqualified to speak about it in front of other people. For that reason, he felt that Tan Paññā was not yet ready to assume the responsibility of a teacher. He did state, however, that it would not be long before the circumstances were ripe for the establishment of a properly qualified Bhikkhu Sangha in England. With that parting assurance, the visitors boarded a plane on June 22 for their return to Thailand.

Two years later, still diligently attempting to establish the Sangha in England, representatives of the English Sangha Trust traveled to Thailand. They intended to beseech Ajaan Mahā Boowa once again to sanction Tan Paññā's return to England, to become a mainstay for the English Sangha. When Ajaan Mahā Boowa refused a second time, they proceeded to Ajaan Chah's forest monastery in Ubon Ratchathani and begged for his kind assistance. The result of that request marks the beginning of the story of the English Sangha up to the present day.

AFTER RETURNING FROM ENGLAND, TAN PAÑÑĀ resumed in earnest the spiritual training that was his life's work. He was now forty-eight years old. In training the mind, the first requirement is to see directly and concretely how different aspects of the mind function in relation to the whole. By reflecting on the knowledge that he derived from listening to Ajaan Mahā Boowa's teachings, and combining that with his personal meditation experience, Tan Paññā probed ever more deeply into the nature of the mind itself. Working skillfully with mindfulness and wisdom, the focus of his awareness sharpened and became more adaptable to the mind's ever-changing landscape.

Ajaan Mahā Boowa referred often to "the one who knows," differentiating the knowing mind from the states of mind that arise and cease. Following the Thai vernacular, Tan Paññā began referring to the knowing mind as the "citta." The citta represented the very nature of mind, its innermost essence, which is absolutely and always untouched by change or death. The mind's true nature is normally hidden beneath layers of defilements and the mental confusion of thoughts and emotions. Occasionally, Tan Paññā uncovered glimpses of that essential nature of mind through meditative insight, thus gaining a deeper understanding and a profound sense of freedom.

Tan Paññā realized intuitively the importance of that stable unchanging essence. It was evident in his practice that mental phenomena came and went—arising and ceasing continually—at almost electric speed. If our awareness of these phenomena were to arise and vanish simultaneously at the same speed, there would be no stable "platform" from which that mental activity could be known or perceived. The mind in its entirety would be nothing more than a chaotic sea of random mental events, with no reliable continuum of awareness to connect them into thoughts, concepts and emotions. For the mind as a whole to function as it does, that platform must exist independently of all the changing phenomena that constitute mental activity.

Transient mental states being the prerogative of the four mental aggregates—feeling, memory, thought and consciousness—the knowing of them must take place outside of the sphere of their activity. However, Tan Paññā realized, that knowing nature was not pure or unblemished. It was permeated by corruptive elements, which distorted the view of the knower and the perception of what was known. The Buddha called these corrupting influences "kilesas." Because one's knowing was corrupted from within by kilesas, one's knowledge of mental activity could not be trusted or true.

Tan Paññā saw clearly that the real enemy was inside. The creator of trouble, the source of all suffering, the destroyer of joy and virtue existed inside of us. Kilesas had a most slippery and unsettling presence in the mind, and they possessed an air of danger which sometimes seemed more charged and intense than any external threat. The kilesas were cunning, greedy, hateful and expert in the games of deception. Under their defiling influence, the chaotic, confused and undisciplined mind again and again fell victim to death and rebirth.

But what was it that died, and what was reborn? Tan Paññā's investigations returned to the citta, the innermost essence of mind. If the citta was the essence of being that wandered from birth to birth, that would explain how the fruits of one's actions were carried along from life to life, to ripen in the future. When corrupted by defilements, the citta manipulated the body and mind to plant the seeds of wholesome and unwholesome actions. It then reaped pleasure or pain as a consequence.

The citta, in a sense, was the foundation of saṁsāra, the round of repeated birth and death. Without the citta to create and store karmic actions and their consequences, saṁsāra would have no basis; it could not exist. But though saṁsāra needed the citta to exist, the citta did not depend on saṁsāra in any way. The two could be separated by eliminating the cause of saṁsāric existence from the citta, freeing it to revert to its pure primordial knowing essence. That cause of continuing saṁsāric existence was none other than the defiling influence of the kilesas. For that reason, ridding the citta of the kilesas was the goal of the Buddha's path of practice.

Reflections on the supreme goal led Tan Paññā to contemplate the truth of the term "arahant." It was apparent to him that "arahant" referred to the citta that had been purified of defilements. The term only applied to a human being by means of that citta's transient association with a physical form. The mental and physical personality lived on as a result of past kamma, but the true arahant—the pure citta—had no form, no characteristics and created no kamma.

IN LATE 1975, TAN PAÑÑĀ COMMENCED WORK on a project that would consume much of his time over the following two years. The perimeter fence built around the monastery ten years earlier no longer sufficed to protect the monastery from increasing outside encroachment. For years the locals had cultivated rice fields right up to the monastery's border. At the end of each year's harvest, they lit fires to burn off the dry stubble from their fields to prepare for plowing and planting the following season. Those unattended fires regularly swept through the boundary fence and burned large tracts of forest inside the monastery. Resident monks were obliged to hastily form water brigades, often in the dark, as they ferried carts of water from the well in an often futile attempt to douse the flames. Beyond that, some of the more recalcitrant villagers had started trespassing on monastery grounds to hunt animals that lived within that sacred sanctuary.

To prevent further damage to the monastery's tranquil environment, ardent lay supporters approached Ajaan Mahā Boowa with an offer to fund the construction of an eight-foot high concrete wall around the entire circumference of the compound. Ajaan Mahā Boowa agreed on the condition that his engineer-in-chief, Tan Paññā, be put in charge of the entire project.

Tan Paññā accepted the responsibility without complaint, but he sometimes wished that the lay supporters would see that there was more to the practice of Dhamma than just making merit by giving offerings to the monastery! People's desire to make merit in this way was no doubt praiseworthy. But he felt it unfortunate that many lay people understood "making merit" exclusively in terms of offering material support, which could at times be detrimental to the proper conditions for spiritual development.

Although doing good deeds is a necessary first step on the path of Buddhist practice, success at that level alone does not lead directly to the ultimate happiness that transcends old age, sickness and death. Leading a life solely based on acting in anticipation of future good results, a person fails to see the cause of suffering concealed in their good intentions. At the time of death, they are bound to face an unavoidable obstacle and be at a loss. Far better that people make a deep inquiry through practice into the Buddha's teaching so that they can go beyond their dependence on an existence that is forever subject to karmic consequences.

Taking up his new task, Tan Paññā designed a wall that took into account the materials that were locally available and the capabilities of the local volunteer labor. He proposed using reusable metal panels to hold the concrete mixture in place for each casting, and had sheet metal fashioned to his specifications. Each section of the wall would be cast on site, so materials had to be portable enough to haul through the dense jungle.

Casting concrete in place was relatively straightforward. First, reinforced concrete piers were constructed to add lateral strength and assure proper alignment of the two parallel metal forms that were anchored between the piers. Once both form faces were tied together and braced, fresh concrete was poured into the forms. That completed one section of the perimeter wall. The concrete batches were mixed by hand on site. Sand, gravel and cement were combined with water in a shallow hand-dug trough and stirred together by villagers wielding long-handled hoes. Other villagers hoisted the fresh slurry to the top of the metal forms in buckets and filled them from a height of eight feet.

Since the circumference of the monastery reached nearly one and a half miles, a total of more than 700 sections was required to enclose the property—a tedious and exhausting project which took the better part of two years to complete.

By mid-1977, Tan Paññā had secured the entire perimeter, with double front gates spanning the final section at the monastery's entrance. He soon turned his attention to remedying the monastery's shortage of drinking water. In consultation with Ajaan Mahā Boowa, the decision was made to construct six large water storage tanks, three on each side of the sala. Tan Paññā calculated that round tanks would provide greater strength and durability. His design was simple: two semicircular steel forms would be butted together to cast concrete rings three feet tall and seven feet in diameter, with five rings stacked and cast one on top of the other to a height of fifteen feet. Three of those water storage tanks flanked the east side of the sala and three more, the west side. For many years, those tanks stored the monastery's only source of clean potable water.

The six new water tanks were fully finished and ready to receive the annual monsoon rainfall in May 1978. By that time, five other Western disciples of Ajaan Mahā Boowa resided with him at Baan Taad Forest Monastery. The influx of new monks, plus a steady increase in English-speaking lay practitioners, meant an increase in Tan Paññā's teaching duties. He had resided continuously at the monastery for nearly eighteen years, rarely leaving the compound except for an occasional trip to Bangkok for a health checkup. He was fifty-two years old and had long since given up the thought of returning to England.

Instead, he adhered to a solemn vow, which he had made years before, to remain where he was until Ajaan Mahā Boowa, who was nearing sixty-four, passed away.

Due to his age and the fact that his competence as a teacher was unquestioned, the junior monks began calling him Ajaan Paññā, ajaan being the Thai equivalent of "teacher." During that period, his teaching responsibilities continued to expand. By then, most of the people attracted to Buddhism were people with an education, and he was seeing more and more monks who had been to college. Their minds had been trained to intellectualize and discriminate prolifically, and as Ajaan Paññā well knew from his own experience, this excess of discursive clutter could be a hindrance for those new to the practice.

Whether his students were beginners at meditation or monastics engaged in a lifetime of spiritual practice, Ajaan Paññā stressed that the development of meditative concentration and wisdom requires adherence to certain universal principles. In essence, that process involved a progression from the external to the internal; from the coarse to the refined; from emphasis on the body to emphasis on the mind; and from a state of activity to a state of quiescence. To be successful, meditation needs to be a discipline that encompasses the whole person and all facets of one's daily life. It is a path of practice that encompasses both cause and effect: a proper foundation leading to proper results. Practitioners cannot simply choose to comply with some aspects of the path and neglect the others; otherwise, all their efforts will ultimately prove disappointing.

Even for those who follow a monastic lifestyle, it is never easy to relinquish the acquired habits that have burdened them since lay life, habits based on personal value judgments that close off avenues to Dhamma in the mind. New monks continue to discriminate on the basis of sights seen, sounds heard, odors inhaled, and tastes savored. They still form opinions about bodily contact and hold prejudiced notions in their minds. It is not easy for monks to let go of those habitual patterns of perception and simply experience things as they really are.

To counter an ingrained tendency to rote learning and discursive thought among new monks, Ajaan Paññā stressed that Buddhist training was not merely a matter of memorizing the words found in the suttas or in the teachings of the ajaans. At the same time, he realized that words must be used to teach people about Buddhism. Although he knew that the true path transcended the distinctions on which language was based, he still tried to put his teachings in terms they would comprehend. His talks used language to make the Dhamma clear to his listeners with the hope that those words would serve as motivation for them to put what they had learned into practice. The purpose of practice was not to increase knowledge, but rather to realize the true nature of Dhamma. However, before they could realize the Dhamma, they would need language as a tool to guide them to a true understanding of the meaning of the Buddha's teaching.

Ajaan Paññā reminded his listeners that although the Buddhist path did not exist in words, this did not mean that they should refrain from reading Dhamma books or studying scriptures. Language's purpose was to point at the truth. Practitioners still had to discover the Dhamma for themselves if they wanted to realize the truth of the Buddha's teaching. Although a lot could be learned from books, they would discover that their actual experiences along the path differed from the descriptions found in books.

From that standpoint, language is an obstacle to practice that is eventually overcome. In Buddhism, statements about truth are never presumed to be truth itself. When Ajaan Paññā introduced Nibbāna to his students, he presented it as an idea, a concept; but it was up to them to transform that concept into a transcendent realization. He conveyed to his students that they must look within themselves for the truth, not in texts or spoken words. The realization of a practitioner's higher aspirations is not so much dependent on accumulating knowledge, but on overcoming the mental hindrances and gaining insight into the truth at which the teaching points.

Ajaan Paññā reminded his students that the solitude offered by the forest environment in which they lived was essential for those who hoped to go beyond an intellectual understanding of the spiritual path, and arrive at a true realization of what the Buddha taught. For that reason, the forest monastery was a natural environment for seekers like themselves who strived to transcend suffering.

He emphasized that when they practiced Dhamma, they had to be prepared for hardships. Even those born with very good kamma were bound to find difficulties at every turn. In his experience, if results came easily, they usually faded easily as well. Understanding the true nature of Dhamma took a long time, and it required great determination to succeed. Those who cultivated Dhamma in the truest sense were few; those who reached the highest realization were even fewer.

Ajaan Paññā impressed upon his students that the practice of wisdom covered a very broad range of mental phenomena. Because of that, they had to search for creative methods to deal with the countless possibilities that might arise in the course of their investigations. They could not expect the right methods to simply appear out of nowhere and present themselves. The right methods, the ones that were most suitable to their needs, could be quite elusive. It was not a matter of merely sitting back and observing awareness as it ebbed and flowed. They would have to search in earnest for the right method or else they would never find it. They had to make a deliberate choice of what facets of the mind they were going to observe, selecting the most salient aspects based on their insights into the Dhamma. For that to happen, they must really care about what they were doing. The investigation had to feel important to them. To be true cultivators of wisdom, they must take the time and the care to properly develop the practice of wisdom. If they did, the highest realization would not be beyond their reach.

That was the gist of the general discourses Ajaan Paññā gave to monks and lay practitioners alike. But he was keenly aware that people's temperaments and abilities differed widely. Just as all people are endowed with their own particular physical features, so is each person's character unique, making for a great variety of temperaments. Due to people's distinct backgrounds and the varying strength of their spiritual faculties, there can be no "one size fits all" teaching which will suit everyone. In private interviews, Ajaan Paññā intuitively tailored the depth and breadth of his teachings to fit the specific needs of each individual, knowing almost instinctively what each student needed to hear.

SUPERVISING BUILDING PROJECTS HAD ALWAYS taken a physical toll in his younger days, leaving Ajaan Paññā little time for deep and sustained periods of meditation. Now that he was older, and burdened with fewer strenuous activities, his daily routine became entirely his own, his heart unencumbered by meddlesome preoccupations. That left the Dhamma as his preoccupation, and Dhamma promoted only contentment.

Sitting peacefully in the solitude of his kuti, Ajaan Paññā enjoyed doing small repair jobs and working alone. He had a knack for cleaning and repairing mechanical watches, a talent he had developed in his youth. Fellow monks fell into the habit of bringing him their ailing watches, and he quite selflessly worked on them without complaint. In the years since arriving at Baan Taad Forest Monastery, he had accepted hundreds of requests for cleaning and oiling, and occasionally for repairs, until he became somewhat of a craftsman in the art of watch mechanics.

He took special care with watches because he knew that a speck of dust or a tiny strand of hair or lint could easily interfere with the precision of a watch's movement. A slow running watch indicated that the mechanical parts needed cleaning and oiling. It was a very common ailment in the northeastern region of Thailand, where fine sandy dust permeated the air during the hot, dry months.

Over the years, Ajaan Paññā had collected a set of essential watch-makers' tools. If he was going to tune and adjust the mechanisms him-self, it seemed natural to him to make use of the precision instruments needed for doing a proper and thorough job. The purpose of tools was a rational one: to do as meticulous a job as possible and achieve the best results each time. So he always made sure his screwdrivers were sharp and all his tools were clean and in good working condition.

Ajaan Paññā viewed proper cleaning and lubrication as one of the most important parts of watch repair, and spent countless hours refining his techniques. When cleaning a watch, he worked not so much to discover something new—although he was always alert for new things—but mainly to reacquaint himself with familiar things. He found it instructive to revisit old terrain. He had cleaned and oiled mechanical watches so many times that he did not have to think much about how to do it anymore. However, even if he had been through something many times, his keen eyes remained constantly alert, look-ing for fresh angles or for anything unusual. He checked the watch mechanism the same way he examined his own meditation practice, never becoming complacent, looking for new and subtle things even though everything might seem the same as always.

When digital watches replaced mechanical ones, Ajaan Paññā re-ceived fewer and fewer requests for repairs. By that time, however, cas-sette tape players and recorders were being used by many monks to lis-ten to Ajaan Mahā Boowa's recorded talks. The dampness of the jungle environment had a corrosive effect on electronic circuits, and Ajaan Paññā took it upon himself to revive those tape players that needed mending. He repaired tape recorders with the same attention to detail as he had with watches. He removed the circuit boards and checked for faulty connections. In some cases, he had to trace and diagram the recorder's circuit boards to work out the correct wire connections between the various components.

Occasionally, he needed to rebuild the circuit board from scratch. Once he had made the schematic diagram, he converted it into a layout that could be fabricated onto a printed circuit board. He meticulously drafted by hand the complex arrangement of wires and circuit components on sheets of paper, using different color pens to represent capacitors, inductors, resistors and the linkages between leads. His drawings were true works of art. The whole layout was transferred to the circuit board which was then immersed in etching solution. After the etching was completed, electric components and leads were mechanically fixed to the board with a molten metal solder. The printed circuit board was then tested for correct voltages and resistances before replacing the defunct system.

Treating every undertaking as a part of his practice, Ajaan Paññā was continually careful to avoid making quick assumptions about the task before him, whether it involved mental activity, watch mechanics or electrical circuits. He approached each task with an open and receptive mind. Ajaan Paññā viewed each task in a way that allowed him to do it precisely and effortlessly, as though the thing he was working on became an extension of his own body and mind. No clear separation divided the external mechanism from the person doing the work.

THE PASSING YEARS BROUGHT AN EVER-INCREASING stream of Western visitors to the monastery. Ajaan Paññā's frequent talks to the monks and lay people usually took place in an informal setting, and often inspired animated question-and-answer sessions. He excelled at the spontaneous back-and-forth of an open Dhamma discussion. He liked to play the devil's advocate in response to his students' queries, taking a commonly-held conventional truth, turning it around and triumphantly declaring the opposite view as being equally valid.

His style of teaching was characterized by taking his students' statements or questions, and recasting them into Dhamma terms that resonated with the heart rather than the intellect. Often, he tried to surprise students out of their mechanical modes of thinking. Bringing them back into the present moment, he thus made them see the issue from a different, more comprehensive angle. Challenging his students' conventional wisdom, Ajaan Paññā forced them to look back to their own resources to find the answers.

Simply sitting in meditation did not mean one was making progress. Ajaan Paññā recognized that the only way for a teacher to determine how much a student understood was to test his wisdom in action. He often discovered this by assigning to a monk a task he had never done before. One with a strong wisdom practice was not easily upset when things went wrong. One whose practice lacked depth was consistently frustrated. He watched and listened to his students to determine how to best help them move forward. Some got the point right away and they were rewarded with encouragement. Others seemed to take forever and were advised to be patient. All were encouraged to carry mindfulness of the present moment into every event of daily life.

Ajaan Paññā rarely discussed the deeper levels of his own personal experiences in meditation. Although meditation was central to his life, he felt that he should not discuss the events of his own practice publicly with his students. He focused his teaching on helping them find the meditation method that best suited their temperament, and on inspiring them to train harder. Certain themes and methods which became more important to him over time received correspondingly more attention.

He would, however, speak openly of his own search to find the truest version of the teaching. In this case, Ajaan Paññā's principal motive for relating his own story was clearly instructional. He believed that this knowledge could help prevent his students from falling victim to certain contemporary teachings that he felt were misrepresenting the time-honored tradition of Theravāda Buddhism.

Ajaan Paññā's teaching was liberating because it spoke about more than just everyday goodness. Addressing the inner workings of the mind and the transcendent paths and fruits with clarity and assurance, it featured some of the most thoughtful and illuminating expositions to be found in present-day Buddhist teachings. Always conscious of the spiritual maturity of his audience, he gave detailed advice on how to deal with mental obstacles such as anger, pain and fear. In their totality, his teachings provided insight into the nature of the human condition as much as they did into the virtues of the Noble Ones.

Due to Ajaan Mahā Boowa's overwhelming popularity in the circle of Dhamma practice, Baan Taad Forest Monastery was soon transformed into a great center of Buddhist meditation. Monks and laity alike gravitated to the monastery in hopes of receiving instruction from a genuine master. The many Western monks who came to learn from Ajaan Mahā Boowa were able to share wholeheartedly in that unique religious experience. Highly revered at home and abroad, Ajaan Mahā Boowa remained actively engaged in teaching both monastics and lay practitioners, elucidating for them the fundamental principles of Buddhism and encouraging them to practice the same bold and incisive techniques that his teacher, Ajaan Mun, had so effectively used.

Throughout that period of expansion, Ajaan Paññā's expertise in the practical application of engineering know-how had allowed the monastic community to keep up with the changing times. From the outset, he was involved in almost every building project carried out at Baan Taad Forest Monastery, often designing the projects and overseeing their implementation himself. Ajaan Mahā Boowa had so much faith in his wisdom and his engineering skills that he rarely questioned Ajaan Paññā's judgment in those matters. Whether the engineering was electrical or mechanical, structural or electronic, he had mastered them all on his own initiative, and could apply them with a skill and grace that consistently amazed his fellow monks. The ease with which Baan Taad Forest Monastery developed from a simple forest monastery into a thriving monastic center is a testament to Ajaan Paññā's ability to manage the monastery's resources while protecting its traditions and keeping its peaceful meditative environment intact.

ASIDE FROM HIS CHRONICALLY SWOLLEN FOOT, and a host of lingering aches and ailments, Ajaan Paññā's health remained predictably stable over the years. The hot and humid seasons took their toll on his physical vitality, but minor operations—on his foot, appendix and prostate—did little to slow him down in old age. He appeared to be ageing gracefully with unflagging vigor. Then, at the age of seventy-seven, in the monsoon days of September 2003, a routine blood test uncovered telltale traces of internal bleeding. A slow and almost imperceptible loss of blood was occurring somewhere within his body. By analyzing the blood count, the doctors measured the loss, but they could not pinpoint its location. Follow-up tests pointed to the colon as the most likely culprit. When a colonoscopy exam discovered a malignant growth at the upper end of Ajaan Paññā's large intestine, the doctors insisted on operating immediately to remove the tumor.

Ajaan Paññā was not noticeably sick; in fact, he felt and appeared quite buoyant. If the doctors had not detected it through a blood test, he would not have suspected a problem. After a period of calm reflection, Ajaan Paññā gratefully dismissed their offer of surgery, saying he preferred instead to treat the malignancy with traditional herbal medicines.

A disciple of his at the monastery quickly arranged for the delivery of a potent Thai herbal remedy, which Ajaan Paññā began ingesting immediately. Appearing unfazed by the urgency surrounding his condition, he carried on with his daily routine as if nothing out of the ordinary had happened. Convinced that the medicine was working, he traveled to Bangkok several months later to get a full check-up. An MRI scan found that the tumor had shrunk from its original length of five centimeters down to only one centimeter. The news was welcome and most encouraging.

Ajaan Paññā took the herbal concoction scrupulously for an additional five months. In early May 2004, he was admitted to the hospital for another colonoscopy. The results confirmed what he suspected: that the tumor had disappeared—no graphic evidence of it could be found. The upper colon appeared blessedly free of cancer. He seemed to be out of the woods.

The question then arose: should he continue with the herbal medication now that the treatment had proved successful? A specialist in traditional Thai medicine advised him against halting the therapy abruptly; instead, he was advised to carry on with it, but at half the dosage. His attendant monks pleaded with him to play it safe and heed the doctor's advice. Ajaan Paññā concluded otherwise. Contrary to the broad consensus of his supporters, he decided to discontinue the herbal remedy, reasoning that it had done its job and was no longer needed. It turned out to be a fateful decision.

Within six weeks, Ajaan Paññā's health seriously degenerated. His students could see that his former vitality and alertness were waning. As time passed, the decline became more pronounced. By mid-July, he experienced an ongoing and severe intestinal disorder. It became clear that he was having a relapse, and that this time he would not survive. The prospect of death hung like a cloud over the hearts of his disciples and permeated the monastic community with an intense awareness of its imminence. In Ajaan Paññā's presence, death assumed a special significance, not as an impetus for melancholy thoughts, but as an urgent reminder that one's time on earth is fleeting. This was the final lesson that he bestowed on all of his students.

Ajaan Paññā's death was not an easy one. His room, filled with the odor of incipient decay, was overwhelmingly silent but for the sound of

his labored breathing. Yet, despite the uncertainty surrounding his po-
tentially prolonged infirmity, he exuded a peaceful inner confidence—
a spirited manifestation of his faith in the training and his fearlessness
of death. That inner refuge enabled him to face death in a way that was
at once thoughtful and serene.

During the final week of his life, Ajaan Paññā's overriding challenge
was the constant fatigue of a body that had spent its karmic energy. He
succumbed to utter exhaustion. His attendants were advised that unless he was induced to eat something, his digestive system would shut
down, leaving him quickly at death's doorstep. Hospital doctors suggested placing a feeding tube through the nose and into his stomach;
he flatly refused. Lay supporters hastily arranged the preparation of
flasks of soup and nutritious broths, which they offered in abundance
each morning. But Ajaan Paññā found it burdensome to force down
even a few spoonfuls.

Unable to eat, he gradually grew so weak that he could hardly
manage even the simplest movements on his own. He continued to talk
and laugh with those around him, but in a voice so faint they strained
to make out what he said. Trying to force down a brew of his favorite
tea, he joked with his attendants that nothing spoiled a good cup of tea
like colonic cancer. When asked how he felt, he murmured softly that
he felt no pain, only debilitating weakness. Several times, the doctors
offered to administer morphine, but his calm and quiet response was
gently dismissive.

Ajaan Paññā remained alert and responsive to his environment
until the night of August 16, when he seemed to let go of the external world completely. His breathing the following morning was deep
and measured, but he evinced no knowledge of the world around him.
Throughout that day and the final night, his breath became progressively shorter and shallower. By the early morning of August 18, his
breathing was soft and smooth but very frail. Soon, it was barely dis-
cernible. Eventually, it became so faint that no one knew precisely

when it stopped altogether. The monks attending to Ajaan Paññā in his final hour estimated the time to be 8:30 am.

Ajaan Paññā's passing was more than simply the death of a good monk. His death was a display of the depth of his realization and the power of the teaching that he had come to embody. In death, Ajaan Paññā made his disciples aware that teachers of his caliber often concealed many exceptional qualities during their lifetime. Sometimes, they showed them fully only at the moment of their death.

Ajaan Paññā's earnest conviction in the simplicity of a bhikkhu's life was evident from the mere handful of belongings that he left behind. Although born at a gold mine, gold was no different to him than dust. He never fell victim to fortune, fame or worldly ambition. He did not have the reputation of a world-renowned teacher, a famous author or an erudite scholar. Nor did he exhibit mystical powers, claim psychic encounters with devas or remain in seclusion for lengthy periods. He simply demonstrated that the truth of the Lord Buddha's teaching was to be found at the very heart of one's being. With grace and humility, he shared his wisdom and his confidence in the power of Dhamma to help liberate the minds of his fellow human beings.

On August 28, ten days after his death, Ajaan Paññā's bodily remains were cremated at Baan Taad Forest Monastery. A special funeral pyre, covered by an ornate Thai-style canopy, was constructed on a broad stretch of ground at the front of the monastery, near a spacious pavilion that was built for use on large and important occasions. However, the pavilion was not nearly spacious enough to contain the thousands of monks and the tens of thousands of Buddhist faithful who gathered from all over the country, as well as from abroad, to offer their last respects to the monk whose impeccable goodness had warmed the hearts of so many people.

The ceremony took place on a bright, cloudless afternoon— a blessed and welcome change from the stifling heat of the ongoing monsoons. For a moment, as Ajaan Paññā's casket was placed atop the funeral pyre, the whole crowd was still. Then, an extraordinary occurrence attracted everyone's attention skyward. Against the clear blue sky shone a fiery, white light from a blinding, seemingly boundless source; a diamond-bright heart radiating outwards and fading to a softly diffused, circular glow. Around this white diamond was a second circle: a ring of rainbow light with an outer border of luminous white down. It was the sun, resplendent in breathtaking purity, encircled by a magnificent rainbow which suffused the translucent, wispy clouds with a prismatic glow. This sudden apparition drew the gaze of the whole congregation and transfixed it on the heavens. A soft, amazed murmur passed through the crowd as the circular rainbow slowly dissipated and faded from view.

Twice more during the course of the funeral ceremony, the natural elements conspired to conjure the same amazing phenomenon. It was as though the power of Ajaan Paññā's spiritual attainment had induced this image to reflect the depth and subtlety of his virtue for all to witness. That vivid testimony to Ajaan Paññā's profound spiritual awakening marked a supremely graceful conclusion to the life and practice of a monk whose kindness and humility radiated softly from his being to encompass the whole sentient universe.

EULOGY

The venerable monk who passed away on August 18, 2004 was beloved both in spirit and in person, an amazing teacher with an incisive, inquiring mind, wise and kind beyond measure. Such was the view of all who were fortunate enough to make Ajaan Paññā's acquaintance. Those individuals met a man who moved with a focused and deliberate gait, limping slightly from an ailing right foot, with steps that never faltered. His neck and broad shoulders stooped slightly, his face sloped forward and was highlighted by a long, fleshy nose and slim benevolent lips. His powerful hands were those of a craftsman. Shorn, silver hair flanked his large flaring ears, while his kind brown eyes glowed with good humor. But what people noticed most about Ajaan Paññā was his presence. His gaze and his bearing were those of a venerable sage.

At the monastery, many people approached Ajaan Paññā to make, or perhaps renew, his acquaintance, addressing him with warmhearted devotion and respect. He was not one to seek out such encounters, but he would accept the deference paid him in a calm and detached manner with a mildly quizzical look of surprise, as if he was not quite sure who deserved the approbation.

Ajaan Paññā had a soft, deep voice, as soothing as a cool forest stream. He would speak quietly to those who sought his presence, his

head leaning affably to one side, inspiring respect and careful attention. Otherwise, content to remain aloof, Ajaan Paññā seldom spoke
except when spoken to, and never appeared to speak too much. He was
unobtrusive and exuded a soothing gentleness that naturally made him
the center of every situation.

Being near him, one sensed his palpable inner peace and serenity.
His gaze was open, calm and benevolent—free of conflict, bias or judgment. With his warmth, his wisdom and his compassion, Ajaan Paññā
personified the nobility of the teachings. By his personal example, the
Dhamma was rendered practical and vibrant with life. His teachings
inspired in others an unshakeable confidence in the Dhamma, and a
conviction in the central importance of a trusted teacher. Those who
encountered his virtuous qualities tended to become acutely aware of
the greed, the aversion and the selfish instincts clouding their hearts.
Earnest practitioners saw in his exemplary manner and freedom from
attachments the special teacher whom they longed to encounter.

Ajaan Paññā's sacred duty to his students was to clearly describe
the coarse and grasping conditions constricting the human heart, while
at the same time making them aware of the pure nature of mind lying
dormant and stifled within. With his words, he transported his listeners into a state of concentrated attention, fully engrossed in and open
to the Dhamma and its boundless potential for liberation.

The people who traveled from far and wide to meet him were often beginners on the path, still flush with worldly attitudes, concerns
and passions. When Ajaan Paññā treated them kindly, they were likely
to respond with emotion. But he was immune to the pull of worldly
relationships. In his monk's life of discipline and renunciation, he had
left behind the emotions associated with family, friends and romance.
He responded to all people with perfect equanimity, having long since
abandoned the entangling relationships that inevitably lead to loss and
suffering. The fires of passion and emotion had been quieted in his
heart.

However, many lay supporters had yet to disengage their minds from attachment to worldly ambitions of gain and fame. They admired Ajaan Paññā's humility, but they also wanted him to receive the prestige and recognition that his exalted character deserved. While he himself had no use for such attentions, it frustrated them that he refused to tout his own merits and take personal credit for his achievements. In the monastic community, however, Ajaan Paññā's combination of humbleness and integrity was highly valued. His fellow monks felt he was someone to whom they could entrust their lives.

Ajaan Paññā learned to accept the circumstances at hand without resistance. He simply allowed the present moment to be, accepting the changing nature of all things and conditions. His fluid understanding of the nature of change came from deep penetration into the truth of the Dhamma. As a teacher, this understanding allowed him to address different circumstances and situations in creative ways.

He cautioned against imposing one's own prescriptive views on the world, particularly regarding those social and environmental issues that often became celebrated causes among his students. He was well aware that cycles come and cycles go, that all things pass away—but with attachments severed, he felt no fear of loss. When teaching the public, Ajaan Paññā sympathized with their commitment to social goals. But he also knew that serving the social community at large did not take precedence over serving the cause of Dhamma. He fervently believed that self-realization was the greatest contribution he could make to his fellow men and women.

Ajaan Paññā never permitted himself to indulge in feelings of satisfaction or disappointment. When things went smoothly, he did not feel especially elated. When encountering obstacles or failure, he was not dejected. He did not struggle against the inevitable; he simply found the means to persevere. The determination to proceed resolutely, regardless of obstacles or difficulties, was a guiding principle in his life. As he approached death, he still kept his feet planted firmly on the Buddha's noble path, never taking for granted that his work was completed.

What was Ajaan Paññā's contribution to the world of contemporary Buddhism? His compassion led him to share the fruits of his uncommon wisdom, enabling those near him to resonate in harmony with the Lord Buddha's teaching. He tailored his teaching methods to his students' social and cultural backgrounds as well as to their unique characters. He made Buddhism relevant to his students by breathing life into the Buddha's teaching, inspiring them to take spirited strides on the noble path to freedom.

Like the Buddha's eminent disciples, Ajaan Paññā taught the Dhamma that was "good in the beginning, good in the middle and good in the end, with the right meaning and expression." With his spare, clear and simple teaching style, he laid out a road map for travelers along the path. For those who earnestly seek the way, his teachings reveal the path to a perfectly contented and purified heart.

Studied carefully and with an open heart, Ajaan Paññā's teachings can help reignite a practice that has stalled after an initial burst of heartfelt progress. For those who have grown complacent in their knowledge of the Buddhist path, the fruits of his wisdom may open the mind to new horizons of the Dhamma and new avenues of introspection. At the very least, he offers a view from the mountaintop to practitioners who otherwise might have only a vague notion of the heights attainable on the Buddha's noble path.

2

DESCRIPTION—SIGNALEMENT

	Bearer—Titulaire	★Wife—Femme
Profession } Profession	~~ELECTRICAL ENGINEER~~ Buddhist Monk	
Place and date of birth Lieu et date de naissance	MYSORE STATE INDIA 19 OCTOBER 1925	Cancelled
Residence } Résidence	ENGLAND	Cancelled
Height } Taille	5 ft 9 in.	ft. in.
Colour of eyes } Couleur des yeux	BROWN	
Colour of hair } Couleur des cheveux	BROWN	
Special peculiarities } Signes particuliers		

★CHILDREN—ENFANTS

Name—Nom	Date of birth—Date de naissance	Sex—Sexe

Usual Signature of Bearer Signature du Titulaire	P.J. Morgan.
Usual Signature of Wife Signature de sa Femme	

3

Bearer (Titulaire)

Wife (Femme)

Recent Photograph of Bearer.

GOOD IN THE
BEGINNING

The path of practice has both cause and effect, a firm basis leading to good results. It takes into account the whole person and concerns all aspects of daily life. We can't simply choose to practice some factors of the path and neglect the others.

———————————

PURPOSE

Have you properly considered your purpose for doing meditation practice? It is important to get the purpose right; that is, the reason why you do it. We start off with the fundamental basis of Buddhism, the fact that we all experience dukkha or discontent which we are trying to cure. We attempt to cure our discontent by using cause-and-effect methods; in other words, we initiate those causes that we believe will lead to the relief of our suffering. In doing so, we search for causes, or actions, that result in less dukkha and greater contentment. Dukkha can be anything from small irritations all the way up to intense suffering. This is fundamentally what we are trying to remedy. It makes no difference whether we are Buddhists or not, we are all driven by this quest to find happiness.

If we're wise and we understand the situation correctly, then we might actually choose the right course of action and manage to get the happiness we are seeking. But because our minds are clouded by defilements, we tend to make the wrong decisions. Due to thinking and acting wrongly, we pile up more and more suffering. Failing to understand the correct way to get rid of suffering, we tend to make the same mistakes over and over again. This is the situation that we are in.

In order to reverse that situation, it is necessary to first turn our lack of understanding into correct understanding. If we can accomplish that, then we truly will get rid of suffering. So the purpose of Buddhist practice is to comprehend within ourselves the right way to eliminate dukkha. This is really the whole of Buddhism: to learn how to think properly, how to behave properly and how to speak properly. Only when we put those factors into practice can we cure the discontent.

In order to learn how to think, behave and speak properly, we must train ourselves. We train ourselves to have a sharp mind, to understand the reasons for the things that happen in our lives, and thus to get to know ourselves properly. By getting to know ourselves, we get to know other people. By getting to know other people we learn how to behave rightly towards them—all because we know how to behave rightly within ourselves.

The means to achieve this is the method that was taught by the Buddha, which is comprised of sīla or morality, samādhi or training of the mind, and paññā or wisdom. If we learn how to practice those three effectively, we can overcome the mental defilements, the kilesas, that cause the discontent we experience. As we overcome the kilesas, the discontent and suffering will lessen and eventually die away. This goal can be achieved. Many have done it already. Countless people have trained in sīla, samādhi and paññā and achieved very good results, experiencing high degrees of contentment and happiness. So the way to happiness is the way of sīla, samādhi and paññā.

The Buddha taught that since the pain and suffering we experience is our fault to begin with, we can therefore free ourselves from it. We can gain release from it by learning to develop wisdom and understanding. We develop this understanding by training ourselves to control our actions, to sharpen our minds and to stop the restless waywardness of our thoughts. When we accomplish that, we can hold the mind still and penetrate deeply with wisdom. At that level, we can use the mind to probe the question of the causes of happiness and suffering.

The Buddha called the quest to solve these problems and overcome our discontent the Path to Freedom. It begins with training ourselves in the way of morality, then developing the mind, and thirdly developing wisdom based upon mindfulness and effort. Mindfulness means keeping the mind in the present moment and thus being aware of oneself all the time. It means restraining the mind from thinking and wandering aimlessly; in other words, not forgetting oneself. This teaching of the Buddha forms the basis of Buddhist practice.

This is how we should understand the purpose and aim of meditation practice. The right understanding gives us confidence to push forward in our meditation. It also gives a method whereby we can work out what we should do and what we shouldn't do, based on our purpose and what we're trying to achieve. If we know that, we can figure out the best method of developing the skills we need to get to our destination.

When we first take up Buddhist meditation, we're not really seeking the truth. The first thing we need to do is develop the faculties which will enable us to search for the truth. It's rather like somebody who's in training for a boxing match. That person has to do a lot of training, but the training itself isn't the prizefight. No medals are awarded for the training. But although the fighter does not achieve his objective while training, the training is, nonetheless, absolutely essential for success in the fight. In much the same way, meditators have to train themselves to develop various essential skills and faculties so that the mind becomes capable of penetrating the cloud of ignorance surrounding it.

As part of that basic training, every meditator should observe at least the five basic moral precepts. One, not to take life; two, not to steal or take what has not been properly given; three, not to engage in sexual misconduct; four, not to lie or deceive; and five, not to indulge in intoxicants that cloud the mind. These five sīla are considered the minimum criteria for being a decent human being. More than that, their practice creates an environment that is most suitable to the development of samādhi and wisdom.

When beginning Buddhist practice, meditators should not start out trying to fathom the most profound truths of Buddhism: they are way beyond the understanding of ordinary people. Because they don't know any better, beginners tend to give them a meaning which is false. It's purely speculation. Whereas, when they start with their current situation and their immediate problems, here and now, they already have a real basis to work with. People can understand the teaching at that level. When you talk about suffering and discontent, everyone can relate to that. They have plenty of experience. When you talk about how we so often misunderstand our situation, thinking our actions are going to bring a good result only to find that the opposite usually happens, people understand that. This gives them a good basis for practical development.

As mentioned above, the Buddhist path of practice is organized according to three basic disciplines: moral virtue, samādhi and wisdom. The two factors of samādhi and wisdom are developed mostly through formal meditation practice with morality serving as a preparatory basis. The whole of Buddhism is practical. The Buddha said that Dhamma is like a steppingstone to get us across the stream; in other words, a practical teaching. As for the higher stages of practice, there is time enough to go on to those privately with your teacher when you reach that level. First, you must learn to calm your restless mind and bring it under control. Only then can you harness its true power.

The training in samādhi consists of learning the art of stopping thoughts and holding the mind still. Thinking is the factor that prevents us from becoming calm. When we can stop our thoughts and hold them still, the results of samādhi will come automatically. Samādhi is quite a natural state. When we stop the restlessness of the mind and keep it still, it will either go into sleep or into samādhi. If we prevent it from going to sleep, it will then drop into samādhi. It's natural. It's not something strange. Were it something strange, the Buddha would not have taught it. In fact, samādhi is inherent to the mind. If we learn to stay clear of the kilesas with the thoughts and restlessness they bring up, samādhi will happen of its own accord.

If we could stop the mind from thinking and hold it still for long enough, we would automatically drop into a state of samādhi. But as soon as the mind starts moving in that direction, the kilesas immediately jump up and begin creating doubt and anxiety, causing that calm mental state to break up. Defilements are constantly disturbing the mind and preventing it from settling down. They act like the wind that blows up the waves on the surface of the ocean. When the wind stops, the waves calm down and quietly recede back into the ocean. The kilesas can also be compared to muddy water. If the water remains still long enough, the mud will settle down to the bottom, allowing the water to become clean and clear.

For most people in the West, samādhi is their weakest faculty. Generally speaking, those people need samādhi more because they live in a very restless and noisy social environment. One of the advantages of gaining a basis in samādhi is a profound change in our social values. The calm and concentration of samādhi will clearly show up the false values of the society around us, and point out what the essential values should be. This change in perspective also highlights the negative side of many things that we tend to cherish and value. It is as though our whole outlook experiences a shift of emphasis.

Samādhi also gives an appreciation of the value of just sitting back, taking it easy and not thinking about anything in particular—an attitude which is so foreign to people in the West. It is almost as if we must learn to do nothing, because, in doing nothing, we are freeing the mind to go its own way. If we do that in the right way, the mind will tend to lead us in a very positive direction. This is valuable because we are learning to listen to Dhamma, rather than listening to our own opinions and the opinions of others. But it can be a hard lesson for people in the West to learn. One of the primary advantages of samādhi is that when the mind is still we can see just how harmful our restless thoughts are. It motivates us with a sense of urgency to try to solve that problem.

Samādhi brings a state of calm. When we do that often, the calm penetrates and gets in deep and becomes part of our nature. When it reaches that level, we tend to be calm the whole time. Then, the kilesas don't come up easily, and when they do they are seen for what they are. In the end, when that calm state becomes continuous, we feel repulsed by behavior that's full of kilesas and don't even want to be associated with it. That's a sign that samādhi is firm and reliable inside. Samādhi must be firm enough to fix our undivided attention on a meditation object, like the senses or the body. When we establish our mental focus on the body, for instance, we must be able to keep it solely on the body.

The practice of samādhi is extremely valuable in its ability to wake us up and sharpen the mind. Samādhi pulls the mind together and concentrates it. But although it fosters a very clear mind, samādhi on its own will not turn into wisdom. Wisdom must be cultivated.

When concentration is firm, it's time to start cultivating wisdom. If you have trained yourself to keep your mind on a single object, like the breath, that training can then come into play when you are investigating with wisdom. You can use the same basic principles in the wisdom practice that you developed in the samādhi practice. You may find it very difficult to attain samādhi. Nonetheless, you should try to do so. And you should use the fruits of samādhi to develop some wisdom. Wisdom, when practiced properly, can be an aid in developing samādhi as well.

There are three levels of developing wisdom. First, there is suttamāya-paññā, which is the wisdom developed through listening to or reading about the Dhamma. Cintamāya-paññā is the wisdom developed by reflecting on what one has heard or read. The third, bhāvanāmāya-paññā, which is the wisdom developed through the practice of meditation, is the most important because it is gained through direct experience.

When you see your own faults internally through direct experience, and realize that they bring you only suffering, you automatically turn away from them. It is not as though you make a mental note to refrain from acting in those ways again; but rather, those faults are like a hot iron that you won't touch with a barge pole. That internal effect occurs straight away as soon as you see your faults with penetrating wisdom.

Withdrawing from samādhi is an ideal time to focus on wisdom and turn that attention to investigating the body. That calm mental state allows wisdom to penetrate without difficulty so that the body's true nature can be seen more easily. You'll notice a significant difference from your earlier wisdom practice, which was much more academic and intellectual, and which the mind resisted doing because the kilesas kept interfering to pull it away. Samādhi frees you from all that. It's a very valuable state if you can achieve it, but it's not easy. There are many barriers to overcome.

There are two main advantages of attaining a deep state of samādhi. First of all, it provides an unshakeable refuge. You know clearly that when you are in that state nothing can harm you. Secondly, when the mind becomes tired from investigating a lot with wisdom, you can use that state to give the mental faculties a rest. In fact, you can use samādhi to refresh the mind at anytime. Samādhi always leaves a very strong aftertaste of calm. The mind is no longer stubborn or difficult, being, instead, completely pliable.

That's the point where wisdom takes over. The wisdom practice uses the calm and concentration of samādhi as an aid to penetrate deeply. But you must develop that calm basis first; otherwise, the mind is constantly scattered. It has no strength. It's like a water nozzle that sprays water out in all directions; the water has no power behind it. However, when you focus the water into one jet, it becomes quite strong. The mind is like that. You need to bring the mind into a very focused state. Then you can deal directly and forcefully with any problems that arise.

Problems arise in meditation practice because our minds are full of defilements. It's as though the mind is pure water mixed with a lot of mud. Because of the mud, the water is not fit for use. Since we cannot find a refuge in the pure water of the mind, we find something else to take refuge in. We seek refuge in our physical bodies, in other people, in places and in other worldly attachments. We try grasping at these things. The trouble is that when we grasp them they never last, they are always changing.

In truth, we cannot really grasp anything properly, because as soon as we catch hold of it, it's gone. We want to somehow make things belong to us and become part of us. But our attempt to grasp these things is based on a false premise. Say we buy an object and call it ours. What in that object has changed by the mere act of purchasing it? Nothing. It is the same after we bought it as it was before. Only our idea of it has changed. It now "belongs" to us. Because this grasping is based on a false premise, we can never find satisfaction in what we grasp. And because of their unsatisfactory nature, we cannot take refuge in external things.

People are always searching for a satisfactory refuge, but they never find one. To begin with, they look inside themselves. But, although the primary refuge exists inside them, they can't reach it because it's concealed by the defiling presence of greed, hatred and delusion. Due to defilements, when people focus inside themselves, all they see is a mess. They find nothing there that they want, nothing to serve as a refuge. What do people do then? They search in the world outside themselves. Consequently, people become interested in all sorts of mundane things that lead them on and on in a fruitless search for the contentment of a secure personal refuge. They end up with only more discontent, more suffering, because they grasp at things that have no real substance, like grasping a handful of air. Yet they keep on grasping, hoping to find contentment but inevitably experiencing the opposite.

The Buddha taught methods that can be used to cure our discontent from within, not out in the world. In other words, we try to counter those kilesas that cause us to suffer all the time. As we begin eliminating the kilesas, we catch a glimpse of the mind's true essence, what we call the citta. And we begin to see how valuable it is. When we begin to understand the true value of the citta, an attachment to that essence of mind begins to manifest. When the attachment to the citta grows strong, attachment to the external world dies away.

The more we eliminate the kilesas, the more we see the value of the citta. Until, finally, when we realize the nature of the citta completely, the attachment to the world entirely disappears. There is no need to make an effort to give up things because at that stage giving up is automatic. This is the true aim of the Buddha's teaching.

In his teachings, the Buddha used the normal conventions of language: similes and metaphors and so on. He spoke about relative truths in the world. The Buddha did not teach absolute truth because absolute truth cannot be described. What the Buddha taught was the skillful means by which we can reach the point where that absolute truth is known. The whole of the teaching is a method to take us from our present deluded state to a state where the mind is clear enough and knows enough to make the "jump" to Nibbāna, so to speak. We have to raise the mind's level up to that point; only then can we cross over. When we try to accomplish it without raising the level of the mind, there is no hope of success.

When beginning the training, we start off where we are—as ordinary people with ordinary understanding. Initially, we have to work with that ordinary understanding and make the best use of it. As we go on, we'll see that ordinary understanding isn't sufficient. So we have to find new methods, new understanding and more subtle ways of looking at things. It's not that the ordinary understanding is wrong, but rather that it's inadequate—it doesn't explain subtler conditions properly.

There are many things in ordinary understanding that can't explain various anomalies that arise in meditation—experiences which don't fit with our ordinary understanding. For that reason, we need to discover a new way of understanding. After we've used that new method for awhile, we'll find that it is no longer adequate, so we develop another way of understanding. By that means, we keep on adjusting our methods as we gradually progress in meditation.

The way of Buddhism leads toward absolute truth. The only way to reach there is to adapt the mind's state accordingly. If we adapt the mind's level to that of absolute truth, then we can experience absolute truth. The purpose of Buddhist training is to reach that point. The absolute truth is Nibbāna, of course. So we have to adjust the mind to the conditions that lead to Nibbāna. When we have incorporated those conditions into the mind, we will eventually reach the goal. Otherwise, we won't succeed. The whole training points the way to Nibbāna.

Please understand as well that the way of Buddhism is not a hard and fast system. The recommendations coming directly from the Buddha are the best because he took the nature of human beings into account. But they are not set in stone. The whole of Buddhism is a method. You can adapt the method to your own needs. You needn't practice exactly according to what the books say. Being a method, the Buddha's teaching is not itself an absolute truth. It is true as far as the world goes, but absolute truth is something utterly beyond.

To begin with, you must start off by using the regular methods, because you don't yet know. But once you've become used to the regular methods, then you can start searching about a bit more. You eventually find out what works and you use it. You must always test new methods by the results they give. Do the results lead to more calm, more understanding? Or do they lead to less calm and less understanding? If the methods lead to more calm and greater understanding, they are probably worth pursuing.

Experiment for yourself to find out the best practice for you. That's the way of kammaṭṭhāna. The word kammaṭṭhāna means "basis of action" or "field of action." The field of action is the whole of what we do in the scope of meditation practice. In practicing kammaṭṭhāna, the idea is to be innovative. You have to think for yourself quite a lot. You must search for and find your own methods. When you come up against a problem in your meditation, you should work out the best way to overcome that problem. Often, people who practice kammaṭṭhāna have their own unique meditation methods which are quite different from those other people use. You must learn to find tricks that help you to overcome the problems you encounter in the practice. Then you can work out the answers for yourself.

The defilements of the mind do not behave in a predictable and orderly fashion. Instead, they create havoc in your thoughts and emotions and in the process cause numerous problems. Because of that, there are times when you have to use morality to overcome a problem, times when you have to use samādhi and times when you have to use wisdom. Normally, it's recommended that samādhi be practiced first to control the mind before developing wisdom. But when a problem arises where it's appropriate to employ wisdom first, then that's the right choice for that situation and you should use it.

The way of developing meditation is not a straightforward, cut and dried process. Each person must find their own way, which means you must be resourceful, and even, to some extent, inventive in choosing meditation techniques. If you encounter a hindrance with no prescribed method to circumvent it, you will have to rely on wisdom to devise a method on the spot. You can't depend only on what the books say. The books are just the bare bones. It's your job to put the flesh on them.

When you have established a true refuge internally, attachment to everything else naturally disappears. The things you do wrong and the problems you create are all concerned with the mind flowing out into the world. It is as though the mind leaks into the world, causing all of its energy to escape. When you keep your attention inside and stop that leakage, you are always in the present and everything is just right.

It is also important to realize that inside your mind there is something that will tell you what is right, tell you what defilement is and tell you the right thing to do. That something is Dhamma. Once you realize it is there, you have to learn to recognize and listen to it. It never forces you, but there is something that will tell you what is correct, and it's often where you don't want to go.

You should learn to know that one very well, because it is an excellent guide. The more you can get to know the Dhamma, the more you have an internal teacher to guide you. You probably have an external teacher, and that is necessary; but finally, you must replace the external teacher with the internal one. When that has been accomplished, you no longer need to be with a teacher. You can practice on your own then. For that reason, you have to learn to recognize the internal teacher, and listen carefully to the teaching of the Dhamma.

By recognizing the internal teacher and listening carefully, you learn to distinguish between the kilesas and the Dhamma. In the end, you find that the kilesas are, in fact, yourself. The kilesas are the ones in charge of everything you do—all of your thoughts, speech and actions. And the Dhamma seems to be separate, something other, something which points the way. You must learn to recognize the Dhamma, which gives a feeling of being something outside yourself. You must come to realize that, while everything else is false, the Dhamma is real. Your task is to get rid of the false things that are the kilesas, so that only the Dhamma is left.

The Buddha said that he taught only two things: dukkha and the cessation of dukkha. Only those two. Similarly, the Buddha once picked up a handful of leaves from the forest floor and asked his disciples which were greater, the leaves in his hand or those in the forest. His disciples said that the leaves in his hand were few, while the leaves in the forest were many. The Buddha said that what he taught was like the leaves in his hand, compared to all that he knew, which was like the leaves in the forest. And, he asked "Why don't I teach you all those other things? Because they do not lead to the cessation of dukkha, they do not lead to Nibbāna."

In other words, the Buddha was saying: I am giving you the method by which you should train and develop your mind. When you follow that method correctly, you will come to Nibbāna. Then you will see the truth for yourself, and all questions will be answered.

PRESENCE

The Middle Way is much misunderstood in the West. People think it means the easy and convenient way of practice. But that idea of the path is merely the way of the kilesas; the way of mental defilements like laziness and complacency. Effort is difficult because it goes directly against the pull of the kilesas. There is an innate desire to just relax, or to go into some pursuit that you feel comfortable with, some habitual activity that is second nature to you and is, therefore, easy and undemanding. Because of habit, the mind finds it very easy to think about such matters. No real effort is involved.

But training the mind to go in new directions is much more demanding, and difficult. Going against habitual tendencies, going against the grain, requires a purposeful effort of mind that must be intentionally brought up and applied. For instance, if a person investigates himself and finds he has a lot of greed for food, he might deliberately take food that's unsavory in order to halt the momentum of greed and bring his mental state back into balance. If attachment to the taste of food is a problem, he may eat only rough, unappetizing food, considering only what is necessary for nutrition. Because the greed for good, tasty food is pulling his mind in the wrong direction, he needs to find a suitable practice to pull it back to the middle again. In a similar way, when we find any state of mind disturbing our meditation practice, we must search for the correct antidote. That is the Middle Way.

The Middle Way consists of practices that arouse energy aimed at correcting habitual imbalances that the kilesas produce. If the kilesas are biasing the mind in one direction, we must place a counter-weight on the other side to bring the mind back to the middle. Only by keeping our mindfulness in the present moment will we be able to see clearly where those imbalances lie. The present moment is the balance point for the mind. The mind rests on just this moment, here and now. Past and future are concepts that the kilesas use to deceive us. They are shadows that we grasp and become attached to, only to suffer the consequences. The past is fiction—it has no reality. And the future is speculation—it also has no reality. The only reality is Dhamma, at this very moment.

I once talked with an acquaintance about past, future and present time. He made the comment that the present is going past very quick-ly. I thought to myself: it isn't. The present doesn't change. There's no movement in the present. The present is just the present, and that's all. The present moment is a personal thing inside oneself. The changes are taking place externally. Changes occur in events and external phenom-ena that arise and die away—but those things are more or less an illu-sion. The present doesn't change. Everything round about is changing, but the present is a deeply-rooted state of mind that doesn't change.

Observing the present moment gives some idea of our internal situation. We learn how much work we have left to do and thus what direction we should take. In seeing the way forward, we realize the scope of our task and where the effort should be placed in medita-tion. In essence, by being present we are cultivating right mindfulness. We become acutely aware of anicca or impermanence. We see sights with mindfulness and we realize that they are constantly changing ap-pearance. We hear sounds with mindfulness and we realize that they are coming and going continuously. We begin to comprehend the all-encompassing nature of impermanence.

Later, we may reflect on how the breath changes every moment. The beginning of the breath isn't the same as the middle of the breath, or the end—each moment it's changing. The moment that passed has disappeared completely into the past; it's gone. It is as though it occurred a thousand years ago. It no longer matters. We can no longer find that part of the breath anywhere. The in and out breaths are in constant motion. The moment of the immediate present is moving along, leaving a path of past moments behind it. The future is always a projection: it never really exists.

In truth, impermanence exists because the mind is moving from the present into the past, which is merely memory. When we see something now, we recall the image of its previous state and, comparing the two, feel that it has changed. In that way, we experience the changing nature of phenomena all the time. If we could remain thoroughly in the present, we would find no change at all. So, we could say that the present is permanent. It's not changing. What changes is everything that whirls around going from past to future and back again.

Change becomes a problem for the mind because we have āsavas or outflows that drag the mind out into the swirling mess, causing us to get caught up in it. We get so carried away by the changing world that we forget about the present reality, which means we are dealing with an unreal situation all the time. We always deal in the past and the future, and forget about the present moment. So keeping the mind in the present all the time, firmly established in the here and now, is an excellent way of developing mindfulness. When we keep to the present, we are anchored in reality. We know our situation. If we are unaware of our situation, we're not in the present. For that reason, keeping the mind grounded in the present moment is a valuable training.

One advantage of being anchored to the present is that we begin to see mental states, and to understand for ourselves how they work.

Once we see how our minds work, we start questioning the whole nature of who we are. It is good to frequently remind ourselves that what is here right now at this moment is all that exists. This is everything. Future and past are not here. We cannot find them. The past is gone and the future hasn't come. Only this moment is here. We keep reminding ourselves of that.

When we experience states of longing for the past or the future, we can remind ourselves that neither of them exists right now. Longing for past and future experience is just a delusion. Being mindful of that will bring you back to the present moment. In the present, there isn't much trouble. Problems are based in the past and the future. Of course, we can still plan for the future as long as we are fully aware that we are doing it quite deliberately now in the present. But, out of habit, we usually forget.

We all have habitual ways of doing things. We use habitual modes of thinking, behaving and understanding. So often these habits determine our mental state, making it difficult to realize what the truth is; making it difficult to be present. Even when we are focused in the present, our habitual ways are hovering in the background. If our attention lapses a bit, they take over straightaway. The only way to overcome that tendency is to continue practicing the modes of training in Dhamma until the situation is seen more and more clearly. Then we begin to realize how delusory those concepts of past and future are; how they are not at all real.

You might say that when the mind is in the present, it is as near to reality as it can possibly get. Whereas, when the mind wanders into the past or the future, it misses reality altogether. The past and the future are not real. The past is always something remembered, so we can never actually be in the past. We can access our memory, but when we access memory we do it in the present; we don't revert to a previous moment in time. Nobody can go into the past; nor can anyone proceed into the future. The mind's projections into the future are just predictions of what may happen based on our experience of the past. Because of that, we can never access the future or the past—we're always tied to the present. This is where reality is. It can't be otherwise. The more we remain mindful, the more we keep to the present and stay with what's real. The key to it all is mindfulness.

The world doesn't really know the present. When we talk about the world, what do we mean? We mean the typical worldly state of mind. A mind that is very scattered and unable to focus for any length of time ends up in a state of half sleep, a dreamlike state. In that state, the delusion is almost complete. We have so much moha, so much delusion, that we are inextricably attached to the normal worldview—to the way things seem in the world—which is rooted in accepted conventions. Being locked into that one-dimensional perspective brings us back to birth again and again. The conventions and the habits that we are so accustomed to are the things that bring us back all the time. So it's important to break up the delusion which promotes that attachment. But we can't do it too quickly. Like everything else in nature, the more quickly something changes the more violent the reaction is. So we must patiently develop and sharpen the tools we need to bring lasting change to our whole perspective. And mindfulness is the passport to success.

When training to develop mindfulness, we try to be aware of what is coming in through the five senses, including our actions, our speech and our thoughts. But that is merely the training for mindfulness; it's not the real thing. The real mindfulness is almost automatic. It is mindful awareness at the mano dvara, the door of the mind. Everything enters the mind through that door, so if mindfulness is focused there, we know whatever comes in. There is no effort involved, it is simply automatic. But reaching the level of automatic mindfulness depends on the prior sustained effort we made to practice mindfulness in all of our daily activities. Only after much concerted effort can we reach the stage where mindfulness is automatic. Only then do we begin to realize that the whole world exists inside the mind, that actually our entire experience is internal. Because everything comes in through the mind-door, there is no need to send the mind out to external objects.

Imagine you are guarding a fortress surrounded by a wall with several doors leading in. When people come in, you must run from door to door and back again to check on them. It soon becomes hectic and confusing. But if you remain in the center and know from that central vantage point, you are aware of everything that comes and goes. Similarly, if, when seeing, you put your mindfulness on the sights, and then when hearing, you put it on the sounds, mindfulness must jump about all over the place. When it's centered in the mind, it knows whatever sensations come in, whether from seeing or hearing or whatever. The whole lot is known easily without any trouble at all. You know what comes and goes there all the time. You don't need to go out to the object. When it's like that, you are aware of everything. Nothing can escape your attention.

When you gain skill in mindfulness, the problems that come up in practice usually sort themselves out in a way that allows you to progress unhindered. When you are stuck and can't find a way forward, mindfulness is usually the faculty that is lacking. Mindfulness provides the data that you need to investigate with wisdom. By being constantly aware of what is happening in the present moment, mindfulness is the awareness that gathers the data that you need to work with. It delineates the parameters of whatever you want to focus on. Once you have the raw data in the form of details, you can begin building up a clear picture as a basis for understanding. In a sense, mindfulness supervises the investigation, but in a passive, not an active, way.

If you can remain truly mindful, then that mindfulness will gradually overcome the delusion. Once you scrutinize a difficult situation to see what it really means, your mindful attention cuts to the heart of that problem. Turning to look directly at a problematic mental state tends to diminish the problem. Diverting attention from it by thinking about something else, or finding some external distraction, merely allows that mental state to remain. Such diversions don't stop it; they merely postpone dealing with it. At best, they're a temporary pause.

Say a person feels bored. What is boredom? Boredom really means you can't fix the mind on anything. Concentration brings happiness. Boredom means that the mind is so dispersed it can't focus on anything long enough to bring up interest and feel contentment. When the mind is like that, it's bored. When you turn to examine that state, you are bringing up something to concentrate on. That concentration itself tends to get rid of the boredom.

Concentration practices entail learning to bring the mind more and more into the present. They accomplish that by using non-analytical methods of controlling the mind. In other words, wisdom is not active so there's no clear comprehension of what's happening. But because samādhi concentration is a present-moment experience that is real, a strong sense of contentment arises. All discontent stems from clinging to either the past or the future. You are attached to what has already happened, or you are worried about what will happen in the future. The present is here now, and it is just right in itself. Being in the present fosters an internal state of equilibrium and well-being.

The training for concentration requires a persistent effort as part of the training. When you train yourself to put forth effort in everything you do, that positive tendency is constantly strengthened. But effort is a neutral power, so it is important that you direct it towards positive goals. Effort will follow our intentions, so it should always be accompanied by a certain amount of wisdom.

We must overcome the status quo, our habitual state of unawareness—the tendency to think and act while being completely unaware of what we are doing. The mind is simply not present. When it's like that, thinking and acting are quite automatic without the underlying knowingness of the mind being really engaged. That is why mindfulness is so important. It keeps the mind focused in the present moment, so that we can see and know what we are thinking and doing. When we are fully aware of what we think and do, we must then put that knowledge into a frame of reference to figure out how our thoughts and actions relate to everything else that is going on around us. From that we can make a judgment, deciding whether what we think and do is good or bad, right or wrong. We can then determine what the consequences are likely to be. This is where mindfulness and wisdom come into play.

Wise effort is the willpower needed to prevent the arising of evil or unwholesome thoughts, and to abandon any unwholesome thoughts that have already arisen. It is also the willpower needed to produce and develop good and wholesome mental states, as well as to maintain and increase those good states already present. That is the way willpower should be used. It empowers the volition to go in the right direction.

Unfortunately, willpower often has the power of the kilesas behind it. When that's the case, it will always push in the wrong direction. When people follow the wrong way until it becomes habitual, it is extremely difficult to turn around and go in the right way. They can reach a point where it's almost impossible to come back. It is not absolutely impossible, because there is no fundamental impossibility for anyone. But they simply have no interest in the things that will turn them around. Because they are only interested in unwholesome matters, they do not want to hear about wholesome ones. When it's like that, nobody can make them reverse course. Only traumatic or catastrophic events can have a sobering effect.

On the other hand, for those people whose willpower habitually goes in the right direction, it becomes increasingly more unlikely to slip back into unwholesome ways. Their positive direction allows them to see the dangers of wrong behavior, and because of that they develop a healthy respect for the consequences of their actions. People who understand the potential for their actions to bring results are fearful of making bad kamma. They know that unfortunate consequences will rebound back on them.

Right effort is the effort that brings you into alignment with the Middle Way. It is the effort that actively works against the kilesas, and undermines their ability to manipulate the mind. This is the true meaning of the much talked-about, and much misunderstood, Middle Way. There is a lot of muddle in the Middle Way. Many Buddhists have the idea that the Middle Way means taking the path of least resistance. But it doesn't. The Middle Way is uncompromising. When the kilesas pull us away from the middle, instead of giving in to them, we must use a practice that restores the proper balance and brings us back to the center.

The Buddha taught that when your mind is biased in one way, you have to counterbalance it to bring yourself back to the middle. He taught three factors that are fundamental to success in meditation: mindfulness, wisdom and effort. Mindfulness keeps you attentive and aware; wisdom directs your attention in the right way; and effort makes you progress further and further along the path. Following the middle path means that you use whichever one is appropriate for a particular situation. The kilesas do not come up in a nice orderly fashion; they come up randomly in their own time. Their arising is unpredictable, so you must be prepared to use whatever means necessary to counter them and bring your mind back into balance.

Most people think that the Middle Way is like a good old English compromise. But that isn't true. The Middle Way indicates the path required to counter the defilements. Because of the nature of their kilesas, some people have to practice the strictest austerities to counter them. For such people, those strict austerities are the Middle Way. Other people, because their kilesas are weaker, can practice with more ease and comfort. For them, that will be the Middle Way. When you go in the direction of the kilesas, you are moving away from the center. Countering the kilesas means bringing your mind and your practice back to the center; that is, back into balance. The Middle Way is a matter of balancing the practice against the kilesas.

REBIRTH

I have always felt that kamma played a big part in my decision to become a Buddhist monk. When you think about it, tens of millions of people live in England, but how many of them have become Buddhist monks? Hardly any. So I think that kamma must have played a significant role. Besides that, as a young man I chanced to read a book on Buddhism which so interested me that I began reading other books as well. I read not only books on Buddhism but books about Hinduism and Christianity too. In the end I reached the conclusion that Buddhism suited me the best. I did consider converting to Catholicism at one time, but the problems that I came up against were the issues of kamma and cause and effect, which seemed to be lacking in Catholicism. I just could not accept a religion that did not include those principles. It just didn't ring true.

It is important to realize that most of the pleasant and unpleasant things that we experience in this life represent the ripening of actions performed in the past, usually in past lives. Those consequences of kamma are programmed into us from birth, causing us to constantly reap the fruits of our previous deeds. Be they good or bad, they are the fruits we deserve. And because kamma is an immutable law of cause and effect, we cannot avoid the consequences by looking for scapegoats. We must accept them as our just rewards.

However, although most experiences in life are the results of previous actions, our responses to those experiences are not predetermined. Instead, they represent new actions which will bear their own fruits in the future. What happens to us now may have resulted from past causes, but it's how we respond to what occurs in the present that will determine what we experience in the future. The underlying intention behind our actions is what determines the nature of their results. In other words, we have a choice. We are the masters of our own future.

So whatever action you may do, even though no one else ever knows about it, you yourself always know because the trace is there within you. That knowledge gets buried within your heart. And when the time comes for that trace to ripen, it will suddenly appear as a result of your previous action.

When the consequence is misfortune, people may lament: why does this happen to me? They do not see the seeds that their previous actions sowed. Because they cannot see the truth, they feel that they are at the mercy of blind justice or God's will or something like that. They don't realize that they themselves have sown the seeds of misfortune.

Such people may even be inclined to deny that rebirth follows death. Or they may hold to the nihilistic view that rejects the possibility of life after death. But such views do not alter the truth. The truth is not governed by speculation, or influenced by people's views and opinions. At the time of death, the supreme authority of kamma and its consequences overrides all such speculative beliefs.

Buddhism asks us to reflect on the truth of our own mortality. It's actually an obvious truth—that we are bound to grow old, become ill and die—but one that we tend to accept only grudgingly. The Buddha was not being insensitive or morbid in calling our attention to human life's inevitable march towards death. In asking us to focus careful attention on matters of birth and death, the Buddha sought to arouse in us a strong determination to turn away from unwholesome states of mind and replace them with wholesome states of mind.

The reason for this is the fact that our actions of body, speech and mind have consequences—both now and for our long-term future. In other words, the consequences of our actions rebound back to us either later in the same life in which the actions are done, or in some future life. Thus, the reason why a being is reborn into a particular realm is because, in a previous life, that being made the kind of kamma that predisposes one to rebirth in that realm.

These two principles—kamma and rebirth—are fundamental to understanding the Buddha's teaching. Kamma means action. When we act, speak or think, those actions leave traces in the mind that are bound to bring results in the future. When we do good actions, good results follow; when we do bad actions, the consequences are correspondingly bad. The traces that are left are not left anywhere outside of oneself. They are internal traces left within the heart.

In Buddhism, we say that causes have effects. In that sense, the actions that we do are causes that will have effects sometime in the future; if not in this lifetime, then sometime after we die. And action, or a cause, creates a force which must find an outlet. The outlet that it finds will depend upon the nature of the action that was done, and the nature of the intention motivating that action. So depending on the nature of the action and the volition, a karmic consequence can arise anywhere at any time, in any realm of existence and in any future birth.

Buddhists have a firm belief in many realms of existence, both above and below the human realm. This range extends from the highest heavenly realms down to the lowest hell realms. It is this hierarchy of existence that constitutes the Buddhist universe. Living beings are being born, dying and being reborn continually. This process is the round of rebirth known as saṁsāra, which implies wandering from life to life with no particular direction or purpose.

Beings wander through this vast and endless universe attempting to find a permanent home, a place where they can feel at ease and secure. In the realms of the devas, they find great happiness; in the realms of hell, great suffering. But their stay in these dimensions is always temporary. No place in the whole universe is permanently secure. Sooner or later, whatever the realm of rebirth, a being will die to be reborn somewhere else. So the search for happiness and security within the round of rebirth never ends.

Direct knowledge of the all-encompassing nature of kamma and rebirth was an essential aspect of the Buddha's enlightenment. As part of his enlightenment experience, his mind traveled back through all of his uncountable past lives. Though his search stretched back incalculable eons, he never saw a beginning to his past existence. He found no beginning and no end. Later he witnessed all the beings in the universe being born, living, dying and being reborn over and over again without end, all trapped in a web spun by their past actions. As a result of that knowledge, the universal laws of kamma and rebirth became central tenets of the Buddha's teaching. In fact, an understanding and acceptance of the principle of kamma and its fruit is an essential aspect of Right View.

The quality of future births depends on the moral quality of our actions now. Relatively speaking, we create ourselves. Kamma means that what we do, we become. We become that because we have acted in a certain way to set up those conditions. So our actions create our own future. If we want our future to be good, we must look very carefully at the kamma we make now.

This is where mindfulness comes in—the awareness of what is right and what is wrong, what is good and what is bad. By practicing in the right way and doing the right actions, you can develop a pretty good future for yourself. If bad kamma prevails, it could be quite disastrous. So kamma is very important.

Where there is kamma, there must be rebirth. We call it rebirth, but actually it is future birth dependent on preceding conditions. Rebirth is just a convenient way of speaking, but it is not strictly correct. No re-birth takes place because there is nothing to be re-born.

To give an example: Suppose you have a box of candles. You light the first one, and then using the flame from the first candle, you light a second one and blow out the first. Is the second flame part of the first one or not? Does the second flame come from the first? You can't say that, because the first one has been blown out and has disappeared completely. On the other hand, you cannot say that they are completely separate, because the existence of the second flame depended upon the flame from the first one.

What happens is this: We make kamma, both good kamma and bad kamma. One of the most powerful mental defilements is the desire for existence, the desire for life. That desire causes us to do actions which promote future existence. By "existence," we mean existence in the form of life, whether it is experienced in terms of sensation or some form of intelligence. When we promote certain actions, those actions must have their results. So the actions themselves produce the next life. When we die, that craving for existence remains.

It is kamma born of craving that passes the flame from one life to the next. That kamma of craving existence creates the re-linking consciousness. We are then pitched into a situation that originates from something we have done in the past. In this way, the grasping for life combines with kamma, which determines the precise destination of our next birth. Once kamma is attached to the new state, then the kamma keeps the ball rolling. At that point, we are at the mercy of our accumulated store of morally good and bad actions.

Many people are hampered in their quest for happiness by their previous kamma. For example, the consequences of killing mean experiencing a lot of suffering. Karmic consequences usually alter the character of the actor. When people do bad kamma, it alters their character for the worse. They may think: "When the time comes, I'll do some good deeds." The problem is, they're slipping down all the time, so when the time comes, they forget about doing good deeds. They simply ignore them—that's the way it tends to go.

When one slips down, climbing back is hard work. It's easy to go down but difficult to get up. That's why it is best to avoid even small instances of bad kamma; they easily turn into habits that become a part of one's character. When that happens, one's character becomes altered, sometimes irreparably.

There is a case on record in the suttas of a man who was a pig butcher. When he reached the age of sixty, he stopped speaking and wouldn't take his food normally. He had to eat kneeling on the ground. He wouldn't use his hands; he just stretched his neck out and ate from the ground. I heard there was a similar case in northern India much more recently: a man who had been a pig butcher did the same thing within the last 40 years. By killing an animal, a person incurs a debt, which can mean he takes on the characteristics of that animal. So one of the consequences of killing animals is that a person tends to assume animal-like tendencies.

People are always creating their own futures. They create now what they will later become. Usually, the future they create is something they don't want. By not wanting it, they actually create it. People worry constantly about things that they don't want to happen, and that very thinking brings them about. The ghost realm, for instance, is created in that way. People's thinking creates that realm of existence, and then they are reborn there.

The coarsest actions, which are bodily actions, bring the most obvious karmic results. Speech is midway. Thought is the most subtle. So kamma comes up in different degrees depending on how it is created. Take anger. If you give way to thoughts of anger, those thoughts are kamma, backed by taṇhā, or craving. The taṇhā is the wanting to get rid of unpleasant feelings, thus arousing anger. The tendency is to try to get rid of those unpleasant feelings by blaming or criticizing someone or something. Those angry thoughts are a type of mental kamma that will come back on you in terms of more unwholesome thoughts.

The taṇhā creates a situation of attachment. In the case of anger, it is attachment to the situation that caused the angry reaction. Because that attachment is still there, the anger can easily arise again. When the trigger is pulled for that sort of situation to occur again—maybe you see the guy somewhere on the street, and suddenly it all comes up—then you have the same problem coming again, and the tendency to make similar kamma by way of speech and action.

When we understand that everything we experience in the present results from past causes, we begin to reorder our priorities. It is obviously not possible to change the past. Consequently, the way we respond to what happens to us now becomes the important matter, because present actions will shape our future. We begin to take responsibility for our situation once we realize that what we experience in this lifetime results from causes we ourselves created in the past. Instead of feeling like helpless victims of an unfair system, we break the habit of blaming others for everything that goes wrong in our lives. In other words, we take full control of our life and our destiny.

The Buddha said that we should use wisdom in everything we do. That means looking at and examining the intentions behind our behavior. Are our actions based on defilements or on Dhamma? We should be very careful of the actions we do in everyday life to make sure that we do not perform bad actions that will cause us suffering in the future. Before initiating any course of action, we must make sure that it is leading in the right direction. We should look to see what we are involving ourselves in, what we are involving other people in, and how that will affect us down the road. Because, in the end, everything we do is creating kamma. We should take care not to unnecessarily build up a store of unwanted results. So we have to be wise and careful in the choices we make.

The important thing is how we respond to situations as they arise. By reacting skillfully, we can change our response from negative to positive. Choice is the positive side of kamma. As human beings, we can make choices based on our innate intelligence. That is one of the reasons why a human birth is so valuable. Animals are basically creatures of instinct, making it difficult for them to have much choice. They lack the means to develop a broader view of their situation. People, on the other hand, have a choice. They don't have to follow their base instincts and react negatively when confronted with the inevitable unpleasantness of life.

Rebirth as a human being is a result of predominantly good kamma from the past. The kamma may have been done many lifetimes before, but more likely it was done in the previous life. A person's state of mind at the time of death is the critical factor in the process of rebirth. At the moment of death, significant good or bad actions performed during that life will tend to arise in the dying person's mind. Otherwise, habitual tendencies or actions performed near the time of death will tend to come to mind. The state of mind at that crucial moment will largely determine the mind's direction as it grasps at future birth.

It's worth contemplating death from time to time. The interesting thing about death is that, after death, nothing of what you can call yourself is left. The body breaks up and disintegrates. No essence remains there. Feelings, thoughts and memories break up as well. All that's left is your kamma.

After all, what is death? Firstly, it's the breakup of one's body. If one views the body as an integral part of one's self-identity, it's the breakup of oneself. Then one's kamma fashions an environment based on one's past actions which is grasped as a ground for rebirth. But the one that is born is not the same one that died. They're on the same continuum, but they are not the same person. Then again, we can't say that they're different either, because they both share the same karmic legacy.

When you reach the time of death, what's going to happen? Try to visualize it. Think of the body. What happens when the body dies? When the body dies, all sensation goes with it—sight, sound, smell, taste, and touch all vanish. So your normal perception of the world disappears. Your possessions all go completely—you won't have control over the slightest part of them. You are totally on your own. You should consider that, and think about what it means. Why do you place so much importance on your possessions? Why are you so concerned about what other people think of you? Why are you so concerned about your social status? Or your position at work? If you are well aware of death, if you contemplate death a lot until you feel it and see it clearly, the importance of these things tends to drop away. Because of that, when they eventually change or disappear, you are no longer affected.

The only possession you keep at death is your kamma. And the best way to make sure that it is good kamma is to do Buddhist practice. This is right kamma. Because it is the direct training for the sake of Nibbāna, the kamma of doing the practice is the best kind you can make.

Even though we are bound by our kamma to wander endlessly from life to life through saṁsāra, this does not mean that the search for true happiness and security is futile and without end. The Buddha himself is the one who found the path and followed it to the end of suffering, thus transcending the world and going beyond the round of rebirth. Because the nature of beings is not absolutely fixed, anyone can follow the Buddha's noble path to the attainment of Nibbāna. That is, all of us have the potential to become noble disciples of the Buddha.

Just like the Buddha prior to his enlightenment, we have all lived through countless different lifetimes before reaching this point. Fundamentally, we all share the same potential for enlightenment that the Buddha had. We, too, can walk the Buddha's path to the end of suffering. That goal is entirely feasible because it was taught by somebody who had accomplished it himself, someone who understood the problems. Right now the problem we face is that our potential remains dormant and undeveloped. It is our job to bring it to light. According to the Buddha's teaching, we are responsible both for what happens to us and for how we respond to it. What happens to us is a result of causes we ourselves have set in motion. How we react to that will determine our future. All that's left is for us to take up the challenge and assume full responsibility for our potential.

BASICS

Now I'll present a short overview of Dhamma, perhaps from a slightly unusual angle. One of the experiences that we constantly have in life is the unsettling feeling of discontent gnawing inside our hearts. We know it—it's always there—but we don't know what it wants or why it wants it. And yet, we know it's there. We can say that everybody experiences a similar underlying discontent. It's a problem people are always seeking to cure. They focus outside themselves looking for some relief: they search for money; they search for goods; they search for power; they search for anything they think will bring them contentment. But no matter how hard they try or how successful they become, the discontent is still there. In the end, mostly they just give up hope of finding a cure. This is what happens so often in life.

It is reasonable that people should want to cure their chronic discontent. They are justified in their desire to remedy the situation. It is the right way. But people invariably misunderstand the fundamental causes of their dissatisfaction. Because of that, people search for contentment in all the wrong places, and behave in all the wrong ways. Discontent is a consequence of wrong actions of body, speech and mind. But people fail to realize that their actions are inherently misguided. Nor do they see the connection between those wrong deeds and their discontent.

Looking at the world we live in, we can see that almost everyone is trying to cure discontent in the wrong way. Instead of looking inside themselves to find a solution, they are searching for happiness outside themselves. Yet they are completely blind to their mistake. The Buddha taught that the fundamental problem is a lack of understanding. We don't know. What we have is a lack of understanding, but we are blinded to the problem by our own ignorance. Being unaware of our ignorance, we don't see the fundamental delusion. Part of the problem can be traced back to the things we learned when we were very young.

At a young age, we learned things from parents, from schoolmates, from school teachers—probably more from classmates than from teachers—and so on. We learned our view of the world from the people around us. At that age, we were not in a position to judge the situation or to think "this is right" or "this is wrong." We just accepted what we were told. We accepted everything from the normal worldly perspective.

Naturally, parents teach their children the best they can. If they are good parents, they teach properly and in a good manner. They teach what they themselves learned from their mentors. But a lot of the knowledge that has been handed down is just views and supposition. There isn't much proven truth in it. Not to blame the parents, but from the standpoint of Dhamma, it's not the correct way to look at things. This misunderstanding occurs because people are convinced that the external world is what really matters. They believe that it's very important to follow the mundane ways of the world. This happens because the defilements are strong, causing people to have more faith in the ways of the world than they do in the ways of Dhamma. As children, we begin to adopt this worldly outlook, which then forms the background of our thoughts and perceptions.

Our background informs our worldview, which is related to memory. This is where the habits of the kilesas enter the picture. Because the factors of greed, hatred and delusion are present, the tendency is to have wrong views and to act in wrong ways. The kilesas are driving those bad habits. Something will trigger a memory, something related to our past, which is part of the continuity of our self-identity. Thinking of that, we reflect on ourselves in the past, which relates to us in the present and pushes our thoughts forward into the future. In that way, our thoughts are always revolving around the notion of self and its relation to time—which means that we think of ourselves in relationship to memory. Whatever comes up is immediately tested to find out: Is it good for me? Is it pleasant for me or not? And we react accordingly.

Quite often, we react in an unwholesome way, which means that our reactions are governed by greed, hatred and delusion. Those unwholesome actions are, moreover, reinforced in memory, strengthening the situation of the kilesas. Only gradually, after a long time practicing Dhamma, do mundane thought patterns begin changing as the Dhamma starts displacing the kilesas as the motivating force behind our actions. But before the Dhamma takes control, the background of the world and its values are entrenched in our hearts and discontent is never far away.

We are always searching for a way to get rid of our discontent. Due to our fundamental ignorance, we normally use the methods suggested by the kilesas, and they don't work. At most, those methods may alleviate one form of discontent, only to create another one in its place. In the end, we are actually worse off than before. If we can reach a state of calm, however, we find that the discontent dies away, at least temporarily. We have not rid ourselves of the kilesas, but they are put to rest for a while because this is a happy state of contentment. As long as the mind rests in samādhi, the kilesas remain quiet. That state of calm can be taken to an even deeper level, where the mind enters into a state of "oneness." Knowing is present, but there is no object to know. That is a state of great contentment.

This contrast between the qualities of suffering and happiness shows up in the first two verses of the Dhammapada, which begin by stating that mind is the forerunner of all conditions. Mind is their chief; all conditions originate from mind. The second verse states that when a person acts with evil intent, pain follows him as the wheels of the ox cart follow the hooves of the ox. The implication here is that pain and suffering are something hard and crushing. It further states that when a person acts with virtuous intent, happiness follows him like a shadow which never leaves. You can see the contrast there: the wheels of the ox cart are coarse, the shadow is subtle. It must be like that because dukkha is going in the wrong direction and the wrong direction becomes heavier all the time; whereas happiness is a result of moving in the right direction, which is bound to be experienced as progressive levels of lightness. However, although you can't point to happiness when it is present, if, for any reason, that happiness disappears for even a short while, you notice that something valuable is missing.

To be successful, meditation practice has to encompass the whole person and all aspects of daily life. The path of practice has both cause and effect, which means a proper foundation leading to good results. We can't choose to be concerned with some aspects of the path and neglect others. If we do, all our efforts will ultimately prove disappointing. For that reason, it's extremely important to address the question of our daily habits and patterns of behavior when beginning the practice of meditation. Behavior and attitudes that lead to tense, stressful relations with others or a nagging sense of regret and remorse invariably have a detrimental effect on our peace of mind. This makes meditation very difficult to develop properly.

That being the case, adherence to the moral precepts is strongly emphasized as a means to harmonize our relations with people in the world. In other words, when we have a firm moral basis, we feel no pull to the world. We do not harbor feelings of guilt in relation to the world, which in turn lead to feelings of discontent that don't allow us to settle down and stay calm. If we have good morality, we can settle easily into the meditation practice and forget the world outside. In that way, the more we meditate, the less our minds tend to go out into worldly matters, and the more effective our meditation can be.

The right way to develop your mind is to follow the well-established, traditional practices that have been passed down through successive generations from the time of the Buddha to the present day, beginning with moral virtue which leads to meditative calm and wisdom.

In the practice of moral discipline, the five precepts are the training rules we observe. Together they constitute an excellent field of training. The five moral precepts are: not to kill, including not only human beings, but animals as well; not to steal; not to indulge in sexual misconduct; not to use false speech, lies, slander, gossip and so on; and not to take drinks and drugs. These five rules of training form the basis of a decent human being. If you can't even adhere to these, you become less and less human. And the end result, well, I'll leave it to you to guess.

Unfortunately, very few people have any real understanding of the way morality works. When people misunderstand the nature of morality, they do all the wrong things, thinking they're doing the right ones. In the West, this tendency is very prevalent now. Lack of moral virtue is a problem that's causing a great deal of trouble. And that's due to a complete misunderstanding of the way morality functions. People say: "Why should we be moral anyway?" Many of them do not believe in any kind of higher moral authority. They think that no repercussions will follow from their actions. Therefore, if they do immoral actions they will get away with them. They fail to understand that they change themselves every time they do an immoral act. They change themselves in a manner that inevitably steers them into a situation where they will receive the consequences of those actions.

When it comes to the practice of Buddhism, it's like the Buddha said: only a few people have little dust in their eyes, only a few. We can't expect most people to be in a position to progress quickly and easily along the path. The best we can expect for most people is that practicing the basic teaching on morality will remove a little bit of the dust from their eyes. In that way, more people will be in the position to understand.

As it is, ordinary people in the world are not capable of much understanding. They go the way of their kamma: they behave badly when they feel inclined to and they are dragged down by it. It's been going on that way for an extremely long time, and the momentum of kamma will keep it going like that indefinitely. Those people who have enough understanding to see the nature of the world clearly realize that this is not a good situation. They know they should try to get free. For them, keeping the moral precepts strictly is very important. They will not compromise on them at all.

In truth, morality is a practice that maintains your status as a decent human being. It maintains that status by keeping your actions within the bounds of what's going to bring you beneficial results in the future. If you choose to do actions that bring unfortunate consequences, you'll just go down and down and down. And the more you go down, the duller and more stupid you become, and the less you are able to see the rut you're in. Acting blindly, you do more harmful actions, causing you to go down further, until the end result is very unfortunate indeed.

Most people are unaware of the direct relationship between actions and consequences. If you want to see some of those consequences, just go into any mental hospital and have a look around. Look at the really burned-out cases and see what they're like. This is the sort of thing that can happen. And this is one reason why people should be moral—just to keep themselves sane. It's mental hygiene.

Normally, people don't eat dirty food or go without bathing until they become filthy. Being fearful of disease, they maintain standards of cleanliness. They worry about diseases of the body, but they don't care a damn about diseases of the mind. And most people have diseases lurking within their minds all the time. More than anything else, these diseases of the mind come from unhealthy states of morality.

Because bad morality originates from defiled states of mind, it is necessary to study the defilements to learn how they operate. After all, the kilesas have always been the enemy of peace and contentment. Reflect on the kilesas as much as you can, and try to see them within yourself. Notice how deep and how subtle they are. Learn what's needed in your own mind to counter those defiling influences. It's not always a matter of sitting formally in meditation; it is more often a matter of observing your mind in the course of your daily life. This is where many people fail in Buddhism. They want very much to do meditation practice, but they do not want to practice virtue to clean up their daily lives. And without a strong sense of morality, meditation will not work.

For example, people tend to think that taking a drink doesn't matter. And it's true. Taking a drink is not considered to be very important. The Buddha said that the real problem is what you do when you're under the influence of alcohol. When you take a drink, you're no longer in full control of yourself. Because of that, you can do things that you would never otherwise do.

If one looks at it from a psychological point of view, one can ask: "Why do I want to drink? What's the purpose?" If you look, you'll find that drink is really an anesthetic. People want to anesthetize themselves to some extent. They want to dull their minds so they don't notice their suffering. This is not the correct way to alleviate suffering. These substances do not take the mind to a higher level, but rather to a lower level. They all distort the mind in some way, creating conditions that are not helpful on the path of Buddhist practice. On the Buddhist path, we need to be sharp so we can see and understand clearly, so as to penetrate to the truth of the Buddha's teaching. Dulling the mind goes in the opposite direction.

Usually people who take drugs are trying to find a shortcut. They're trying to enter a certain mental state through the back door. What they don't realize is that the attainment of a meditative state can only be correct if there's hard work behind it. You must go about achieving it in the right way. When you attempt to cut corners, even if you gain something, you'll lose it just as quickly. It's not something that is truly a part of your nature. When you penetrate the domain of the mind in the orthodox way, by means of the practice, then you experience something genuine.

The nature of moral behavior is rather interesting. Morality in general is a relative thing. But it's not relative in the way they thought of it in the 1960's in America. It's not relative to the individual. It's relative to the human being as a human being. It is the set of conditions that relates directly to the human being, which means it comprises the virtues of human status. So to break those precepts is really going against one's own human nature. Take an animal like a tiger, it has a different set of precepts. It has its own kind of precepts, the precepts of its nature. Its nature is that of the tiger. If it acts within the bounds of what a tiger is, then it keeps to that state. It's that way with most animals. The nature of a tiger, or the nature of a human being, or the nature of a dog: these are different levels and forms of nature.

The human being is a very high form of nature, so we should at least try to honor that by keeping the five precepts. It is important to understand, however, that morality does not mean only the five precepts. It also means right behavior and good manners in general. It means being careful in speech and action, doing things in a seemly and proper way. All of this comes under the heading of moral virtue.

The main pillars of morality are, of course, the five precepts. These five are the most important ones to practice. But there is a lot more than that to the practice of morality. You can see the general aspects of morality in people's behavior. Some people behave in a very coarse way, and it shows. When a person behaves in a coarse way, we refer to them as a crude person. Whereas, someone who behaves in a refined way we call a refined person. Because their actions initiate from their minds, these two people will tend to think and act quite differently.

When what flows out from the mind is good, then the resulting actions will be good. Those actions produce the type of kamma that will always redound to our benefit. So we should pay attention to our ordinary behavior as well as the specific actions covered by the five precepts.

Actions of body, speech and mind are forms of kamma. Kamma literally means action; but, more specifically, it is volitional action initiated from deep within the human heart. That volition may remain purely mental as thought, or it may be expressed outwardly through bodily and verbal actions. The resulting kamma then creates a potential to bring forth results that correspond to the nature of those actions. When internal and external conditions are suitable, kamma gives rise to the appropriate consequences.

There are three types of kamma: thought, speech and action. Thought is the most subtle. Speech is more gross. Action is the grossest. The Buddhist position on morality is that it concerns speech and action only—not thought—because thoughts are too subtle for people to control. Because they are so difficult to control, the Buddha said that our first duty is to get everything right outside—and outside means speech and action. Even though you're turbulent inside, get it right outside first, so that you don't upset the world around you. When you upset the world, the world reacts negatively. Then your situation is not peaceful, so you can't focus properly on any of the other practices. You must first set right your responsibility to the world without lingering feelings of regret or remorse. Being at peace with the world, you are free to forget worldly concerns and focus inside.

Because actions and speech are on public display, they directly impact the world around you, defining your relations with other people by the reactions they cause. Thoughts, even when they concern other people, arise in such a way that those people are unaware of their content, so they have no cause to react. Because of that, the level of thought is higher than those of speech and action and so doesn't come under the heading of morality. If you look at the five precepts, they are all concerned with speech and actions—none of them concern the mind itself.

However, training the mind is very important because if you think wrongly, that harmful mental attitude tends to go out into speech and action. In those circumstances, you very easily engage in misconduct. Those who constantly do immoral deeds tend to slide down below the level of a human being. This is very unfortunate, because it's easy to go down but very difficult to get back up. So you should be vigilant in maintaining the precepts.

In practicing the way of Dhamma, one must start from the level of moral virtue. One needn't be a recluse to practice meditation, but moral integrity is needed. For a householder, practicing regularly at home can be very valuable. Although the meditation may not go terribly deep, it still has significant potential. But first, one has to overcome all the difficulties that living in the world presents by using mindfulness and self-restraint. All day long one is either driving or catching buses or shopping or working a job. Through all that, the mind is constantly jumping about to all sorts of things. When one sits down to do meditation practice, the thinking continues unabated. Because of that, it's very difficult for a person living in the world to slow down enough to do serious practice.

Those who have done sufficient training to achieve some control of the mind can practice more effectively in the work-a-day world. But it usually takes a lot of hard work. Chiefly, one must learn to control one's thoughts. And that means words, words in the mind. Cutting off the inner dialogue allows one to gain a lot of control over the mind. But that is not easy. It's as though when a thought comes up, that thought seems terribly important at that moment. There's a voice inside which says, "Oh, you should think that out first before continuing with the practice." But this is just the kilesas whispering again—that's the way they are, always putting up stiff resistance.

We must come to know the kilesas because they are the adversaries of Dhamma. When we know the enemy we get some idea of what we're up against and how powerful their resistance is. Both Dhamma and the kilesas are located in the heart. The two are mixed in together, both vying for center stage. At one moment Dhamma may come up; at another moment kilesas come up. But for the ordinary person, it is inevitably the kilesas that have the upper hand. For that reason, practically everything we do is infused with kilesas. We're never free of them. We can see this in our own practical experience. Our general outlook on the world remains constant over time. Because that outlook is infused with kilesas, it's as though we're always wearing a pair of tinted spectacles. The whole outlook is colored by them, distorting everything. Because we never get to remove the spectacles, we never have a chance to see things clearly.

If we had enough clarity, the kilesas would stand out sharply in our minds. But because we never see the other side, it seems as though the defilements are not even there. We can catch them only when they become more obvious: as when anger comes up or greed comes up. When the kilesas become active, then we can catch a glimpse of them. We may not see them at the time they arise; but afterwards, on reflection, we realize that the kilesas came up. When that happens, we should question ourselves: "What brought that up? How did it come up?"

When we analyze this process until we see clearly how the kilesas arise in our minds, we can then watch them much more closely. It's still a very long task to overcome them; even getting some control over the simpler ones is hard. We must use all the methods of Dhamma at our disposal to rein them in. But the more we can subdue the kilesas, the more happiness we experience and the more freedom we feel. We can see that we are achieving something that matters, which gives us the feeling that we're people of importance. I don't mean important in the sense of big in the world, but rather a sense of something inside which has real value.

Previously, we seemed to be just like everyone else, but as the kilesas diminish, it becomes more and more apparent that mentally we feel a bit different from other people. We find that this inner freedom is far more worthwhile than anything else, simply because it's real, and it lasts. It isn't something that just comes and goes. It remains vibrant in the heart. That inner stability is what we are aiming for.

Most people have very little understanding about what happens inside their own minds. This is something that we should try to remedy. Otherwise, life will pass us by and we will have lost the opportunity to do something about it. It is very important that we have a mind which is well-trained in mindfulness and knows its situation at all times. Mindfulness is essential. As long as we have mindfulness keeping a close watch on our mental state, we can be pretty confident in our speech and actions.

The only way we can prevent negligence in our actions is to be mindful. When mindfulness is present, we are aware and watchful to make sure that a harmful negative reaction does not come up. By careful observation, we realize what is wrong and stop the reaction before it can arise as speech or bodily action. When we do that, we bring more and more of the Dhamma into our lives. The more Dhamma comes into our lives, the more our minds incline to Dhamma, which leads to harmony and peace. That state of harmony and peace then increases the amount of happiness and contentment that we experience. Conversely, when we go against the Dhamma, we promote negative reactions which clash inside the heart. When these internal battles are going on, there's a feeling of constant dissatisfaction. That is a way the kilesas cause suffering.

When examining our minds, we'll probably find that they are whirling about much of the time. Stray thoughts pop up in a rather random fashion: thoughts, ideas, pictures, and so on. The mind is just spinning aimlessly; it's out of control. This is not a beneficial state, but it is there in practically everyone. Very few people have proper control of their minds. In order to stop the restless whirling of the mind and establish some control over it, we must develop a meditation practice. When we can control the mind and bring it to a state where mindfulness is in charge such that the internal situation is clearly understood, one can then be more or less confident of the future. In that way, we start to change the haphazard way the future seems to just overtake us and we begin to develop control over circumstances as they occur.

Begin meditation practice by focusing your attention on one object, like the breath. Mindfulness of the breath has long been considered one of the most effective means of helping beginners to develop mental calm and concentration. Seated comfortably in meditation, preferably in a quiet and calm environment, simply remain aware of the normal cycle of breathing, the in-breath followed by the out-breath, focusing on each breath as it passes the tip of the nose—breathing in, then out, then in again.

While doing that practice, you'll find initially that the mind has a strong tendency to jump away. You focus your mind on the breathing, and the mind stays there for a short while. Then, oops, it's gone. It jumps away. This is the mind's natural tendency. You can never really get the mind to stay still; it just won't stop. The mind is always moving, but its movement has different qualities. If it is moving in just a haphazard way, it becomes very weak. So, to strengthen the mind, you have to bring it into a single channel. Then, it becomes strong, and it becomes capable of thinking properly. Also, you find that the mind becomes calmer and experiences a sense of contentment that it has never known before. This contentment is very important, because when it comes, there is no reason for the defilements of greed, hatred and delusion to arise. Normally, they are the forces agitating the mind and causing discontent.

When you get good results from your practice, the resultant happiness will bring up more energy to continue with the meditation. At first, it's hard work; but when the happiness comes, that positive feedback supports the practice. Generally, when you fail to attain good results, the fault is too many thoughts going on in the mind: too much thinking. And even when you manage to stop thinking for a moment, the mind quickly reverts to its discursive ways. This means that the mindfulness is not strong enough, so it requires quite a sustained effort to keep the mind on the meditation object. Otherwise, you'll notice the mind being pulled away often.

When your focus is firmly on the breathing, then only the breath is known. When something comes up, trying to distract your attention in some way, tugging at it until you lose the breath, that's the kilesas interfering. They keep striving to wiggle free by bringing up all sorts of distractions to drag the mind from the discipline of the meditation object. Be aware that this is just kilesas coming up and quickly pull the mind back to the practice, using concentrated effort to hold it there. Mindfulness is the key. Mindfulness means "attention;" keep your attention on the breath.

Once you have learned to discipline the mind, try to get your focus more precise. When you have your attention fixed on the breathing, you should know not only when the breath goes out and comes in, but every moment of it coming in and every moment of it going out. When you do this, your attention is more and more absorbed in the breathing. As your attention follows the out-breath until it stops, you must be vigilant at that point because that's exactly where the mind tends to jump away. So watch that point and hold your attention there until the in-breath comes. With the in-breath, there is a similar tendency to jump away, but it's not so pronounced. The point is, you want to train yourself to make your concentration constantly more precise.

When you reach a stage of sufficient calm and strength of mind, you should then turn your attention to developing wisdom. This means, first of all, contemplating the physical body, observing it, thinking about its characteristics and questioning your assumptions about it. Look at the body closely. It's very important to understand its true nature.

People often use their bodies as a means to satisfy their desires and find gratification. But what they desire is usually quite harmful to them. Using the body in that way only causes more trouble. It is harmful for the body, and it is not good for the mind either. So, we have to look at the body and see what it's actually made of. Seeing the body in that light, we realize it's not really so attractive or desirable. It's made of physical matter that is very perishable. Its existence is uncertain. Being susceptible to disease and old age, it is always fragile and unstable. In the end, it cannot be relied upon.

When we die, the latent desire for bodily existence leads us to grasp another body. That is the way the round of rebirth continues. We have gone through all this in the past—we don't know how many times, maybe millions. Having reached the point of birth, we go through life, suffering sickness, old age and finally death, only to be reborn and start the cycle all over again. Birth, life, sickness, old age and death, just going on and on and on. And, all the time, there's suffering and discontent. The only way to break this circuit is to sever the attachment that causes it.

The attachment can be cut only by means of wisdom. In the beginning, we investigate the body to find out that this body is not me. It's not mine. This body came from the earth. It is made up of earthly substance. It relies on the earth for its sustenance, and, in the end, it goes back to the earth. So, really, the earth is the owner of the body, not me. I've just grabbed it for temporary use, and that's all.

By seeing that truth in a profound way, we lose a lot of the fear of death, realizing: "Oh! This isn't me. I don't die. I go on, but the body doesn't." The body will die. And with the body, the faculties of feeling, memory, thought and consciousness will also die. That which is left we call the "citta"—the essence of mind that knows. Knowingness does not depend on material substance. It is something that is very difficult to define, but it's the one that matters. The citta is really important because within it are the defilements of greed, hatred and delusion, as well as the Dhamma, the right way, the truth. A tug-of-war-like tension exists between the two. It just depends on circumstances which side comes out on top.

Mostly, the defilements are on top. They're the boss. It is only when we begin to see things as they really are that the Dhamma starts getting stronger. As the Dhamma gains strength, the defilements have less chance to interfere. By persisting diligently in the practice of Dhamma—and it's very hard work—one can eventually break through to a natural state of total freedom. The Buddha called it "Nibbāna." Nibbāna is what we all really should be. It's there within us all the time, but we just don't recognize it. If we can clear away all traces of ignorance and defilements, what's left will be Nibbāna.

In Buddhism, we are not aiming to become saints or to attach labels like "arahant" to ourselves. We are simply aiming to become normal people who have straightened out the crookedness in our hearts; people who have tamed those inner demons we call the kilesas, allowing us to lead ordinary lives happily, instead of at the dictates of a mass of emotions, sensations and other influences all tangled up inside our hearts. Surely this is our birthright, so to speak, rather than some exalted special status such as the word "saint" brings to mind. It is what we ought to be, a state of normality. But to reach that state we will have to fight and defeat the demon properly. At present, we have the ideal opportunity to do just that. We are now face to face, as it were, with the demon. We have the weapons of the Buddha's teaching, the protection and help of our Dhamma teachers and the good will of all our Dhamma friends. All that's left is to clench our teeth and set up the determination to carry on, however difficult it may be and however long it may take.

GOOD IN THE
MIDDLE

Buddhism is not a path of gaining so much as a path of relinquishing. The goal is not reached by striving to go higher. The goal is there already. We uncover it by getting rid of things; not by gaining something, but by relinquishing everything.

———————————————

BODY

Of all the meditation subjects that the Buddha recommended, body contemplation is probably the most unpopular with Western practitioners. Although body contemplation is very worthwhile, for some strange reason it's not encouraged much in the West. Very few teachers even mention it. Why is that? They must not realize how valuable it is.

Contemplation of the body is an essential component of the Buddha's teaching. This may seem strange in an age when people know all about the world, but know very little about themselves. They've studied science, so when you ask them the reason for doing this or that, or how something works, they can go into great detail. Even if they themselves don't know, they can easily find out by asking someone who does know, or by looking it up in books or online.

But when it comes to the human body, what do they know? Even if they know physiology, in the medical sense, all they've done is study someone else's body or pictures of the human body in a textbook—not their own body. But surely our bodies are extremely important. If we didn't have a human body, how would we experience the world? The human body allows us to access the world. It is our outlet into the world, so to speak. Surely, to know the body's true nature is essential to our well-being.

In order to comprehend its nature, we should ask ourselves: What actually is the human body? What's it composed of? Is it a pleasant thing or not? We can put aside our preconceived ideas about it, and just ask objectively: Is the body something attractive or not? Let's have a look. Most people in the world seem to think that the body is very attractive, that it's a most desirable thing.

But let's look at it and see whether that's true. What happens if we don't wash it for a few days? We've got to keep washing the thing; otherwise, it stinks before long and becomes unbearable. Let a few strands of hair fall into a plate of food, and we quickly lose our appetite. Why? Head hair and body hair are inherently filthy, which is the reason that we have to continuously wash them. In fact, nothing that comes in contact with any part of the human body remains clean for long. Due to the dirt and the smell that accumulate on our bodies, our clothing and bed linen must be constantly laundered. Even the food we eat, once it's ground between the teeth and mixed with saliva, becomes filthy as well. There are many such aspects of the body that we must look at to determine whether it's a pleasant thing or not, whether it's beautiful or not.

You should search for the truth of the matter. After all, most people think that they are their bodies. If that's the case, surely you should want to know something about yourself. When you are so interested to know everything about the world, why do you leave out the one thing that is the most important of all—yourself? Why not try to get to know yourself?

The first step in trying to get to know yourself is to question the nature of the body, because the body is the grossest part of who you are, or who you think you are. However, as you probe more deeply into body contemplation, you begin to realize that the body, in fact, is not you. It comes from the world, and it returns to the world. It's simply a part of this earth. It consists entirely of atomic structures—atoms, molecules, chemicals and so on. And it's nothing apart from these things—it doesn't go beyond the state of physical matter. When you look at it properly, you can see that it isn't really you. It doesn't belong to you; you can't even control its destiny. The body at birth is derived from the world; at death, it returns to the world. There's no way to stop it from rejoining the earth as organic matter.

When you cling to the body, it's almost as if you are confining yourself in a prison house. The human body becomes a prison that restricts you to certain conditions from which you cannot free yourself. So you must understand the body's true nature and realize that the body is not what you really are, that clinging to it creates undesirable consequences. Search and find the truth of the matter. After all, why not examine the body? It's such an obvious thing to look at.

When you do, you begin to see that your whole outlook on the world depends on the body. Consider any aspect of life and you'll find that nearly every one of them depends on the body. Houses are built according to the needs of this body; cars and towns are based on the shape and size of the human body. All the things you use are designed to fit bodily dimensions.

Because human beings are attached to their bodies, they have to put up with the vicissitudes of bodily existence, most of which are quite unpleasant. The body has its own momentum; you can't control it. It gets sick, and you can't prevent it. It grows old, and you can't prevent it. Eventually, in its own time, it dies, and you can't prevent that either.

The body belongs to the earth. It originates from earthly substance and then returns to the earth. In fact, the body can only live in a physical environment that is suited to bodily existence. The body requires earth to stand on, air to breathe, water to drink, food to eat, energy and heat to function, and so on. All these things come from the earth. Because of that, this body is really just part of the earth. But still we insist on grasping at it and claiming ownership of it. Once we own it, we also own all the difficulties that come along with bodily existence, which we find we don't like. We don't like being sick, we don't like growing old, we don't like dying.

The body is something that we are familiar enough with that we can take parts of it in our mind and keep our attention on them, turning them around and thinking about them to see their attributes and their associations, and to see their cause-and-effect relationships. Because we know so much about the body already, it's a very good basic subject for meditation.

Body contemplation takes two basic directions. One is the way of samatha, using calm and concentration as a basis; the other is the way of vipassanā, using insight and wisdom as a basis. To practice the way of samatha, you keep your attention on one aspect of the body, like the skin, without thinking much about it. Just keep the skin fixed in your mind as much as you can. One advantage of using this method is that the mind becomes calm and focused. And because the focus of your attention has been concentrated on a part of the body, it's easy to then turn and investigate that body part to develop a deeper understanding of its true nature.

The vipassanā way of doing body contemplation begins by questioning the nature of the body. What is the nature of skin? Where does skin come from? What is it composed of? What happens if I don't wash it? Suppose I cut off a piece? What lies underneath it? What internal organs is the skin covering up and what are they like? Consider all aspects of the parts that make up the body. This is the way of developing wisdom—questioning all the time, searching for what's really there.

To begin with, take the body as the body; that is, take it in the way you normally experience it in your life. You are not attempting to superimpose a radical new view on the body. Rather, you want to go more deeply into what is right there in front of you and expose some obvious truths about it. You are trying to see this body in what might be called "the light of truth"—trying to see what bodily existence means in such a deep and profound way that you realize the body is not you. It is not yours. This is the important point. Later on, you can examine the body as a mental image. At the beginning of body contemplation, however, you must look at the body in the way you normally do. Otherwise, the investigation becomes too nebulous and the practice doesn't progress properly.

The first aim of the practice is to discover for yourself the body's repulsive nature, repulsive in the sense that it doesn't reflect the nice image you have of yourself. This discovery counters the normal view that the body is an attractive and desirable part of who you are, a part that deserves your constant fondness and attention.

On the other hand, you also understand that the body is a necessary and valuable instrument, because without it you do not have a physical basis for your mental faculties. Without a physical body, you would not have access to the faculties of thinking and recollection. There'd be just bare knowing, and that's all. Therefore, you must have the body to function. So, although it is seen as undesirable, you are also aware of its necessity. As long as you maintain that balanced view of the body in your practice, you can avoid negative states of alienation and aversion.

Although it's up to each individual to decide the best method to use for body contemplation, starting with hair of the head, hair of the body, nails, teeth and skin usually provides a very good basis. If you feel you would rather investigate the body as arms, legs, head, organs and so on, that's quite a legitimate practice too. Reflect on how the human body is merely a combination of various parts; it's not a completely homogeneous entity at all. Apart from the head, most bodily parts can be cut off and the body will continue to function. An enormous amount can be removed from the body without death occurring. Then you can reflect: "If I refer to this as my body, what about this arm, is it mine? If it's cut off, is it still mine?"

So you begin body contemplation by focusing on the parts that make up the body: head hair, body hair, nails, teeth, skin, bones and so on. You can either mentally visualize each one or focus your attention on the location of each part, whichever you prefer. This exercise is the training for wisdom, not the wisdom itself. When you keep practicing in this manner, probing and questioning continuously over a long time, you will suddenly see one of the body parts from a totally different angle. It's as though you see the full implications of it in relation to the realms of mind and matter.

Take skin, for example. You know its characteristics and its basic functions. Skin is a thin layer of surface tissue that is necessary to protect the internal organs from exposure and maintain the life of the body. You are aware of all that, but what are the implications of skin as far as your notions of self are concerned? This is what the training for wisdom is trying to uncover. In the end you realize that skin is just part of the world; it comes from the world and it goes back to the world. It isn't you. There is nothing of you in it. How could it be you? What you cling to as an integral part of your self-identity is merely a perishable physical substance. When you see these implications clearly, it feels almost as though you are giving up a cherished part of yourself. Seeing the implications and letting go of the attachment is the work of wisdom. It means knowing directly that the skin is not self, not merely thinking about it. Skin couldn't be self; it has no relation to self.

That is one method used to overcome attachment to the body. Without developing your faculty of wisdom, you are unaware of how much attachment you have for it. You don't realize how much your self-identity is bound up with the body. For your own physical and mental welfare, it's very important to overcome that attachment.

Another effective method for overcoming bodily attachment is the asubha contemplation. The asubha contemplation entails focusing on the human body's inherently impure and loathsome nature. Much of our discontent comes from taking the body as the basis of who we are. It's a central feature of our self-identity. Because of this deep-seated notion, we project a definite sense of self into all our actions. We deliberately plan our whole lives around desires related to the body. By contemplating the body's impure nature, we can experience it as inherently unstable, impermanent and repulsive. In that way, we can reduce the craving built up around the body, until eventually we are able to free ourselves from the strong sense of self associated with it.

Because the skin so easily fools us with its deceptive appearance, it deserves a very careful examination. This thin layer of tissue covers the flesh and internal organs of the body. Although at a glance it may appear clean and attractive, closer inspection shows a scaly, wrinkled layer that exudes sweat and grease. Only constant washing and cleaning make it bearable to live with.

After thoroughly investigating the outer layer, mentally strip off the skin and investigate the internal organs, following whatever method best suits your natural temperament. As you contemplate the body, certain parts or characteristics should begin to stand out and catch your attention. You should focus special attention on those parts. When you investigate deeply into just one body part until seeing its true nature clearly with wisdom, you will be able to extend that understanding to include the entire body, because all bodily substance has the same nature: it's filthy, disgusting and repulsive through and through. No desirable and satisfactory personal identity can be found there.

But you must understand very clearly that the objective of this contemplation is not to stir up aversion for the body. That would be wrong. You only want to see its loathsome nature. It's rather like opening your refrigerator and seeing a rotten piece of meat that has been there the last five weeks. You'd feel it was repulsive, but you wouldn't feel hatred for it. You'd just take it out and drop it in the garbage. That's all. Likewise, with the body, it isn't hatred you want; that's wrong. You want the experience of loathsomeness, a feeling of dismay that you've grasped this body at birth, that you're bound to this body and that you have to live with it until it dies. Still, while you remain in the body, you have an opportunity to see the Dhamma. In that sense, it's quite valuable. You must use it in the right way to overcome your delusion. This is the true purpose of body contemplation.

After practicing the asubha contemplation intensively, you may later feel irritable or even angry for no apparent reason. This is a reaction to the body contemplation itself. When your deeply-ingrained views of physical identity are probed and questioned, the internal forces of delusion build up a feeling of irritation or annoyance. You may feel like a bear with a sore on its head, as they say. In order to quell those negative emotions, you should combine body contemplation with another practice like ānāpānasati or mettā to calm down and cool off. This is consistent with what the Buddha taught. He said that when one does body practice, one should do ānāpānasati as well.

The body is an interesting object to investigate. You can divide up the body in various ways. Another way is to investigate the body in terms of the physical elements of earth, water, fire and air. The natural world around us appears to be very real and solid. But it only appears that way because our bodies are also composed of the same natural, material elements. Fundamentally, there is no difference between the makeup of the human body and the makeup of the physical world. In modern terms, they both consist of atoms and molecules. You should look at the body from that angle and reflect on it.

You should also look at the body with the understanding that the four elements of earth, water, fire and air are actually just symbolic representations. In examining matter, scientists have never found an "earth element" anywhere. Nor have they found air, water or fire elements. They do not exist as actual physical properties. In fact, contemplation of the four physical elements is a psychological method of analyzing matter. And mind is the main requirement for making the analysis—you have to contemplate those characteristics subjectively. The mind uses concepts about earth, water, fire and air to represent material qualities such as solidity, fluidity, heat and motion, so as to understand the body on a more subtle level.

Another interesting approach to body contemplation is to ask: how is the body known, how is it experienced? The answer is that we know the body through feeling. It's feeling that informs us about our bodies. It's difficult to experience the body any other way. Of course, we can think in terms of the body's constituent parts and so on. These are things we know about because we can see them. But from the perspective of an internal experience, we actually know the body through feeling and sensation.

Because of that, the body we know is really a feeling-body. That feeling-body is a subtle body that's projected into our physical form. Our minds contact the physical body through that projection, so we don't actually know the physical body directly. When we want to investigate our bodies, we must turn to sensations to guide the way. The internal makeup of the physical body is known only by means of a mental image, a concept that comes from seeing pictures depicting what the various parts look like. All of those parts combine to make up the physical body, but that is not the body we know internally.

When we contemplate the body by examining those bits and pieces that make it up, we are working with a mental picture of the body. When we contemplate the corresponding feeling-body, we may find that the feelings inside paint quite a different overall picture of the body—and quite a different understanding of what makes up the body, as well. That's why it's important to realize that feeling is the most important aspect of our knowledge of the body.

For example, when you feel a pain in your foot, the source of the pain appears to be located in the foot. In fact, sensory impulses are transmitted from the foot to some mechanism in the brain which projects the experience of pain onto the image of the foot in the feeling-body. So the experience of pain takes place in the mind's image of the body which is mentally superimposed on the physical form. We feel the painful sensation in the foot only because our instincts tell us it must be there. In the same manner, the whole body is mirrored in a network of sensations. For that reason, the feeling-body is very important. It's the one we know. It is the source of our perceptions of the physical body.

If the above method of investigating the body works, then use it. By analyzing the body in this way, we are seeking to see this body for what it really is and drop our attachment to it. In doing so, we realize that our physical body is not so important. It's just a conglomeration of material substances that will one day be reabsorbed into the physical environment. The question then is: why do you grasp at it?

People grasp at bodies because they imagine themselves to be secure in bodies, even though the body is not a secure refuge. It is always subject to the uncertainty of disease, old age and death. At the same time, the body is a very sensitive organism. It relies upon a suitable environment, which means it must have air to breathe, temperatures that are reasonable for human life, and protection from dangers in its environment. All of these factors are necessary. If they are not available, or if they change, the body will perish.

Because our bodies are so inherently vulnerable, we should really be looking for security in other ways. When we realize that, in fact, the body does not offer us the security that we want, we should examine the nature of that insecurity to see if there isn't a better way to find a secure refuge than grasping at the human body.

When people identify with their bodies, they become concerned about them. Because the body is the basis of their life, they're afraid of losing that base. The body is like a home, a home they can come back to. When their minds go whizzing off somewhere, they can always come back to home base. It anchors them, so they feel secure. If the base wasn't there, where could they come back to? There'd be nowhere to return to. When people feel they are drifting, they want to find a foothold, an anchor to hold them firm.

Because every part of the body is constantly changing, it is not reliable enough to provide such a secure refuge. Our personal stake in it puts us under its unstable influence. Whatever happens to the body is then experienced as happening to "us." When it becomes sick, we become worried and depressed. If the body gets injured, we're distraught. We're distraught because we're attached to the body, thinking of it as an integral part of who we are. When it dies, we're suddenly homeless. Because of our attachment, whatever happens to it, happens to us.

Once we realize what the body's true nature really is, we are freed from our attachment to it. Then what happens to the body is something that happens separately, externally. It's as though somebody else's body is injured or sick. Pain is experienced in the body, but there is no concern about the pain. It isn't me. It isn't mine. Because it isn't me or mine, it never again has the same sway over our emotions. It no longer pulls us along with it. The mind remains separate and free. Being separate and free, it is also secure. It knows that delusion has been at least partially eliminated. It knows that whatever happens, it won't go in the wrong way. It won't fall back. This is the result we are working for in body contemplation.

Once you have examined the body and realized that it is not yourself, when something happens to the body, you are not concerned about it in the same way as before. You know that it's not happening to you. You realize that, although it's happening to the body, that body is not you. Although the physical condition may be unpleasant, the unpleasantness is merely the body's unpleasantness. You are not affected.

The purpose of body contemplation is to realize that the body is not you, nor does it belong to you. The body belongs to the natural world. You have grasped at the body, and continue to grasp at it by maintaining it in good condition. But the time will come when that body has to return to the world of nature. When you truly realize within yourself that the body is merely a temporary home—something you have on loan, so to speak—then concern for the body drops away. Fear of death also drops away, because you realize that death is simply the death of the physical body. This understanding is not a matter of being alienated from your physical body; rather, it is seeing with wisdom the truth about its natural state.

There are many different forms of body contemplation, but regardless of which method you use, the basic purpose of the meditation practice is to learn to see the body in "the light of truth," and thus understand its true nature. This is the crux of the matter. By seeing it for what it is, you realize that it isn't self. That fundamental realization transforms your whole perspective. Having realized that the body is not self, you simply drop it. Eventually, you see that all of life is just shadows, like images flickering on a cinema screen.

The knowledge you gain from seeing the truth is very powerful. At the time of death, when the body dies, you know that it's not you that dies. By bringing you to this realization, body contemplation gives you a great deal of spiritual and emotional strength, and relieves the mind of an enormous burden both now and in the future.

MEMORY

When we were very young and still trying to make sense of the world around us, our minds struggled to absorb all the diverse information that they received through the five senses and to organize it in such a way that we could retain it for future use. We gradually learned to lump similar sorts of things into categories under headings for easy access. Eventually, these general categories began to represent an array of variations on a common theme, referred to by a certain name or word.

Take trees, for example. Very early on, we began to recognize shapes of light and color which we could distinguish from other visual forms. We knew they existed but we didn't know how to tell them apart. Finally, someone pointed out a long brown stem with a green bushy top and called it a "tree." They made us repeat the word over and over until the sound stuck in our mind. Pretty soon, the sound of the word "tree" became a symbol in our mind for all visual images that had a similar shape and color. As we discovered more and more trees in our world, they were all placed under the same iconic symbol—tree. In the same way, we soon learned to distinguish and then recognize all the visual objects in our environment. They, in turn, were all given words to symbolize their unique characteristics.

Symbolizing is a way of simplifying. For the most part, it's necessary for the mind to simplify the great variety of incoming sense data.
Mental symbols are nature's way to store an enormous amount of information, knowledge and understanding within a very limited mind
capacity. In other words, creating symbols facilitates the task of dealing
with a lot of complex information.

When we group a large amount of information under one symbol,
like "tree," we can then deal with just that symbol without the need to
consider the totality or the complexity of what it represents. We have
a name for it and that's enough. The complexity can be devilish, but if
we can name the devil, we have defeated him. In other words, we have
been able to grab a hold of him in some meaningful way.

Any object of consciousness is made up of bits and pieces, called
sankhāras, that act like pixels on a screen. We don't see the individual
pixels; instead, what we see is a mental object distinct from its background. But the object that we distinguish in this way is, in fact, just
a symbol representing the complexity of all the bits and pieces that
comprise it. We use such symbols all the time; our minds are absolutely
riddled with them. They are part of the fundamental way we think. We
have to use symbols for thinking because the complexity of phenomena is so vast that the mind just isn't capable of holding it all at once.
So we focus on certain prominent aspects of every experience and turn
those into symbols representing the whole.

But these objects are more than just visual images in our lives.
They also have a certain emotional impact on us, often associated with
the experiences we had in relation to them. Sometimes the experience
was positive, sometimes negative and sometimes neutral. In whichever
case, our future perceptions are then colored by an emotional overlay
as well.

With more time and more experience, the complexity of our
perceptions increases. Depending on our emotional state and other
conditions, seeing a tree might make us feel happy or frustrated or in-

different. The symbol is still the same but it has multiple shades of meaning. And because no two individuals are exactly alike in the way they perceive things, the words and symbols that represent those objects may have significantly different meanings from one person to the next.

When we are first introduced to a new place, much of what we perceive is unfamiliar. So we begin to look around and observe the general nature of that environment until we can mentally consign the whole of it to a symbol for convenient future reference. It's like putting all of our observations under one heading in a directory. Then we need only access that heading when we want to refer to that place. There will be a word symbol, but there will also be emotional content within ourselves.

Creating symbols is essential because it frees memory to be used in all sorts of other ways. Otherwise, if we had to remember everything, our brains would have to be enormous to hold it all. But there is also a fundamental disadvantage to mental symbolizing, because, in the end, we tend to deal only with the symbols and not with the reality. As a matter of fact, we begin to give the symbols a reality that they don't possess. This can very easily be a cause for more delusion.

For instance, we take something very complex, like another person, and give that person a name. Our notion of that person revolves around the emotional reaction his name tends to evoke. That notion is a very static view of another human being. In truth, the reality of human beings is very complex. We have a general idea of the people we know, but that idea doesn't take into account the changes that are constantly taking place inside them.

We have symbols for everything, including our emotional states. When a particular emotional state comes up, we recognize it because we remember it under a certain symbolic heading. It's hard to define these internal symbols. Often they are just feelings, but we know them quite distinctly. That is, we know what the feelings symbolize to us. But that doesn't mean that we know their reality. We often think we understand something, when in truth, instead of catching hold of what's really happening, we've merely caught hold of a symbolic representation of it.

What actually happens is invariably quite complex. What's really happening is more like a whirlpool, a whirlpool of constant change. If we try to resist change and remain static, we will miss the truth every time. If we can just watch it closely, we will see that everything is part of this whirlpool of changing phenomena. So we let it follow its natural tendency.

We should try to be aware that there is a vortex of activity occurring in and around us all the time. We experience this, but because our minds are not quick enough to catch up with the constant arising and ceasing of phenomena, we have to reduce the whole lot to something simple enough for our minds to latch on to. Thus we create a symbol. For instance, a motorcar. The word "motorcar" is just a symbol. What is a car actually? It's an assemblage of 100,000 different parts. Nevertheless, we represent it with that one symbol. Similarly, a "house" is composed of countless bits and pieces. We refer to it as a house because our minds just aren't capable of handling the complexity of what's really there. We just can't hold it all in our minds at the same time, so we have to simplify.

The symbols in our minds change and adapt according to circumstances. We have a range of symbols that can adapt to fit different situations. Part of the symbol is the form, part of it is the use and part of it is the location. Symbols go even further by isolating an object and separating it from the whole of its background. For instance, we identify one tree out of a whole forest. Why do we identify that one particular object as the tree and the rest as the forest? It's just our way of grasping the situation in terms of cause and effect.

The same principle applies to internal objects, like emotions. We try to get a handle on them by giving them a name. By that token, we think we understand them. But it is important to realize that the naming and labeling of such things does not truly represent their reality. Internal phenomena like emotional states must be carefully observed. We should always be willing to question them within ourselves. We mustn't simply dismiss them by saying: "That's hatred. That's greed." We must look at them as they occur inside. Look at those mental states just the way they are, regardless of what we call them. Try to understand their real nature apart from the name.

We should look at the symbols in our minds and try to understand how they distort reality. Being mere symbols, they do not represent the truth. Therefore, they are, in a sense, false. By investigating the symbols, we come to realize that we have views about those mental constructs which we are very attached to. This attachment sets up a tension in the mind based on the possibility that they may fade from memory.

Thinking about people and events in the past is a way of refreshing the memory. We do this because we don't want to let go, because we have a lot of attachment to them. I am growing old now and my memory is not as good as it used to be. I find some advantages in this because the past seems to be rather vague, so I don't think about it much. Because of that, the attachments are dropping away. Having a fading memory is a disadvantage in some ways, but it also has its good points.

The symbols we accumulate to structure the world around us are bound up with the faculty of memory. Memory is a database of all our previous experiences that runs like a continuous thread through the pattern of our mental activity. The data from memory comes in through the five senses; it's the senses that tell us what to remember.

An enormous amount of our thinking is based on memory. When we see or hear something, we identify it by comparing it to remembered impressions. Our present experience may be associated with external sensations, but those sensations have to be identified and interpreted in the light of past sensations. Once we recognize a particular sensation, we think about it, which again relies on the faculty of memory. For that reason, memory is an essential part of all of our perceptions.

We can observe how some symbols in our minds tend to fade over time. They may be little used or outdated. But as soon as they start to disappear, up comes our self-identity, saying: I mustn't let that one go. So we begin to think about it, in the process strengthening and reestablishing it in the mind. We refresh our memories by thinking. Quite a lot of our discursive thought is directed towards that aim.

We build up our view of the world from the internal sensations we experience. The impressions we receive are stored in memory. We've accumulated an enormous amount of data dating back to when we were children. As we grew up, we became very concerned about learning everything we could about our environment, mainly for the sake of our own security in the shifting landscape of life. When we know something and can put a name to it, we find reassurance in that knowledge. If any changes occur in our world, we immediately recognize them and make note of them, because changes may signal imminent danger. We instinctively want to be on top of every deviation from the norm that takes place. In the process, we are constantly updating our memories with fresh information.

As new changes occur, old information immediately becomes part of the past. Memory references the past. Because of that, memory itself is the basis of our concept of time. The time that we know is the past. We don't know the future; we predict that. We only predict the future on the basis of what's happened in the past. And we can access the remembered past only by reflecting on it in the present. So we can say that memory is at the center of our views on time.

We rely on the past for a sense of security in a changing world. We become very attached to what we remember because it gives a sense of continuity to our lives. It's as though, if we can remember something, it still somehow exists. Although we can't actually go back in time, there is comfort in recalling the memory of it. Memories easily become a refuge from the uncertainty of impermanence. But such a refuge is based on neither truth nor stability. We have to accept that nothing is permanent, that everything is constantly changing from one moment to the next, and therefore, we should not be deceived into thinking that our memories contain anything in which we can put our trust.

Instead of getting caught up in the content of our memories, we should examine the nature of the faculty of memory itself to understand how the process works. Memory is made up of an alphabet soup of images, concepts and symbols that compare incoming sense data with past experience in an attempt to "recognize" where it belongs in the inner world of known perceptions. In other words, memory matches present perceptions to past experiences and labels them accordingly. We recognize a tree because we have the characteristics of a generic tree stored in our memory. This, in turn, is based on a commonly shared interpretation of what that particular form represents. But the designation "tree" is merely a symbolic substitute for reality, not the reality itself. We suppose that by naming it, we understand what it is. But the reality is quite different from the name.

When it comes to discussing a topic like meditation, difficulties in communication are bound to arise because we all have our own ideas and our own unique inner experiences. In using language to convey our meaning, we have to turn those concepts into spoken words. Words are sounds that others pick up and turn into meaningful concepts inside themselves. They take the spoken sound, the word, and refer it to memory to find out their own understanding of it. That understanding depends largely on the listener's background. Even with a similar background in Buddhist practice, we can never be sure that any two people will understand a word in the same way.

One of the greatest difficulties in explaining mind development to people in the West is that they don't have the advantage of a Buddhist background to help them grasp a basic understanding of common

Buddhist terms and concepts. The English language just doesn't have the words needed to properly explain the teaching to them. That is, the words and the concepts for what's being discussed just aren't stored in their memory.

Language is necessary for communication, but it is also a minefield for misunderstanding. It's useful to study how language works, how it conveys meaning. Basically, language is a symbolic process. When we think of an object, we are reminded of the word for that object, which has specific connotations attached to it. But the connotations for the same word may differ between the speaker and the listener, which easily causes misinterpretations to arise. The same word, the same symbol, conveys different shades of meaning to different people.

When speaking about physical objects in the world, like trees, the differences are unlikely to be a problem. We can point to a tree. But when it comes to concepts like virtue or concentration or wisdom, there's nothing concrete that we can point to. Because of that, it is very easy for people with limited genuine experience in these matters to misunderstand the meaning of these concepts. Because they've never seen virtue, concentration and wisdom as objects, most people are bound to develop wrong views about them.

When a student is unfamiliar with the terminology, the teacher must carefully explain the path of practice, step by step, and gradually build up an understanding of the basic concepts involved. However, only someone who has really mastered the practice and knows what he's talking about can teach like that. Otherwise, the teacher will be left to explain the practice according to what has been handed down in the Buddhist texts. Because of a lack of profound personal insight into the Dhamma, the teacher is using concepts that he does not fully understand himself, which easily causes misunderstanding to arise in his students as well.

When practicing on one's own without a teacher, the Buddhist texts can be a useful reference. But we should not depend on them too much. Following the texts as a guide to meditation has its drawbacks because our inexperienced minds are not equipped to unravel their deeper meaning. So we should use the technical terms in the books with caution, as it is very easy to misinterpret their intended meaning.

Like any technical subject—for example, engineering—we cannot make use of the technical terms properly unless we understand their meaning relative to the whole subject. The definitions of Buddhist terms developed from ancient times are not the precise types of definitions we are used to seeing in scientific subjects, so they rely even more on a comprehensive view of the practice. Their meanings are more like descriptions that depend on background knowledge from the student in order for him to understand their significance within the context of practical training and self-transformation. They are not concepts that most of us have ready equivalents for in our memory. The only way we can find the full meaning is by experiencing it directly and seeing how it fits in with everything else, like a central piece in a jigsaw puzzle. When that piece fits in snugly all around, then you know what it means in relation to everything else.

Similarly, the true meaning of the Buddha's teachings found in the suttas can be very difficult to understand simply by reading and reflecting on the translations available to us. There is no harm in reading the suttas; they are quite inspiring. But we must be careful of the language used in the English translations because the words chosen can be misleading. In most cases, the translations are made by people who do not have a proper understanding based in the practice. Because of that, the translations are not necessarily very accurate.

Many aspects of the teachings cannot be understood properly until we have developed an understanding of Dhamma in our own practice. Only then can we realize the various subtleties of meaning implicit in the texts. In that case, we may clearly comprehend a profound experience here and now in the present, but the experience may be such that it does not relate to any conceptual symbol we have stored in memory.

For that reason, we often cannot verbally explain experiences of profound insight satisfactorily. The language is simply not there.

In the Thai Forest Tradition, a distinction is made between saññā and paññā. Saññā is traditionally translated as "perception." Although that is not entirely incorrect, the best translation of saññā is "memory." Paññā is best translated as "wisdom." The difference between the two is similar to the difference between appearance and reality; supposition and truth; or intellectual understanding and direct insight. In other words, saññā is analogous to the intellectual understanding arrived at by thinking; whereas paññā is the direct knowing of essential truths.

To give you an example: Thoughts are usually formed in words, which are symbols stored in memory. A thought that comes up in words originates from a nucleus or seed of that thought located deep inside. When you trace the thought process back to that original seed, you will find that the entire idea expressed in that thought is contained in the seed. Thinking attempts to express that idea in a dialogue. But on a fundamental level, the idea behind that thought is complete in the seed. Realizing that, you also realize that you know the fully-formed idea already, so there's no need to think about it. In fact, thinking about it at length merely dilutes the essence of it and distorts the meaning.

Discursive thinking takes appearances, thinks about them, comes to an intellectual understanding and then supposes that the understanding represents the truth. When we sit down to meditate, our tendency is to try to verify that understanding by searching for evidence of it in our experiences. In other words, our search for the truth is already prejudiced by our suppositions. We expect to find what we suppose to be there. We then interpret our meditation experiences in the light of that expectation.

Consequently, our minds are constantly referring present moment experiences to the past—our memory of what should be there—and thus overlooking the true nature of what arises here and now. Because we have figured out in advance the nature of what should take place along the path, we want to check the validity of present moment experience by comparing it to a conceptual understanding already formed in our minds. This is the nature of saññā: recognition, interpretation, supposition. And it's a big cause of deception.

Paññā or wisdom is knowing and understanding, but in an active sense, as in the act of knowing or the act of understanding. Although that knowing is usually based on the Buddha's teaching, it does not rely solely on conceptual interpretations learned beforehand to recognize the truth in meditation experiences. A thorough conceptual understanding of the teaching is useful as a background to the wisdom practice, but it should not assert itself as the main player when wisdom's direct non-conceptual insight is active.

As a spiritual training, wisdom shines a light on the nature of present moment reality in an intensely focused way which allows no time gaps for fact checking with our intellectual understanding. This is the nature of paññā: cause-and-effect understanding grounded in the interaction between present moment conditions.

When you start practicing meditation, your mind is out in the world ninety percent of the time. You have accumulated a storehouse of knowledge about the world around you. You have extensive knowledge of the external world, but you know nothing about what goes on inside your own mind. As you learn how to investigate the nature of your mind to see how it works, you come to the conclusion that your view of the world is fundamentally wrong. You realize that the symbols you have accumulated to structure the world around you are false. That realization comes, not from remembered concepts, but from the insights that gradually change your understanding. By using wisdom to analyze and investigate, you will begin to illuminate the true nature of things. The insights that arise from that effort change your overall understanding of Dhamma.

As you progress in the practice, you should investigate with wisdom repeatedly until you become skilled in its use. Avoid speculation or conjecture. Don't allow thoughts of what you *should* be doing, or what the results *might* mean, to interfere with your present-moment focus. Just concentrate on the truth of what wisdom reveals and let that truth speak for itself. In this way, you can maintain a proper balance between memory and wisdom as you advance, stage by stage, to the attainment of purity of mind and freedom from suffering.

FEELING

raving is the root cause of attachment. Because of that, to free your mind of attachment you must go directly to taṇhā, or craving, and eliminate that. If you overcome craving, you'll overcome attachments. But you cannot deal with the attachments directly. Trying to overcome attachments by sheer determination or willpower won't work. The only way to overcome attachments is to get rid of their cause, which is craving. This is stated clearly in Paṭiccasamuppāda or dependent origination: "Dependent on feeling, craving arises; dependent on craving, attachment arises." Craving being the condition for attachment, when craving is destroyed, attachment cannot arise.

Because craving is dependent on feeling, when you aim to destroy craving, you have to first focus your attention on feeling. This is a critical point, because exactly at the juncture between feeling and craving you can place a barrier. Feeling is just feeling. It is a result of past kamma, whereas the taṇhā is new kamma. So by allowing the two to link up you are creating more kamma. If you can turn away at that juncture and prevent that new kamma from occurring, the situation gradually improves. But Paṭiccasamuppāda does not give practical guidance on how to do that. It reveals how the process unfolds, but it does not indicate the way to unravel the entanglement. In order to unravel it, you must learn to find the feeling. Examine feeling and see how feeling gives rise to taṇhā.

Paṭiccasamuppāda is an account of the sequence of causes that condition the arising of suffering and, in reverse order, the cessation of suffering. The Buddha's purpose in teaching dependent origination was to point out the general pattern of conditions that causes beings to wander endlessly in saṁsāra, and to show how that causal sequence can be brought to an end. The Buddha emphasized that he was able to attain enlightenment because he was able to bring dependent origination to an end within his own mind.

Because Paṭiccasamuppāda is a realization that the Buddha came to on the night he gained enlightenment, as a teaching, it can be difficult to clearly comprehend. For that reason, the conditional factors of Paṭiccasamuppāda should be used as meditation subjects with considerable caution. The Buddha laid out a practical teaching. For example, Paṭiccasamuppāda explains the process of what happens to create dukkha, but it does not give the method of how to cure dukkha. In order to discover the method for curing dukkha, you must practice the Noble Eightfold Path until you understand the Four Noble Truths. That notwithstanding, a basic understanding of the process laid out by Paṭiccasamuppāda can help quite a lot in meditation practice. It details a process that can be understood at different levels of subtlety.

Due to those subtleties, the factors of Paṭiccasamuppāda are difficult to interpret using conventional language. My understanding of them goes something like this: "avijjā paccaya sankhāra" means avijjā is the fundamental ignorance within oneself, a cloud of delusion which is extremely deep and all-pervasive. Ignorance produces the kamma that leads to all the conditions for birth. Dependent on the existence of those conditions, or sankhāras, viññāṇa arises. Those first three factors—avijjā, sankhāra and viññāṇa—are not dependent on physical human existence. They are most certainly mental states.

The viññāṇa factor in Paṭiccasamuppāda is always referred to as "paṭisandhi viññāṇa." This is not the normal type of viññāṇa that we refer to as consciousness. Rather, it is the re-linking consciousness that connects one birth to the next. That re-linking consciousness forms the connection between past and future which leads to grasping at the moment of conception. Paṭisandhi viññāṇa is said to be "free of doors," that is, free of the sense doors.

To understand paṭisandhi viññāṇa you should put aside the word "consciousness," which can be quite a misleading translation. My understanding of the word viññāṇa in this context is that the prefix "vi," meaning "divided," is combined with "ñāṇa," meaning "knowing." In other words, "divided knowing." The one mind splits into two, subject and object, and instead of being pure unlimited knowing, the mind is driven by avijjā plus kamma to discriminate so that it becomes "this" knowing "that."

A duality is thus established in which the "this" becomes nāma and the "that" becomes rūpa. Thus viññāṇa is the condition for the arising of nāma-rūpa. Although avijjā, saṅkhāra and viññāṇa are conditioning factors, those factors all arise simultaneous to the split into duality. No time interval is involved. It's like a railway engine pulling a train: the engine is the cause but none of the cars move independently.

So viññāṇa is a condition for nāma-rūpa to arise. Nāma-rūpa is a difficult factor to interpret. Nāma literally means name; in other words, putting names to things, designating and defining. And rūpa is the form; that is, the thing that we make concrete with the name. When we make forms concrete with names, we divide them out from the whole. Looking at the forest, we see leaves, trees and flowers. We call them leaves, trees and flowers merely to define certain aspects of what we see. But they are only *our* aspects—they do not exist as such there in the forest. The forest itself is one whole; it is we who differentiate the various aspects.

In reality, our perceptions do not exist as separate entities at all. We separate the forest into various parts so that we can bring some order to our perceptions. This is how nāma-rūpa works. It is the dividing out of certain aspects of our perceptions of nature which accord with the previous sankhāras. In other words, we are defining our world according to our own past tendencies. So we create a world in the present based on data from the past. This loops back to avijjā paccaya sankhāra, with sankhāra being the karmic conditions from the past that determine rebirth.

Nāma-rūpa in turn conditions saḷāyatana, which is the breaking forth of the sense fields. The senses are the fields of sight, sound, smell, taste and touch, with the mind as the field of cognition. It is not so much that the senses are faculties we acquire, but rather that the senses are productive faculties. The sense fields produce sights, sounds, smells, tastes and tactile sensations as internal phenomena, which means they are very actively involved in generating those sensations.

In the Paṭiccasamuppāda formula, saḷāyatana conditions phassa, or sense contact. The sense fields allow contact between sense objects and their corresponding sense bases. So the sense bases are a precondition for contact to occur between the mind and its perceptions.

Phassa gives rise to vedanā; that is, sense contact conditions the arising of feeling. In the context of Paṭiccasamuppāda, the arising of feeling is a resultant process that is caused by consequences of actions done in the past coming up in the present. The feeling may be pleasant, unpleasant or neutral.

Feeling is a condition for taṇhā, or craving, to arise. Based on feeling, a personal, emotional judgment is made as to whether a feeling is considered pleasant, unpleasant or neutral, which leads directly to a craving for the pleasant, an aversion for the unpleasant and a dull indifference toward the neutral. In other words, there is a tendency to react with either greed, aversion or delusion. These reactions are all aspects of the kilesas, with feeling as their condition. Feeling arises, and then the kilesas arise.

For example, you hear a sound you don't like. Based on that sensation, an unpleasant feeling arises. That unpleasant feeling is a feeling of aversion. Thus, aversion arises dependent on circumstances. Feeling is experienced first and, if we don't like it, that feeling then brings up aversion. Because that feeling is dukkha, a desire to suppress it arises. The tendency then is to search for scapegoats. You try to find something, like another person or a sound or the heat or whatever. You straightaway blame something like that for the unpleasant feeling. Then the anger goes out to that. This reaction is quite wrong because that anger generates a lot of thought, and that thought is kamma. That kamma will revert back to you later and produce the feeling again.

But the feeling of aversion isn't the emotion of aversion. There's no aversion in feeling. It becomes aversion when you start thinking, criticizing, blaming and so on. That's where the trouble comes—in the thinking. Feeling is a result of the past; but when you think, that thinking is kamma. So it's the thoughts that keep the anger going. It's there in Paṭiccasamuppāda. Dependent on phassa—the contact of sensation—feeling arises. Dependent on the arising of feeling, craving arises. So the craving comes dependent on feeling. But the feeling is a result of the past, so it's just something you have to put up with. Whereas thought is taṇhā, the craving to get rid of that unpleasant feeling, which is the making of new kamma.

Taṇhā has two aspects: craving to have pleasant feelings and craving not to have unpleasant feelings. Craving, in turn, gives rise to either attachment to pleasant experiences or distaste for unpleasant ones, which is the reverse side of attachment. Because of habitual emotional patterns, we usually get caught by feeling when it arises, and immediately up comes taṇhā, the craving. The only way to overcome that is to learn the method of going inward to investigate feeling.

Suppose in the past you have been angry, and that anger triggers the arising of feeling in the present. That feeling is a feeling of imbalance; your mind is out of balance. Feeling out of balance, you try to restore a sense of equilibrium within. If the cause is anger, the habitual response is to blame something or someone. If the cause is greed, the response is to go out searching for sense gratification. These are the normal ways that the kilesas seek balance.

Instead of restoring equilibrium, the kilesas become the causes of more defiled actions. When those actions bring results, the consequences of those actions then act as fertile ground for more defilements. In other words, seeking balance in defiled actions creates more kamma, which only makes the imbalance worse, because the consequences rebound back to you later on. In this way, the round of rebirths continues to revolve without end. As long as ignorance and defilements are calling the shots, kamma will continue to bring results and suffering will continue to accumulate. Only when ignorance and craving are destroyed will the chain of dependent origination be broken and the end of suffering be reached.

To summarize in reverse order: attachment depends on craving, craving depends on feeling, feeling depends on sense contact, sense contact depends on having the sense bases, which in turn depends on having mind and body. Mind and body depend on viññāṇa, the consciousness without doors, which arises due to the ignorance that produced the kamma, leading to all the conditions for birth, ageing, sickness and death.

The point where we can have the greatest impact in breaking this cycle of birth and death is at the nexus between feeling, craving and attachment. It is there that we can start unraveling Paṭiccasamuppāda. Feeling is a critical link in the chain of dependent origination because it is between feeling and craving that you can erect a barrier to prevent the evolution of the process. It's at this juncture between feeling and craving that we have an option to either accept or reject the kilesas.

Craving's reaction to the arising of feeling is not predetermined. The arising of feeling simply means that the conditions are present for activating the kilesas. Whether the kilesas spring into action at that point or not depends on our state of mind. The kilesas don't have to become active. We have the option of accepting or rejecting them. That's where our freedom of will comes in. It comes in at the juncture where feeling conditions craving. When we do that, we start to dismantle Paṭiccasamuppāda until we reach the cessation of suffering.

So let's examine feeling. Feeling is a result of past kamma. Feeling is based upon something that we've seen, heard, smelled, tasted, touched or thought in the past. If we examine it, we'll see that the feeling is just based on a form or a sound or a smell or a taste or a contact or a thought. That's all. But, because of memory, we then associate that sensation with some past experience. If the experience was pleasant, we like it. If unpleasant, we don't. And because we associate it with something in memory, a reaction takes place. We want it if it's pleasant. We don't want it if it's unpleasant.

So when some object is presented to us, through any of the senses, which we either like or dislike, we should try to notice the accompanying feeling—the feeling of attraction or repulsion—and how the tendency is to react with either greed or aversion. It is the reaction that's important. The feeling arises down in the heart region, and the reaction arises down there too. But the reaction is often supported by a lot of thinking, which is up in the head. Feelings are results of kamma from the past, which is felt as pleasant or unpleasant, good or bad. When pleasant kamma comes up, it brings a feeling of "I want that," which is triggered by greed. When aversion comes up, it triggers a response of "I don't want this feeling. I want to reject it."

In trying to reject the feeling, we may think, "Oh, it was that person's fault. He did it; he caused this unpleasantness." So we make excuses and think critical, angry thoughts. Those angry thoughts are the reaction to the feeling. When angry thoughts come up, they are a form of present kamma that tends to bring up the same feeling in the future when something triggers it. So when watching feeling, it is important to pay close attention to the reaction that feeling brings about when something sets it off. That's where we can easily go astray.

For example, feeling may be set up through the senses: we hear a sound or we see or smell something, and that will bring up a memory from the past. That past situation comes up in the present as a feeling similar to the one in the past. We then react to that in the same way we did then, thus making the same type of kamma which set up the feeling originally. So the wheel goes rolling on, round and round.

Usually, the contact and the feeling arise so quickly that we have great difficulty in distinguishing them. Contact giving rise to feeling takes place so fast that it is almost impossible to separate them. So it's difficult to see that distinction. But feeling is the important factor to look at. We know that feeling comes from contact. Normally, the contact is automatic; it takes place without any deliberation. Following that contact, feeling arises. It's a resultant process that is caused by consequences of actions done in the past coming up in the present. When that happens, mindfulness should be focused on watching the feeling to make sure that a negative reaction does not take place. In other words, when it's an unpleasant feeling, we tell ourselves: "This unpleasantness is my own fault; it's a result of my own kamma. I've got to put up with it." We must always avoid blaming someone else.

The feeling of aversion is an unpleasant feeling. We must learn to turn inwards and look at that feeling. If we can turn inwards and look at it, we won't let it escape and turn into bad thoughts. So we defeat the kilesas at that point. Mind you, we only defeat them a little bit at a time. To get rid of aversion completely, we'll probably have to do it many times, until it gradually, gradually goes.

To accomplish that, we must look within ourselves to find out where these feelings are; and we must discover what sort of feelings give rise to what sort of mental states. It is very important in meditation practice to look for feeling, to get to know it—particularly feeling in the solar plexus region. Because when we're upset in one way or another—it's always felt down there. And it's always there that the kilesas, the defilements, originate.

Thoughts, speech or actions that follow the lead of the defilements create kamma. The kamma that results will come back to us as feeling in the future, starting the cycle rolling again. When we short-circuit the whole process at the link between feeling and craving, the momentum will slowly lessen, and the offending defilements will gradually die away, bit by bit.

The benefits won't appear suddenly; old habits don't die easily. But with persistence, over time they can be reformed. What's important is developing the good habit of being mindful of feelings as they arise and assessing their potential danger to us. It's almost like seeing a red flag come up, warning us to be vigilant. We immediately turn inward then, thinking, "I mustn't let this get out of hand." This is a fundamental part of the training in sense restraint.

So the way to deal with feelings is not so much a matter of deliberately not reacting to them, but rather one of being mindful of them. When we are mindful, not reacting will take place automatically. Mindfulness is a kind of monitor that checks what's going on without interfering with it. With mindfulness, we sometimes feel like we are standing back and watching the feelings, as though from a back seat inside somewhere. Observing from that back seat, we can see clearly what's happening, but we don't interfere in any way. Pleasant and painful feelings are just happening, and that's all. It's that sort of attention that is required.

So pay close attention to feelings. When unpleasant feelings arise, examine them at the point where they occur. Don't let those feelings turn into thoughts about blaming others. Think only about the feeling, not other people. In other words, if you keep the mind inside, no harm is done. Trouble comes only when you let it escape out into thought, speech or action. By allowing the mind to go out and blame things externally, you make kamma, and that kamma comes back to you in the future in the form of the same sort of feeling. So the wheel just keeps spinning. If you don't learn to correct this recurring cycle, you will never get free from it.

To correct it, you must do the right thing by not letting the mind go out. You must focus inward—every time—to look at those unpleasant feelings. And accept them. Accept that this is your own fault. Because you have done unwholesome acts, unpleasant feelings arise as a result. So you are to blame for the result. When you accept that it's your fault and don't let your attention go outward, then that debt is paid and your difficulties become a little bit less. Each time you do it, they are reduced. Through that, you find a certain joy and contentment arising within. You feel happy. That happiness is a result of the work you've done—because you have learnt how to cure the defilements to some extent. The more you go on in this way, the more you feel buoyant and light. This result points out the right direction. It shows that you are taking the correct path. The more you experience happiness, the more you know that you're headed in the right direction.

The kilesas come up because of feeling; feeling is the goad which arouses them. So if you can put a barrier between the feeling and the craving, you stop the kilesas and they can't become active. By being aware of the kilesas, you can see them when they come up and not react to them. Because they come up in connection with certain feelings, you know that particular feelings are the conditions for the arising of particular kilesas. When that feeling comes up, you know that certain kilesas are lurking in the background. So keep a watch out. Keep the mindfulness strong. If you watch that process, the kilesas don't get a foothold, and the mind naturally calms down and becomes peaceful.

SENSES

Our situation—not only in this world but in all realms of existence—is a situation which is always ruled by the fundamental ignorance of avijjā. Avijjā is a basic lack of understanding that clouds the mind and deceives us into thinking that we actually do understand. We think we know things, but really speaking, we don't. We have a veil of ignorance which prevents us from seeing the true nature of things. Our ignorance makes us believe that there is nothing beyond what our senses can perceive, nothing else but the world we live in. In truth, there's a great deal more.

Intuitively, we suspect that there is something better than this world, but we don't know what it is. So we search for it. Because we have an array of senses to work with, we tend to focus out in the direction that the senses lead us, and look for happiness there. Of course, that's the wrong direction—true happiness does not exist out there at all. This misunderstanding occurs because we have the five external senses and the internal senses of feeling, memory, thought and consciousness. Our natural tendency is to mix them up, using the internal state to deal with the external objects that we see, hear, smell, taste and touch—which represent the external world. This leads the focus of our attention outward. Going outward, we never find the truth.

Because of not knowing the truth, the mind's attention is drawn to perceptions in the world. In focusing out in the direction of the senses, the mind becomes attached to sensory experience and builds up so many attachments in the world that it becomes completely entangled in worldly ways. It becomes so trapped in its own delusion that it can't see anything else.

People easily get caught up in craving experience of the world through sense contact. When that happens, there is absolutely no hope of reaching the end of suffering until they can learn to overcome the wanting that pervades their minds. When wanting is subdued, then attachments are overcome. Once attachments drop away, there is nothing to stop the mind from going in the direction of freedom from suffering.

The question is: How can we subdue our craving for sense experience? The mind is constantly detecting objects that are coming in through sight, sound, smell, taste and touch. That causes it to buzz about all the time, chasing after sense gratification. But what are the senses and how do they work? And why do we give them so much credence?

In fact, our sense perceptions are deceiving us. Their story goes something like this: Our senses display information related to the world around us, which the mind receives and interprets in its own fashion. In other words, impressions that come in through the senses are subject to individual interpretation. Our experiences of sights, sounds, odors, flavours and tactile sensations are based on the mind's interpretations of incoming sense data. We could say that everything is filtered through the "black box" of the mind. This means that everything we know via our senses is filtered through the mind, which then recognizes and interprets all that data in its own peculiar way.

The interpretation is what we know. We don't actually know the reality of the things out there. We have our way of interpreting them, and that's as far as our information goes. We know the information stored in the black box, but we don't actually know the true nature of what's on the other side of the black box. Because we have to use the black box as an intermediary to access the world, we don't know what the truth of things out there really is. Everything reaches us filtered through the black box of the mind.

When it's like that, we don't really know the truth of our external environment. If we investigate it, we have to accept that the world is a very mysterious place. It isn't quite what we think it is. People assume the world functions in a certain manner because they learn which effects come from which causes. Seeing something happen there, they notice certain results appear here. Having worked out a theory to explain why that is, they then predict that if they do this, they should get that. Because it seems to work most of the time, they feel confident that their theory is correct. But that isn't necessarily the case. All they know is that by applying that theory they can get certain results from those causes. Because it seems so effective, people feel that it must be right. In fact, it's only right within the scope of the method that was followed.

Because people nowadays believe in the explanations of science, they believe they know all about the world. One of the fundamental assumptions in science is that the senses tell us real things, that our senses give us a true representation of what's there. In truth, it is impossible to really understand the world outside—because our senses have no means to contact it directly. After all, how do we know the world outside? We know it through sight, sound, smell, taste and touch, all of which are experienced internally. We assume that physical matter is made up of atoms because that theory seems to work well. But even then, we don't really know for sure what's there.

The whole of science is based on an interpretation of experience. Scientists are quite successful at working things out according to cause-and-effect relationships. But, truly speaking, all the scientists can say is that when they do something, it works. They don't know exactly why.

They don't take into account that everything we know happens inside us. The whole of it depends on the mind.

From physiological evidence alone, science is aware that the mind works like the simile of the black box, which mentally brings together all the senses and their interpretations. For example, people perceive colors in different ways. Not everybody interprets colors identically. In other words, a color is experienced differently from one person to the next. That natural bias is known by science.

But the scientific picture is much more complicated because scientists are seeking only impersonal, objective information that can be measured and arranged into general theories. Buddhist practice, on the other hand, seeks direct insight into the nature of specific phenomena as they arise in the mind of the individual; that is, insight into how the mind itself affects the interpretation of sensory input. Since science cannot measure the interpretations that the mind puts on incoming sensations, it has no means to analyze them. But the subjective suppositions we make about sensations are crucial factors in how we perceive the world.

Simply by using our basic powers of reasoning, we can go a long way toward developing a clearer understanding of how our minds work. This is possible provided that we are ready to accept, or at least seriously consider, whatever conclusions our reasoning leads us to. If we have fixed and rigid views, opinions or beliefs, it may be nearly impossible for us to question that "world of supposition."

The most effective way to analyze our situation is to start with our understanding of the external world, which we are convinced we have a firm grip on. So, how do we know the world? The only way available to us is via our senses: sights, sounds, smells, tastes and tactile sensations. This suggests where our investigation should start.

All five senses work in much the same way, in that they are sensitive receptors that react to stimulation caused by contact with external objects. That contact, in turn, sets up a train of electro-chemical pulses that travels through the sensory nerves, terminating in the brain. This, in brief, is the regular scientific view. So it is convenient for us to accept it as a suitable starting point.

Let us analyze one sense faculty, sight, as typical of them all. Say an object, such as a tree, is seen. Light reflects off all the relevant parts of the tree, and a small part of this light enters our eyes. Due to the geometry of optics, this light displays a small image of the tree upside down on the retina, much as a camera acts in taking a photo.

The image selectively excites the retinal cells, which transmit nerve impulses down the optic nerve to the brain. What then happens in the brain is either poorly understood, or not yet understood. The significant point is that, from all of this, we experience the image of a tree. But, where does the experience of seeing a tree take place? Is the tree we see, in fact, out there in the world? Or, is it the image on the retina that we see? Or, is there some coded image in the brain that we see? In fact, as our entire experience of sight is of the same sort as our seeing of the tree, our perceptions of visual space and location cannot be defined except in terms of the confluence of visual objects, eye contact and eye consciousness. Therefore, the best that we can say is that the tree is seen in the realm of seeing; and it has little meaning to ask where the realm of seeing is located.

In the act of seeing there are three factors: visual object, eye sense organ and eye consciousness, with eye contact being the coming together of the three. Those three do not occur in consecutive order, but rather they represent one visual moment, which means that all three of them operate simultaneously at the moment of contact. When they function together, eye consciousness occurs. You might say that a moment of eye consciousness is like a single pixel on a computer screen, of which there must be hundreds and hundreds to build up an image. That can give you an idea of how fast eye consciousness works. Eye contact is actually the confluence of all three factors meeting together, which enables the whole process to produce visual images.

That process culminates in the brain, which changes nervous impulses into visual imagery, though we don't quite know how. From that process, seeing happens. However, because seeing is an internal process based on the mind's interpretation of sense data, we never truly know the intrinsic nature of the object we see. That's hard for us to grasp because we have such a long history of thinking of people and things in the world as being "out there." In truth, the world we know and everything in it are all internal. In that sense, the whole world is a world of mind.

This becomes clearer when we realize that the external stimuli that contact the eye are not actually what we "see." For instance, the lens of the eye is sensitive to electromagnetic radiation. Although the eye picks up electromagnetic radiation, it does not transmit electromagnetic radiation back to the brain. It sends a nervous current that initiates a biochemical process, which is then converted by the brain into what we interpret as light and color. From that process, visual imagery arises inside of us. Those mental images are what we see. For that reason, all seeing is composed exclusively of internal imagery.

So we see sights internally, not externally. In the world outside, there is actually no light and no color; there's only radiation. We refer to light and color, but those references are just analogies used to explain our experiences. In reality, light and color are also internal phenomena, not external ones. We don't actually know what's outside. All we know is what appears internally.

The other senses work in much the same manner, each in its specific mode. Take hearing. The experience of sound takes place inside. Out there are only vibrations of various frequencies. When those vibrations contact the ear, that stimulation excites the auditory nerves of the inner ear, which transform the stimuli into nervous impulses. Those nervous impulses are transmitted to the brain, which processes that data in some mysterious way that causes sound to arise—within us. Truly speaking, all sound happens within us; it doesn't happen outside at all. What's out there isn't really sound—it's merely vibration. It turns into sound when it gets inside us.

The same is true of smell. Out there in nature are only chemicals, not odors. When chemicals in the air contact the nose, nervous impulses are sent to the brain. Only when the sensation gets inside of us does the experience of smell occur. So our sensory experience represents an interpretation of input from the external environment, not the external environment itself. All we know is an internalized version based on our personal viewpoint, the perspective of the knower. The knower inside can never actually contact the world outside, because contact takes place between material substances, like chemicals and bodily tissues. The internalized sensory imprint is as close as we ever get to the physical world.

Our sense of taste is similar. Say you have roast beef with chili sauce: there is no taste in the beef or the chili. They are made up of chemicals, not taste. When those chemicals contact your tongue, they cause a reaction. From that reaction, you get the taste. So taste arises only after the resultant chemical reactions are processed within us. We say that the taste is in the food, but it isn't: the taste is in us.

The sense of touch is just contact caused by pressure or variations of temperature, which turns into feeling only after it is processed within us. Touch works by sending information to the spinal cord, which forwards messages to the brain where the feeling is recognized and interpreted. But feeling is not present in the objects of contact themselves.

To summarize, we know the world we live in by means of the sense fields: sight, sound, smell, taste and touch. We then incorporate that sensory information into our thinking, which organizes it in such a way that we experience it as external to us. In other words, we see the world as being out there in relation to us, because that's the way it appears. And we, the ones who know the world, appear to be inside. But if we investigate the senses closely, we'll see that the entire world actually arises inside the mind.

Although it's not difficult to understand this intellectually, in practical everyday terms, I am not sure this knowledge makes much difference, because most people will still act as though the world outside is something real. It appears like that to people because they have been brought up to think that way. But, from the point of view of investigating and learning about ourselves, this knowledge is important. We can learn that the way we think and the ways other people think are not actually the same. We see things in a certain way, but somebody else sees them in a completely different way. It's not necessarily the case that either one is wrong; both may be right. It's just that the experiences we base our interpretations on are different.

If we want to understand the senses on a deeper, more personal level, we need to analyze the whole process more carefully. However, contemplating the senses is a challenging practice. The problem is that we are very strongly conditioned to see the world as existing outside ourselves and having a reality of its own. When we start investigating the senses, we can see intellectually that the outside reality is an illusion; that actually everything is internal. However, this understanding is still of an academic nature. Although it is quite valid at that level, we must go beyond that intellectual understanding and actually realize it for ourselves. We must realize with total certainty that the realms of the senses are things existing solely in our own minds.

Seeing things in this way makes us realize that the world is not quite the place we thought it was. When that realization strikes home, our interest in the world of the senses starts to wane. We begin to see that the world out there is merely a kind of magic show, lacking any real substance. The value of that realization is a lessening of attachment to external things. We no longer view them as worth craving. Having understood with insight the true nature of sensory experience, we know that everything we perceive in the world actually arises internally. Because perceptions arise inside us, they are actually a part of us;

so why should we want to possess them? That kind of seeing begins to break down our attachment to external objects.

This insight is invaluable because we see with a very clear mind what the world is. We no longer receive sensations in the usual, familiar way. Usually, we are so familiar with the world that we don't think about it very much. In a state of insight, however, we see it clearly. Seeing clearly, we learn a great deal. The value is in the lessons we learn about the world. And when we learn enough about the world, we let go of the world. We realize that attachment to it is a major cause of suffering.

This is the aim of the practice of wisdom: to understand the true nature of the world, mainly for the purpose of uprooting our attachment to worldly things. When we truly comprehend the nature of the world, we realize: "Oh, it's all inside the mind." With that knowledge, our attachment to the world weakens. When that happens, things that occur in the world don't affect us so much; they have less impact. We sort of shrug and say dispassionately, "That's just the way of the world." We let them go. As the mind detaches from external things, the focus turns more and more inside, more and more toward seeing how sense consciousness influences our perceptions of the world. It's a complicated process.

As an example, consider this: Wisdom entails seeing the past and the future from the perspective of the present moment. We cannot be aware of a visual object until after the visual data have contacted the sense base. And between the moment of vision and the moment of recognition there is a time lag. A momentary time gap exists between the arising and ceasing of one and the arising of the other. Because of that, the past moment of vision exists only in memory. The sights, sounds, et cetera that we experience are always in the past and filtered through memory. The mind seeks images and symbols from the database of previous experience to recognize and interpret incoming sense impressions and thus "understand" them. In this way, the practice of wisdom unravels the entire process of sensory experience.

There is also another way to investigate this process. When we sense things, there is the one that senses and the thing that is sensed. In seeing, there is the thing that is seen and the one who sees it. From that, we get the notion that "I see that." So, immediately a self is assumed. This self comes up in relationship to all the senses in the same way. But, in each case, it is a different "self." The self that relates to seeing is not the same self that relates to hearing. The one that relates to the external senses is not the same one that relates to thinking or memory. Each time, it's a different self. In the end, when we follow the way of Dhamma, we have to give up the attachment to all ideas of self.

This problem of self-identity arises because we have a fixed idea of our own reality. Being attached to this fixed idea of a personal reality, we cannot see the relativity of the world. We do not understand how relative our existence is, and how changeable. We don't like that uncertainty, so we create a self-image as a refuge, and make it appear very real and important. That precipitates a clinging to this fixed idea of self. And there is the dislike of letting go lest that self be swept away in the whirlwind of changing phenomena.

But in the final analysis, the way of Dhamma is to see all perceptions as just phantoms, phantoms of your mind. That means that you know another person only in your mind. Therefore, that person is really a part of your mind. So when you're angry with that person, you're really angry at your own mind. Things that person says are heard internally. Because you hear them internally, they belong to you. The belief that they come from another person is just a delusion.

The way of Dhamma is to truly realize that the whole fault is in you; the fault is your own, every time. It's not that other people don't cause trouble—in the ordinary worldly sense, they do. But you are at fault when you believe that they are causing *you* trouble and react accordingly. You are to blame because your mind has been deceived by its interpretation of sense perceptions, deceived because it knows wrongly.

All we actually do know are sights, sounds, odors, flavors, feelings and thoughts. When we understand this, we realize that what we know as sight is just form, light and color; sound is just vibrations; odors and flavors are just chemicals; and touch is just feeling, whether pleasant, painful or neutral. That's all we know. Those sensory experiences vary over a certain range, and that's all we can say. Our whole world is composed of that sensory input. When we know all that, we know everything. People think of the world and the universe as being immeasurably large, but they're not. Actually, they're no bigger than our senses. The really big universe is within us, but most people are completely unaware of its vast potential.

When you persevere in questioning everything, sooner or later you'll come back to the mind, because that's the center. You should question any sensation arising through the eyes, ears, nose, tongue, body, mind, feeling, memory, thought, consciousness or anything else. Is there anything you don't need the mind for? You need the mind for everything. Because of that, the mind is the true essential. Everything you work on in your wisdom practice will eventually come back to that one fundamental truth.

GOOD IN THE
END

Like a tornado, the mind is a whirlwind of changing phenomena without any real substance. The mind's existence is merely that whirling, dynamic movement and nothing more.

———————————————

SELF

Each of us has a worldview built up inside since we were born, informing us about the nature of things in the world. This worldview of ours is like a map located within, which tells us where everything is. We feel secure in this view because we know where we stand in the world and how we should behave in the world. Behind that view is a belief that it represents something real. At the center of it all is our self-identity. Not only do we have a view of how things are now in the present, but we also have a view of how they became like this. In other words, we have views about both the present and the past. We also have a view which is projected into the future telling us what we think things will be like.

Our views of the world and our place in them are, in fact, false. The very nature of our self-identity makes them false. Because of that, most of our delusion is located in these views. And the trouble with delusion is that it prevents us from seeing what is real and what is not. So we continue viewing the world in our habitual way, even though our worldview is untrue.

Delusion creates our worldview, which includes all our beliefs, our ideas and our opinions about everything. This information is saved in our memory. We remember things and situations because we crave security. For example, when we come to a new place, we search around to find where the things we need are located. Having found them, we remember where those things are. When we need them we'll know where to look. And we check our surroundings quite frequently to make sure everything is where it should be. In this way, we update our memory all the time. If something has changed, we question the new order and then we adjust memory accordingly. We always want the assurance that things are more or less permanent.

We're always seeking permanence—permanence in the sense that memory reassures us that things are as they were previously. We have developed an idea of permanence that we superimpose on the world. Then, when our world alters dramatically, we are really upset. The world seems to have suddenly changed, but actually it has been undergoing change the whole time. Our minds just gave it the appearance of permanence, that's all.

As such, we tend to be deluded in the way we see and understand. We go along with that understanding because we crave security. Without that feeling of security, false though it is, we would feel the need to be constantly watchful of everything in our environment, and that would make us feel uncomfortable. Thus, we're always trying to fix in place the world around us, our environment, so that we know it and feel unthreatened by it. We lull ourselves into a false sense of security because we are deluded into thinking that our world remains unchanged when, in fact, it does not. Everything is constantly changing. Even if we fail to see everything changing, the changes are taking place.

We must realize that change doesn't mean just change out in the world; it also means change in ourselves. When we see something from a different angle or at a different time, we see that the object has changed. But the change is largely in oneself, the one who sees it. That's the real meaning of anicca: everything is changing within us the whole time. We remember seeing something, but by the time we see it again it has aged. More than that, in the meantime we have learned more about all sorts of things, so internally the thing is not seen in the same way. It seems to have changed when, in fact, it's we who have changed more. The changes inside us are much more relevant to us than the changes outside. These changes occur in our minds, attitudes, understandings and so on.

Change also occurs in the self that we think is so permanent and stable. This is an area where delusion blinds us to the truth. It's not the case, as many Buddhists believe, that the self does not exist. Actually, a self-identity does exist for all of us, but it's constantly changing and so has no permanence. That being the case, the idea of self is not incorrect, as long as we realize that the self is not a permanent entity. Actually, there's bound to be a self—that's what we all experience. But when we examine it, we'll see that our self-identity doesn't remain the same for two consecutive moments. It is changing continually.

The Buddha never said that there is no self. He said that no permanent entity exists that we could call "self." In the suttas, it is stated: "All things are anicca. What is anicca is dukkha. What is anicca and dukkha is anattā." This indicates that in the Buddha's time it must have been obvious to everyone that the true nature of "self" must be absolute happiness. In other words, if it was not permanent happiness, then it could not be self. Time after time in the suttas, this formula comes up. It must have been taken for granted by the average person at the time of the Buddha, in a way that it is not by people nowadays. So the relationship between happiness and a belief in self must have been common knowledge. It was this belief that the Buddha was countering with the doctrine of anattā.

Whatever is anicca is dukkha, and whatever is anicca and dukkha cannot possibly be the permanent happiness that the concept of self implies. Therefore, not-self means there is no permanent self which equals permanent happiness. Because everything is changing, nothing can be satisfactory; and because everything is changing and unsatisfactory, no permanent self-entity exists anywhere in the universe. The Buddha was not saying that there is no self-perspective in the whirlwind of changing phenomena. He was saying, instead, that there is no permanent unchanging self to be found. The Buddha said that the self can be body, the self can be feeling, the self can be memory, the self can be thought and the self can be consciousness. One's self-perspective can jump between any of these aggregates of personality. It is constantly moving about.

Our delusion is not so much that we experience everything from a personal self-perspective, but rather that we deny change and cling to that sense of self as real and permanent. Our sense of self is so firmly established that it serves no purpose to deny its existence. On the other hand, as long as we continue to deny change we will never see the truth of not-self. The delusion of self is completely bound up with the delusion about permanence.

The fundamental delusion of self is deeply ingrained, and therefore, critical to the way in which we interact with the world. The Buddha called this delusion "māna diṭṭhi," the idea of "I am"—I have views, I have ideas, I have thoughts and so on. In our ordinary interactions with the world, the idea of self is actually necessary because we need a reference point to compare ourselves to other people and to objects in our surroundings. We must have some reference point to function in the world. So our minds devise a self-perspective. That's alright; it's necessary. But then we cling to a very firm belief in the reality of that self and assume it to be a fixed entity.

The delusion really starts when we believe in the permanent reality of that self and react from a self-centered viewpoint. We then harbor opinions of ourselves as being more or less exalted, as being right or good or entitled. What are those ideas attached to? They're attached to our views of self, a self which is virtually an imposter. At best, we can say this imposter is a necessary evil. But it's not a true thing. So the whole basis of our thinking is delusional.

Ignorance and craving are the factors that create the delusion of self-identity. They create the delusion that we exist in relationship to something else, meaning a self must exist in relation to what's not-self. The kilesas convince us that what matters is the advantage to self, and they do whatever they can to promote a strong self-image. Ultimately, the troubles we experience are all caused by believing in that self.

When there is self, there is also that which is not-self; and there is the relationship between the two. In the relationship, that which is not-self defines self, and that which is self defines not-self. The two sides work together. Without not-self, the self just disappears, it means nothing. Not-self must always be there, always pointing to self, to "I am."

The belief in an immutable entity is the background to the idea of self, the idea that the self has a fixed, independent existence. The self exists—everybody has a self-identity—but the self is an endless series of changing phenomena that whorls about continuously, forever changing appearance, like a chameleon. It's not that self doesn't exist, but that it's a bundle of dynamic change. So we cannot pin the self down and say it is this or it is that, because as soon as we pin it down, it immediately becomes different.

Because of that, the eternalist's belief in an immutable entity is quite wrong. If something is entirely unchangeable, that must be Nibbāna. Nibbāna is certainly not an entity. Where we have entities, we have comparisons between different entities. When we have comparisons between entities, then those entities must be impermanent in order to exist.

The nature of existence can be expressed as a paradox. We can say that the fundamental characteristic of existence is constant change. Existence depends on change. At the same time, anything that changes is not real, because it does not last. The fundamental characteristic of reality is permanence. Thus the paradox: what exists is not real and what is real does not exist. Reality and existence cannot, therefore, be coincident. The world of our sensual experiences is an aspect of existence because nothing remains the same from one moment to the next. Nothing we experience is fixed and immutable; all is flowing and changing. Nibbāna is the one permanent reality that does not change.

So we can say the self exists because it is constantly changing. Most people misunderstand the Buddha's basic teaching on anattā. Buddhist conventional wisdom has it that there is no self. But truthfully speaking, we cannot claim that we don't have a self, since we've already created it. It's there. We refer to it. That reference, in fact, brings it into existence and maintains it. The self-perspective exists. But certainly there is no entity of self, no permanent self. The personal self is merely a product of delusion.

I visualize the self like a whirlwind, a tornado. It comes buzzing across the plains, whirling violently, creating havoc and damaging everything in its path. But when we examine it closely, we find it is only air, and nothing else. And when the air stops whirling, where is it? We can't find it. It's gone. In other words, there's no substance there. There's no entity to be found. Its existence is merely that whirling, that dynamic movement. The self is very much like that: a whirlwind of changing phenomena driven by mental defilements.

The self is a reference point, and that reference point is created by the kilesas. Actually, we talk about self in terms of subject and object. When we sense things, there's the one who senses and the thing that's sensed. We see things: there's the thing that's seen and the one who sees it. We say, "I see that," having assumed that there's some self that sees it. "I hear it" or "I think it"—a self-perspective is always coming into our experience. But in each case, a different self arises. The self that relates to seeing is not the one that relates to hearing; the one that relates to the external senses is not the one that relates to thinking or to memory, et cetera. With each new mental state a different self arises, a different reference point. And every reference point is bound up with kilesas.

Bad states of mind obviously involve the kilesas; but good states of mind also involve kilesas. Like fish in water, we are so immersed in kilesas that we never know any other perspective. Just as fish know only the experience of water, so we have no idea what life without the kilesas is like. Because they are always there, we know only their side of the story. Their side of the story is the fiction of individual personality, the imposter that we call self.

The self is a very elusive thing. Because it's shifting about all the time, we seek confirmation of its objective reality. A lot of our thinking is done for just that reason. In fact, that's the reason we do so many things; the reason why so many of the kilesas get involved. The self is an illusion that the kilesas conjure up to push their way on us. Since I have a self, I should know who I am. To know who I am, I must have objects and people surrounding me to tell me who I am. Views, attitudes and emotions also help define who I am. I am this type of person; that is, the type of person I believe myself to be. I may appear very different to other people, but I hold to the belief: "I am this type of person." I wish to reinforce that belief, so I act in ways that I think that type of person would act, and often make a fool of myself in doing it.

If we could just drop the idea of self, we would be all right. Here, I am not saying we can drop it just like that—we can't. People can't just drop self. If they dropped self in one way, they'd just take it up in another way. The only positive action we can take is to work on the meditation practice. Cultivate sīla, samādhi and paññā until the mind develops wisdom. When the mind develops wisdom to a sufficient level, the dropping of self-identity will happen automatically. There will be no need to actively try to let go. When the deception of self is clearly comprehended, the desire to cling to a self-identity will drop away on its own.

Letting go of self-identity is not like having given up cigarettes but still constantly craving them. In truth, a person who gives up cigarettes like that has not given them up properly. As long as the wanting remains, they have not really been given up. On the other hand, the giving up of kilesas leaves no residual wanting behind. It may happen that certain desires have so thoroughly disappeared that suddenly one day you realize: "Oh, the kilesas don't come up like before. I am not interested in them anymore." The interest has dropped away. This is the way the breaking of attachment should be—it should be automatic and final.

It's not so much that the way of practicing meditation is very difficult; it is the overcoming of those things that are blocking the way that's really difficult. In a very real sense, we are our own worst enemies in meditation. We tend to get hung up on all the wrong things. It is not just a matter of doing the right things, but more a matter of going in the right direction. When we go in the right direction, we start uncovering the wrong things that we do and begin to correct them. By going in the right direction, we slowly cut away at our delusion. Then we learn not to do harmful actions in the future.

The barrier to achieving that, of course, is attachment to our self-identity. In order to breach that psychological barrier, we must give up a part of our precious self. We must accept that, at a certain level, we can no longer make a distinction between ourselves and other people. Most people are not prepared to go that far. By accepting that, we would be forced to relinquish many of our personal motives and ways of behavior. For instance, we couldn't consider other people as enemies, because when no distinctions are made, hating others is equivalent to hating ourselves.

Also, it isn't that we destroy the self through meditation, but that we come to understand that the self is an illusion. No destruction of self takes place because there's nothing to destroy. It's rather like trying to destroy a shadow. Seeing through the illusion, on the other hand, reveals the mind's true nature. Fundamentally, the element of Nibbāna is there within us already. It must be there; if it wasn't there already we couldn't possibly reach it, because Nibbāna is not subject to arising. The Buddha stated very clearly that whatever arises must cease, which means that Nibbāna must be there within us all the time. Otherwise, it would have to arise at some point in time, which is incompatible with its nature of being unchanging.

This is the true nature of Dhamma, the Dhamma in the heart. The heart always experiences a pull in the direction of Dhamma, but its pull is not like the pull of the kilesas. It's not like the pull of the child who must have a sweet right now. That's the pull of the kilesas. The pull of Dhamma is a longing to get back to something that we know is real; it's a longing to go home, in the true way, where everything is just right.

In the end, following the way of Buddhism back to our true home means giving up all attachment to our ideas of self. Our journey home begins with examining all of our attachments in the light of the three marks of existence: anicca, dukkha and anattā. Anicca is impermanence, constant change, the tendency for nothing to last. Dukkha is discontent and dissatisfaction. We see that everything is always changing; nothing lasts long. We get something that seems very good, and before long it's gone. That's not a basis for lasting contentment. And that which is changing and unsatisfactory is anattā because it cannot be a basis for a viable self. How can there possibly be a self in what's changing and unsatisfactory? When all is changing, the self does not remain the same for two consecutive moments.

The way of Dhamma is to realize that this is the case, that all of existence is characterized by these three marks: anicca, dukkha and anattā. Seeing those in a profound way cuts away our attachments. Seeing those marks clearly, we won't experience attachment to anything because, how can we be attached to something which doesn't last? As soon as we grasp it, it's gone in the same moment. It's like trying to pick up water with a sieve—it just falls straight through.

That which we call self and think of as self is bound up with the delusion that we exist as individuals in this world. That which is Dhamma appears to be something other—something outside the domain of self, but something which can come and help. Like delusion, Dhamma also resides in the mind; the two exist side by side in the mind. Delusion is the factor that creates a sense of duality and then tries to secure that perspective in place. Because of that, we experience nothing but pain and suffering. No matter how tightly things seem to be fixed in place, those things always undergo change because they are anicca. So we suffer because the one we think of as self is constantly trying to resist the inevitable.

That one, the self we think we are, can never know the truth. That which appears to be the other is the truth. While the self cannot help us to realize the truth, the other—which is the truth—is not really separate from us at all. We must learn to recognize that within us there is the truth of Dhamma that will always tell us the right way to go, both in terms of which actions are morally right and wrong, and in terms of which meditation techniques are best suited to countering delusion. We must learn to trust the voice of Dhamma within us. The more we trust it, the more its power grows within us and the closer we come to reaching our true home.

CITTA

Kruba Ajaans of the Thai Forest Tradition have always placed a special emphasis on what they call "the one who knows." In doing so, they make a fundamental distinction between two very different aspects of the mind: the unchanging knower, and the fluctuating states of mind that are known. Because we fail to understand the difference, we take transient mental states to be real, to be the mind itself. In fact, they're just changing conditions that never remain stable from one moment to the next. The knowing essence of mind—the one who knows—is the only stable reality.

Mostly, we group all mental functions together and refer to them as mind. But in truth, states of mind exist in conjunction with the knowing of them. When we see that distinction clearly, a realization occurs that mental states like good and evil, happiness and suffering or praise and blame are conditions separate from the awareness that knows them. The knower occupies a neutral position between dualities like happiness and suffering. One simply knows them. If we can see this clearly, we can put down the whole lot and let them go.

The Pāli word "citta" is often used when referring to "the one who knows." The word citta itself is very difficult to translate. When discussing the nature of the citta, language has its limitations. Attempts at translating a word like citta into English always lead to misunderstanding because no comparable English equivalent exists which encompasses all aspects of its true meaning. In fact, the true nature of the citta cannot be expressed in words or concepts. Concepts such as mind, soul or spirit all miss the point. All words carry certain preconceived notions that limit their definition. But the citta is completely unlimited. Because it encompasses everything, the citta has no boundaries by which to delineate it.

For that reason, the word citta is best left untranslated. It is far better for people to struggle to understand an unfamiliar term than for them to completely misunderstand that term due to a misleading translation. Misunderstanding disguised as knowledge never leads to the truth.

The term citta is usually translated as "mind," but this is quite misleading. What we generally refer to as the mind is different from citta. The mind incorporates the mental faculties of feeling, memory, thought and consciousness, and is usually considered to be that which thinks and remembers. Those mental faculties are inherently unstable: they all constantly arise, remain momentarily and die away. The citta, on the other hand, does not arise and does not die away. It exists entirely without reference to time and space.

The citta is difficult to explain, mainly because it does not represent a material object. Because the citta is not something that can be pointed to or examined in any way, from the world's viewpoint it does not exist. You can know the citta, but you can't see it. It doesn't resemble an external object. It's not a sensory thing that you can contact. You can't perceive the knowing essence because the knower and the knowing are the same. For the citta to perceive itself, it would have to split into two, and it can't do that.

In beginning to understand the nature of the citta, we should realize that it has various aspects. On one level, there is the citta of ordinary life. This citta is rather like the movement of the waves on the surface of the ocean, in contrast to the still depths below. We might call the one that moves on the surface the superficial citta. The superficial citta knows the five senses of sight, sound, smell, taste and touch. It is the one who makes decisions, the one who makes kamma; in other words, the one who is active. This is what we mean by the citta in ordinary life.

This superficial citta has qualities and faculties that are changing all the time. It is never without change. When the citta is associated with the aggregates of body and mind, it is bound up with the world of constant change. The citta changes because it must change. Because the aggregates are part of the world, they are inherently impermanent; so the citta cannot remain fixed in that situation.

However, the superficial citta is always grounded in something we call the "original citta," or the "primordial citta." Unlike the ordinary citta, the original citta is something which is vast and unfathomable. It is like the depth and breadth of the ocean, as opposed to wave-like sensations rippling on the surface. The waves are not separate from the ocean, but they do not really affect the ocean either. At the same time, the waves can be quite turbulent and full of motion. They are never still. The basic condition of waves on the ocean's surface is constant change. The depths, however, always remain as they are: still and unchanging.

The mental aggregates, or nāma khandhas, of feeling, memory, thought and consciousness are also bound up with the surface motion. The fundamental ignorance, or avijjā, which permeates the ordinary citta and influences its knowing, uses the functions of these mental aggregates to perceive objects, such as seeing forms and hearing sounds. When the citta is modified in this way, we call it consciousness, being that function which acknowledges sensations. The citta is modified in that way because avijjā, which has been infused into the citta, usurps the citta and uses the citta's power to its own ends.

One of avijjā's primary aims is to experience sensations. The reason it wants sensations is to prove its own existence—its self-identity. The only way that the citta with avijjā can verify its identity is by relating itself to other things through sense experiences. So consciousness is necessary for the citta infused with ignorance to relate to other things, thus reinforcing its own self-existence.

Consciousness is necessary to experience the duality of subject and object, but it is completely extraneous and unnecessary to the original citta. So from the point of view of the reality of the knowingness which is the true citta, consciousness is superfluous because the true knowing is always present in the citta, even after all the physical and mental aggregates have disappeared.

Because of that, we cannot really say anything definitive about the original citta at all. Although its scope is immeasurably large, it remains for us a mystery, an unknown quantity.

For that reason, the citta always causes people great uncertainty. But it's also the one that is most valuable, the one that really matters. Its subtlety makes it difficult to fathom. We can say that the citta is the essence in a person—everything else is peripheral. In that sense, citta is life, the essential component in what it means to be alive. Because of that, anything that lacks citta isn't alive—it's just inert material substance and nothing more.

The citta is the active one. It creates the five aggregates of body and mind; it creates vedanā, saññā, saṅkhāra and viññāṇa. It creates everything. You mustn't think of the five aggregates as being five different rooms that the citta enters one after another. It's not like that. The citta creates a moment of viññāṇa, which then dies away. Then it creates vedanā, and that dies away. Then it goes to saññā, and that dies away. Then saṅkhāra, then viññāṇa again. It performs the duties of feeling, memory, thought and consciousness. They're all the jurisdiction of the citta, the whole lot. It performs multiple tasks.

To give an idea of what the citta's nature is: We see, hear, smell, taste and touch things, but how do we know those sensations? Where is the knowing located? Suppose we see something and we know perfectly well that it is such and such an object, and we know its purpose and so on—there's something in us which knows that sensory input. But when we search for that which knows, we find it very difficult to catch hold of the quality of knowing independent of what is known.

Say we know a sensation. The knowing is not the same as the sensation. Knowing is not a sensory experience. Sensation is an object of awareness, something that is known. But the knowing itself is never an object of awareness; rather, it's awareness itself. Normally, whatever we experience is perceived through the senses. But we can never experience the citta in this way because the citta is actually that which knows all sensations. The citta is the center, everything else is peripheral. Basically, it is the knowing essence within us.

But you should approach the knowing with caution because, although the citta is the one that knows, it does not always know correctly. That's normally the case when its knowing is contaminated from within by mental defilements such as greed, hatred and delusion. The citta still knows, but it knows falsely. What ensue from that wrong view are unwholesome actions of body, speech and mind.

The body and the mind are simply mechanisms. The citta is the force that controls their behavior. The citta exercises the powers of intent and volition. That intention, in turn, creates kamma. Because the body and the mind cannot act independently of the citta, only the citta can be held responsible for kamma and its consequences. When the kilesas usurp the citta's power, they tend to make body and mind act in ways that promote greed, hatred and delusion.

The real power of the citta is neutral, but the kilesas are biased, so they harness the strength of the citta for unwholesome purposes. The kilesas want this and want that. All the time, they are grasping at something. And they push the citta about to make body and mind strive to attain those things. In the end, the citta reaps the consequences of those actions, which is why there is so much pain and suffering.

When the citta, under the influence of the kilesas, wants to go in a certain direction, it makes the body and the mind do its bidding. Body and mind simply follow, carrying out the dictates of the citta. Because of that, neither body nor mind is really essential. The essential thing is the citta. But in order to free the citta of kilesas, we must have both the body and the mind as the mechanisms necessary to see the kilesas in action. The kilesas are located in the citta, but they express themselves through body and mind.

Body and mind are comparable to a computer: the body is the hardware and the mind is the software. The person using them is the citta. The computer must be there for the person to use it, just as body and mind are needed for the citta to function in the world. A person can use a computer with good or bad intentions. Either way, the computer simply follows commands. The intentions are found in the person, not in the computer.

Similarly, the kilesas are not found in the body or in the mind; the kilesas are located in the citta. When a person dies, the mental aggregates die along with the body and disappear. But the citta—the knowing essence of mind—does not die. That means that after death the kilesas remain with the citta. They don't disappear—and neither do the results of kamma created by the kilesas nor the tendency for them to arise in the future. Because the kilesas and their consequences are still there, a new birth will take place. Kamma is then reactivated in conjunction with the next body and mind.

The citta is the very foundation of saṁsāra. It is the essence of being that wanders from birth to birth. That wandering is governed by kamma and its consequences. And it is the citta that carries the kamma from birth to birth. This would seem to imply that the citta is some kind of entity, like a soul. But it is not an entity at all, just as the vastness of space is not an entity. The citta is simply a reality that knows; a vast knowing essence at the depths of one's being that knows the nature of kamma and its appropriate consequences from one birth to the next.

The kamma that determines the next birth will then dictate the citta's level in that plane of existence. That's the level at which the citta normally functions—what it tends to always revert to. If you investigate often, you can locate the level that it seems to revert to inside yourself. We call this "the ground of the citta," meaning the level of the citta.

In the cycle of rebirth, the citta can experience many different levels. Our cittas are on the human level, but there is quite a lot of variation even on this level, from people who are extremely low and coarse to people who are very high and near to the deva realms. It's quite a broad range. We should investigate to discover our normal level within this range. This is important to know. If we can gain some understanding of our own level, we can better understand where our faults lie, and how we can go about correcting them.

Due to various circumstances, the level of the citta can change at times, but it tends to revert back to its basic level. If a person practices in good ways, or in bad ways, and they go on doing that for a long time, the level of the citta can reestablish itself. That is, the ground of the citta can change. For example, if a person who is normally quite friendly gets into a long-lasting situation that causes a lot of anger to come up, that anger can take over and become the citta's basic level. We also see the same thing in people who have mental trouble. When they become stuck in that mental state for a long time, that state becomes the level of the citta.

One of the problems we have is that we all tend to think that things are fixed inside. That's not so. States of mind change all the time, going this way or that way. It depends entirely on the conditions that produce the state. Conditions that occur very frequently can bias the citta in a certain direction. To put it in another way: When we develop habits, those habits tend to take hold of us. When we become thoroughly involved in those habits, they can be so strong that they become part of us. Habitual involvement can change our whole mental outlook.

The most effective way to shift the ground of the citta in a positive direction is to put the Buddha's teaching into practice. Constant, sustained meditation practice develops good mental habits. Good habits lead to a sharper mental focus and greater degrees of calm and concentration. When the citta is raised to a sufficient level of calm and concentration, the knowing essence within becomes more apparent. In truth, that knowingness is so very refined compared to our physical form that its true nature becomes apparent only in a state of meditative calm.

Although the citta is bound to the physical body from birth, its presence is so subtle that normally we are unable to detect it. The citta's knowing is actually dispersed throughout the body in such a way that we can't pinpoint its exact location. Only the practice of meditation can identify its presence and separate it from everything else associated with the body. In samādhi meditation we can experience that separation, seeing the citta as the knowing and the body as the known.

In order to reach that stage, we must first discipline the mind to overcome the resistance formed by accumulated bad mental habits. In other words, we have to train the mind to calm down and stay at home. When the mind is very calm, it is easy to direct it inward. It will be content to stay inside and go deep until it understands things clearly. Whereas, if we try to do that with our ordinary consciousness, the mind will jump about and will not stay fixed on one object, because it is still hungry and unsatisfied.

The mind is always hungry and searching for something to satisfy its appetite. So it seeks satisfaction in sensations, which is searching in the wrong direction. It jumps around all over the place like a monkey, but never receives any satisfaction. The way to cure that is to temporarily halt sensory experience—clamp down and block it off.

In meditation, this means keeping the mind focused on only one object. You undercut the feeling of dissatisfaction by allowing the mind only one object, using mindfulness to hold the object in place. This anchors the mind and prevents it from drifting. Because it can no longer jump about, the restlessness gradually subsides. In the Visuddhimagga, the restless mind is compared to a calf that is taken away from its mother and tied to a post with a rope. At first, it brays and jumps about, trying to escape. Because the rope prevents that, it eventually gets used to the situation, calms down and goes to sleep by the post.

When you anchor your mental focus on one object for a long time, the mind will calm down and fill with inner peace. Eventually, you'll get to a point where the citta is so fully satisfied that it no longer searches for sensations. When that happens, the citta goes still and quiet. When the citta becomes still and quiet because it no longer wants to experience external sensations, you can begin to see its true nature. Seeing that, you realize how rarely the citta is in harmony with itself.

Meditation is a process of going inward. Essentially, this process moves from external to internal, from coarse to subtle; it moves from an emphasis on the body to an emphasis on the mind, from a condition of activity to a condition of stillness. In other words, it involves a movement away from the realm of the known and into the realm of the knowing.

Once the mind becomes skilled at achieving calm and concentration, it begins questioning its relationship to the known, the objects of awareness. The body is made up entirely of inert material substance, physical matter that on its own has no awareness. Since physical matter is incapable of knowing itself, what is it that knows the body? Where is that awareness located? Feelings don't know themselves; they are known. What is it that's aware of feelings? Memories, perceptions and thoughts are objects of awareness. They are known as they arise and cease, but they themselves have no innate awareness. So what knows them?

If body, feelings, memories, thoughts and perceptions are all known, there must be an independent knower that encompasses all aspects of body and mind. There is, of course, but the problem is that ignorance weaves a web of delusion around the knower, distorting the knowing in such a way as to cloud the difference between that which knows and that which is known.

In that respect, the phrase "the one who knows" and the word "citta" are used by the Thai Forest Tradition in a way that other Buddhists might find difficult to comprehend. Sometimes, this understanding may seem at odds with what we read in the early Buddhist texts. One of the standard formulas found in the suttas states that a full comprehension of the five aggregates results in the destruction of greed, hatred and delusion. This statement represents a simplified view of a very complex experience. The implication is that the five aggregates encompass the entire world of human experience; that nothing—including an independent awareness—exists outside the domain of the five aggregates. If nothing exists separately from the five khandhas, then everything that exists must be included within their domain.

That is actually true, but not in the way people normally think. It hinges on what is meant by "existence." Change is the essence of existence and everything in the five khandhas is constantly changing; therefore the five khandhas are the domain of existence. Without change, there is no existence. On the other hand, changing phenomena are not real, because reality never changes. Thus the five khandhas exist, but they are not real. They are not reality because reality is not impermanent. Because it never changes, reality is not known through sensation; and because we can't sense reality, it's not associated with the five khandhas. However, reality can be known: We know it by being it.

We can put it like this: everything in the world is impermanent; everything is constantly changing. Again, change is the very nature of existence. Without change, there is no existence. Everything that is impermanent is unreal. It never has any time to be real; it's changing all the time. What we have here is a fundamental lack of reality.

The citta, on the other hand, is the exception to the rule. Existing separately from the five khandhas, the citta is comparable to the unfathomable vastness of space. Just as space is the medium without which nothing could come into being, the citta is the stable conscious continuum without which nothing in the realm of the five aggregates or the six sense bases could come into being. The citta is the unchanging reality in which everything in the world arises and then ceases. Because the citta does not change, it does not exist—but it is real. Being awareness itself, it is that all-encompassing presence in which arising and passing are known.

In truth, there is nothing really wrong with the citta. Within itself, it is naturally pure already. It's the defiling influences infiltrating the citta which cause it to experience happiness and suffering, gladness and sorrow. But the true nature of the citta has none of those qualities. Moods like happiness and suffering are not intrinsic to the citta. They merely deceive the untrained mind, which follows after them until it forgets itself, forgets its true nature.

Really speaking, the citta is already still and unperturbed: just like the ocean. When the wind blows, the surface water ripples. The ripples are due to the shifting winds on the surface, not to the ocean itself. The ocean depths remain unmoving and unaffected. When thoughts and perceptions arise, the surface of the mind ripples; when sense impressions arise, the surface of the mind ripples. The rippling is due to the thoughts and sensations. When the mind follows its surface activity, it loses sight of its true nature. If it doesn't follow after them, it can know fully the fluctuating nature of mental activity and still remain unmoved.

Our practice should be focused on seeing that which knows thoughts and sensations as they arise and pass away. We must train the mind to know all aspects of mental activity without getting lost in any of them. By doing that, the natural peacefulness of the citta will stand out clearly and remain unperturbed by happiness, suffering, gladness or sorrow. If we can experience this distinction with clarity, we can relinquish all aspects of existence and let them go their own natural way. Ultimately, this is the goal of Buddhist practice.

NIBBĀNA

Recently, I read Maurice Walshe's introduction to the Dīgha Nikāya. He writes very well. He made an interesting point about the Noble Eightfold Path. He said the eight factors of the Path are divided into three parts: sīla, samādhi and paññā—but the order is different. The wisdom grouping of Right View and Right Attitude comes first, followed by the morality grouping of Right Speech, Right Action and Right Livelihood, and ending with the concentration grouping of Right Effort, Right Mindfulness and Right Concentration. He surmised that wisdom must come first before there can be morality and concentration. To some extent this is true, but the real meaning of the Path is quite different.

The essential truth of the Noble Eightfold Path is that the Path can only arise when all eight factors reach a sufficient level of development to bring about the path moment. At that moment, all eight factors should converge simultaneously, each lending support to the others. By that definition, it becomes a true Path only at the path moment, which is the experience of Sotāpanna, Sakadāgāmī, Anāgāmī or Arahant. The Path proceeds from a lower state of purity to a higher one. It culminates at very specific path moments, when all the path factors coalesce at a certain level of perfection. Until those path moments arise, the work of a practitioner is only preparation for the Path.

People have a lot of misunderstanding about the Noble Eightfold Path. When Westerners begin to learn about Buddhism, they often start by studying the Noble Eightfold Path. But it's not the right way around. In the suttas, when the Buddha gives a discourse concerning the Noble Eightfold Path, he always mentions it at the end of the discourse. After talking to people until he gets them into the right frame of mind, he then explains the Path.

We must understand that the Noble Eightfold Path is not a path that we practice a little each day. The Noble Eightfold Path means that all its eight factors are Right: Right View, Right Attitude, Right Speech, Right Action, Right Livelihood, Right Effort, Right Mindfulness, Right Samādhi. They are all Right, and by Right is meant perfect. And being perfect, they provide a path which is capable of taking the mind, step by step, to the final goal. In other words, they initiate a path moment, the moment of Sotāpanna, Sakadāgāmī, and so on. This is the true meaning of the Noble Eightfold Path.

Of course, we must steadily practice to perfect each factor of the Path; that's necessary. But simply practicing the Noble Eightfold Path a little bit here and a little bit there won't get us to the goal. Today we'll do this, tomorrow we'll do that and so on. The Noble Eightfold Path is, in effect, the path to Nibbāna. This means that it culminates in perfection at a very deep level within the mind. It's not simply a journey from one stage to the next; its fruition requires a practice of meditation that has gone very deep, to the point where all these factors coalesce with equal strength and purpose. Only when the time and conditions are right does the path moment take place. That being said, the Noble Eightfold Path is not simple textbook Buddhism. That is something which has been misunderstood.

By the same reasoning, the Noble Eightfold Path is not a path that one travels along as one would a road or a walkway. Rather, the Path is set up as a mode of transcendence. When we have done the work to set the Path up correctly, it acts like a channel for transcendent states of mind to arise—Sotāpanna, Sakadāgāmī, Anāgāmī and Arahant. Because of that, all the path factors arise simultaneously. It is a difficult feat to accomplish because we must get all of those factors just right at the same moment. Having done the work, when the right conditions arise, they will all come together and bring forth the path moment.

In order to accomplish this, we must gradually develop all of the conditions which are necessary for that moment to take place. It involves not only formal meditation practice but all of our activities throughout the day. Effort and wisdom must be present at all times in order to turn every situation into Dhamma.

To begin with, we should first develop the path factors individually. That's necessary. When those factors are well developed, then our practice will be strong. When it is strong enough, the factors can join together to act as a bridge crossing to the other side—for example, from the path moment of Sotāpanna to its fruition. Although it is necessary to develop the factors of the Path individually, we mustn't think that those factors themselves are the Path. The Path only arises when all eight factors have been perfected. Emphasizing that all the factors are "Right" in effect means they are perfect. Once they are in perfect harmony, the path moment takes place.

Maggasāmaggī is the condition where all the path factors come together simultaneously to become a transcendent path. All eight of them must be present at the same time. It's not as though we practice sīla, then samādhi, then paññā in that specific order. Nor is it simply the good results we accumulate by practicing those factors over a long period of time. We can impose that meaning onto it, but it doesn't actually mean that.

In the Sāmaññaphala Sutta of the Dīgha Nikāya, when the Buddha taught King Ajātasattu, he began with dāna and then went to sīla and so on, up and up until he finally came to the Noble Eightfold Path. In other words, the Noble Eightfold Path came right at the end of the Buddha's discourse. After the Buddha had gone through the factors of the Path, the king—who was very moved by what he heard—paid his respects and departed. The Buddha then told the monks present that if the king had not killed his father, he would surely have experienced the Path. This suggests that the Path couldn't form at that point because the king's sīla factor was weak, which prevented all eight factors from coming together with equal strength.

So in order to fully realize the Path, we must train ourselves in all of the path factors until they are strong enough to go beyond. But the Path is a lot more than just a way of training, for it is through the Path that the goal is directly experienced. Eventually we reach a situation where the goal is known, but not necessarily realized. In other words, we may know that the goal is there, and know the general direction to take to reach it, but there's nothing we can point to, no object we can see up ahead representing the goal.

Actually, the goal is not something we reach by striving to go higher and higher. It's not like that. In truth, the goal is there all the time. What we must do is get rid of the things hiding it from view; not gain something, but relinquish everything. So we must get rid of all our wanting, all our attachments, all our wrong views and all our delusion. Developing the path factors eventually gets rid of all attachment to anything connected with the world. When we do that until we let go of everything, the goal—Nibbāna—is there. Then nothing is left for us to do. Therefore, Buddhism is not a path of gaining so much as a path of relinquishing.

When all the factors of the Path are Right, they act like a bridge leading one from an ordinary mundane state to the state of Nibbāna. At first, the realization of Nibbāna takes place momentarily because the pull of the kilesas is too strong for the mind to remain there, it falls back to mundane consciousness again, where more work must be done. The long-term effect on the mind is a stable foundation. We can say that when the mind attains any of the paths, it has known Nibbāna for a moment. An aftertaste of that realization of absolute freedom remains with one, making it impossible for the mind to deteriorate below a certain level.

Each of the four stages of the Aryan Path is a very distinct and clear-cut experience. Whether or not we can put a name to the experience is not so important. We simply know that experience, and we never forget it. After attaining Stream-entry, for example, we will know very clearly that something extraordinary has happened, causing a big change in our fundamental makeup. Looking back, we'll be aware that since that time a noticeable difference has occurred.

With Stream-entry, we secure an absolute faith in Dhamma, because at the moment of Stream-entry the truth is seen with absolute clarity. Having seen the truth, doubt about the truth can no longer arise. We also see clearly that the physical body is external to our personal identity: it is not us, it does not belong to us. And understanding arises that the ritual ways of behavior and the ceremonies that people use to improve their situation are not the way to find the truth. At the same time, we realize the absolute necessity for practicing moral virtue. Because we see these truths for ourselves, nothing can shake our faith in them.

At the path moment, we have an unshakeable certainty that the Path and its fruition are leading away from the world. When the world is finally transcended, the conventional nature of relativity breaks down. It is as though the mind goes into emptiness, an emptiness of all that we know. It goes to a reality which we call Nibbāna. This reality is of such a nature that it has no relative characteristics. Because nothing like it exists in the relative, conventional world, we cannot accurately describe it. When we reach that level, then that's where we are meant to be; that's all we can say.

Interestingly, the momentary realization of the Path is such that it leaves no traces in normal memory. The ariya puggala cannot remember precisely what happened at that moment because there is nothing in the experience of Nibbāna for memory to latch on to. Thus, when Nibbāna is known for a moment, a situation is set up where the goal is known, but it is not known in any concrete manner. We know with certainty that the goal is in that direction. Knowing that, we understand how other practices, like worship and ritual, are all illusory. Those practices do not lead directly to Nibbāna. It becomes absolutely clear that the way to Nibbāna is the way that the Buddha taught, the Noble Eightfold Path.

At the moment of Stream-entry, we will experience our first taste of Nibbāna, a taste of liberation that will beckon us to strive for complete fulfillment. Being able to name and describe that experience is of little importance. Even the terms we read about in the Buddhist texts do not necessarily lead to a better understanding, mainly because we read them from a background that is unsuited to understanding. We view the picture they present from the perspective of our ordinary life. But that is a false picture where Stream-entry is concerned. People like to discuss the four stages of the Aryan Path, but language mostly misses the truth.

In fact, only that first taste of Nibbāna can resolve the issue. After that first taste, after the attainment of Sotāpanna, the Path becomes a causeway crossing to the other side, with each stone located in its rightful place. Only when those factors are all properly in place can we cross over.

The texts say that the way of Sotāpanna is the way of discovery. In other words, wisdom arises. Sakadāgāmī, Anāgāmī and Arahant represent the way of effort. Once the right direction has been discovered, effort must then be put into getting rid of the kilesas in order to go the rest of the way. In practice, this means that we must develop all eight factors of the Path until they reach a perfect condition. Then the mind transcends the conventional world, and fruition occurs automatically.

With the Path, the question arises: Must all the path factors be at a hundred percent strength for the path moment to arise, or does its arising depend on the strength of the path factors that are sufficient for a certain individual? Personally, I think the strength of the path factors is an individual matter, dependent on a person's specific needs. The requirements for a certain individual may lean heavily on some factors and less so on others so as to bring about a perfect overall balance. What's needed is sufficient overall strength in them all. For example, when wisdom is strong, you don't need so much samādhi, though some samādhi is still necessary. With the other path factors present, the samādhi will inevitably be Right Samādhi because each factor of the path is a supporting condition for the other factors.

But regardless of individual temperament, Nibbāna is equally accessible to everyone. I'd say that Nibbāna is already there in everybody and everybody knows it, but they don't recognize it. Intuitively, we know that there is something better than this world, but we don't know what it is. So we search for it. Because we have an array of senses to work with, we tend to focus out in the direction of the senses, looking there for true happiness. Of course, that's searching in the wrong direction.

When we go out in the direction of the senses, we become attached to sensory experience and build up attachments to worldly gains. People nowadays think life should be about world development. But development in the world means deterioration in the mind, because people's minds are always out in the world and never inside themselves. The way of Dhamma is just the opposite: it's about getting rid of all mundane attachments and thus getting rid of our concerns about the world. When we practice in that way, the path of Dhamma will steadily lead us to greater and greater freedom, until eventually we arrive at the ultimate goal. But, because our attachments are very sticky, it's not an easy task.

The ultimate goal, Nibbāna, is beyond the world, beyond attachment. The nature of Nibbāna is emptiness. When our consciousness is rooted in this world, however, we cannot become aware of emptiness. We have no means to know what it is. Instead, we hold tightly to perceptions of "me" and "mine," so the world we live in is bound by artificial conditions. We are attached to a world of conditioned reality.

Nibbāna, on the other hand, is totally unconditioned. At that level, there is no difference between one person and another. Because of that, knowledge and understanding at that level can be conveyed directly, heart to heart, without the need for verbal expression. But such direct communication requires somebody who is at that level to fully comprehend it. Other people might be able to gain some understanding in this way, but they will experience difficulty turning that knowledge into ordinary thoughts. Because of the kilesas, their thinking will distort the meaning.

There is the mundane way of communication, which is ordinary speech; and there's a higher way of communication, which, although more accurate, is also elusive and formless. Trying to communicate direct understanding in the higher way, using metaphorical terms, can be more confusing than using the ordinary way of speech. In ordinary speech, we use logic, reason, experience and memory. Although the explanations are a bit makeshift, they can gradually lead to understanding. But when the ordinary person tries to explain Dhamma in high-sounding metaphors, the explanation usually turns out quite messy because there's so much scope for the kilesas to intrude and distort one's thinking.

Nibbāna is described as being empty of all distinctions. But we mustn't make the mistake, as many people do, of saying, "We are all one." That's merely another form of distinction. On the one side, we are many; on the other side, we are one. But who is this "we?" When we talk about one, we can also talk about many—in which case, all ideas of oneness disappear. When it comes to Nibbāna, all words and concepts cease, completely.

Some people believe that peaceful states of mind are a foretaste of Nibbāna. This is not true. Nibbāna is a total break from every type of conventional experience. It is a revelation of something which has always been there, though we have never known it. When the mind reaches the stage where it is not anicca, not dukkha and not anattā, it has completely transcended the conventional world of our experience. It has gone totally beyond. Because of that, Nibbāna can never be explained in conventional language. In the Sutta Nipāta, Venerable Upasīva addresses the Buddha and asks him to explain the state in which all conditions cease. The Buddha replied that when all conditions cease, all ways of speech cease as well. Nibbāna is the Unconditioned, so we cannot use conditioned ways of speech to speak about it.

The word "enlightenment" is often used to describe attainment of Nibbāna. But enlightenment, used in this way, is a contradiction in terms, because the experience of light for a highly advanced meditator is a manifestation of avijjā, or fundamental ignorance. The final level must be absolute emptiness. Nothing is there to perceive. Anything that manifests is an attachment. Light, for instance, is an attachment. One must go beyond all attachments to get to Nibbāna. So the word "enlightenment" signifies a subtle state of delusion, rather than a state of awakening. Although manifestations of pure radiance indicate a very high meditative attainment, they in no way represent the final goal. The final goal is empty of all conventional characteristics.

To experience Nibbāna means to know the truth in a deeply profound way. This knowledge is not something superficial that you can contemplate and think about. You can't think about Nibbāna because everything you think about must be relative. Thinking means duality: *you* thinking about *that*. The non-dual nature of Nibbāna has neither subject nor object. So what is there to think? Nibbāna cannot be pinned down with words.

For that reason, the Buddha did not expound an ultimate philosophy. Instead, the Buddha taught practical methods to achieve the unconditioned state. For instance, he taught that everything is anicca, dukkha and anattā. However, he did not say that the ultimate reality was nicca, sukha and attā. He said that the ultimate was not anicca, not dukkha, not anattā—which is very different. Nicca, sukha and attā are the opposites of anicca, dukkha and anattā; whereas the ultimate, the Unconditioned, cannot be bound by any qualities that define it in any way. All definitions are wrong. The Unconditioned is just that: totally without conditions—meaning no words can possibly describe it. It's not something that language can identify clearly. Like the vastness of space, Nibbāna is unbounded and immeasurable. Having reached it, all words cease. They must cease, because all words are bound up with conditions. The Unconditioned can only be known by being unconditioned.

This brings up a familiar question: Is Nibbāna still a possibility for us today? The answer should be obvious. Dhamma exists and the Paths exist, and you can see the reasoning behind them and the methods needed to get there, so why shouldn't your efforts bring results? The Buddha's teaching was designed for human beings, and human beings today are not much different from what they were at the time of the Buddha.

The view that the attainment of Arahantship is a thing of the past is a silly view. It's like saying that if you mix salt and sulfuric acid you can no longer get chlorine; it worked in the last century, but nowadays it can't be done. It's that silly. Arahantship is a fact of nature; a state that is there in us all the time. It isn't as though it's something new to us. Because it is there, it can be known. What we have to do is clear away all the rubbish hiding it from view. When we've completely cleared away the rubbish, that state will appear.

Nibbāna is not something that can arise. If Nibbāna could arise, it would cease as well. So it must be there the whole time. Nibbāna is there in everyone, but it's covered up by the messiness of the defilements. Your job is to get rid of that mess. When you've gotten rid of the worst of it, then you can clear away the last little bit and break through. There is nothing to stop you—except yourself. Those who say it can't be done nowadays are essentially creating a barrier for themselves. For them, Nibbāna becomes impossible because the belief that it can't be attained makes it impossible. If someone fully believes he can't become an Arahant, he'll never try. Those who believe they can, will at least try; and if they persevere, they may well succeed.

In the final analysis, if you try to understand Dhamma and Nibbāna without attaining them first, you'll be left with mere concepts and ideas, which won't be the real thing at all. They will just be ideas and symbols in your own mind. To actually know for yourself, you must get to that state.

The stages of Sotāpanna and the rest are stages where Nibbāna is experienced, if only briefly. Withdrawing from those attainments, you can't remember anything about them, because there's nothing to remember. You can only remember things that are relative, and that state is not relative. So withdrawing from Sotāpanna, for example, you wouldn't actually remember what happened. All you would know is that there has been a change. When Nibbāna is first experienced, the truth of Nibbāna is known, but later only the aftertaste of that truth remains. The aftertaste means that you have complete faith in it. With complete faith, you do not doubt the Buddha's teaching at all. Because you've experienced Nibbāna, you know without a doubt that it is the true way.

In the end, Nibbāna—the final cessation—comes when you can find absolutely nothing. You cannot even find the one who's found nothing. All distinctions disappear. It's not so much that you attain something, but rather that the one who does the attaining has disappeared. When that happens, talk about qualities like humility and equanimity misses the point, because no person is there to be humble or equanimous. Such qualities are merely conventional designations for constantly changing mental states. The comings and goings of mental states in no way impinge on the pure, unconditioned essence of Nibbāna.

In Theravāda Buddhism, one epithet for reaching Nibbāna is this: to come to the end of all questions. This doesn't mean that all questions have been answered; it means there are no more questions that one can possibly ask—because the basis for asking questions no longer exists. No one is there to ask the questions, and there is nothing to ask the questions about.

The quest for Nibbāna begins with our search for lasting happiness. Having failed to find that happiness by attempting to satisfy our desires, we see the danger in becoming attached to things that are unreliable, unstable and constantly changing. As long as there's attachment to things that are changing, disappointment and suffering will occur when they cease to be what we expect them to be. No matter how hard we try, we cannot find anything in the world which is permanent and stable, thus we always fail to find lasting happiness. The Buddhist path is the path of getting rid of craving, giving up attachments and letting go of everything. When we practice in that way, Dhamma will steadily lead us to more and more freedom, until eventually we can arrive at the end goal, the highest happiness, Nibbāna.

WISDOM

Wisdom, as understood in the Buddhist sense, differs from wisdom in the worldly sense. In the world, wisdom usually means clever or skillful thinking that leads to understanding. In Buddhism, wisdom is more closely connected with deep contemplation. It's more like a deeply probing mental faculty firmly based in a calm and concentrated mind. Wisdom is not restless; instead, it carries with it a sense of peace and happiness, and has about it an almost joyful quality. This is the wisdom state we are aiming for, though it's not so easily attained. Some people take to it naturally, but most people remain stuck at the level of discursive thinking.

Wisdom is a mental faculty that must be cultivated. Even those who possess innate wisdom will not be able to use it properly unless their mindfulness is strong enough to support and direct its activities. Wisdom doesn't mean mere intelligence. It represents an ability to understand that is developed through spiritual training. For that reason, the first necessities of spiritual training are the attainments of good mindfulness and a calm mind.

Wisdom resolves problems and puts things right. But, it's no good trying to master wisdom without first developing a basis of calm and concentration. Otherwise, it won't be true wisdom; it will just be discursive thought. Discursive thought is superficial; it jumps from one concept to another without ever going deeply into any of them. Wisdom is different. It acts on a deeper and more penetrating level than mere thinking.

When the mind is calm and free of distracting thoughts, body contemplation is an excellent place to start cultivating wisdom. From body contemplation, you can then progress, step by step, to investigating the subtleties of the mind and mental phenomena. The body is easier to start with, though, because it's more tangible. You can see and feel the body. You can look inside of it, either by seeing another person's body or by looking into your own body and examining what's there. Being gross, it is not difficult to grasp. The mind, on the other hand, is very subtle, making it difficult to get a hold on, difficult to comprehend. Due to the degree of difficulty, you must develop wisdom to quite a high level before you can really tackle the mind in the right way.

The path of wisdom practice—investigating inward from the coarsest objects to the most refined—is exemplified in the Four Foundations of Mindfulness or the Four Satipaṭṭhāna: body, feeling, citta and dhammā. Here we have a path leading progressively from the external to the internal. The body, being external, is the most obvious. Going inward, feeling is represented by the more subtle feeling-body. More subtle still is citta or states of mind. Lastly, there is dhammā, which is the content of the mind—the subtlest phenomena of all. Each of these four is a domain of personal experience, and each is a mode of establishing mindfulness.

Our contemplation of the Four Satipaṭṭhāna must start off with the most visible and tangible aspect of our personal identity. When we gain some understanding of the grossest aspect, the progression to the more subtle aspects can begin. In order to find out what we are, first we have to find out what we are not. If we eliminate what we're not, we'll get a better idea of what we are. So we look to see what we're not. One of the things we're not is the physical body.

To begin establishing mindfulness in the body, we focus on the physical body in the normal way we understand it. Without going into abstract ideas of embodiment, we simply examine the condition of the human body as we experience it. What is the human body and what is it composed of? Investigating truthfully, we see that the composition of our physical bodies and that of things in the material world are of a similar nature.

The body is made up of the same physical elements that are found in material substances everywhere. In other words, it consists of atoms and molecules, et cetera. Because the body is born of the physical world, it must depend on the world for food, air, heat, light, and so on. In truth, the body belongs to nature. And in the end, when the body dies, it decays, disintegrates and returns to nature. In respect to its composition, a living body is not fundamentally different from a corpse.

The body's impermanent nature notwithstanding, we still identify with our bodies as being a very real part of who we are; we see them as being ours. This is how we perceive bodily existence. But by what means do we actually *experience* the body? It's our own personal experience of the body that should be the determining factor. Aside from others' descriptions of the body's makeup, how do we know the body from the inside?

We can surmise that the human brain contains knowledge of the whole body. It is known that the body is laid out in sensory areas of the brain according to where the nerves end up. The brain has areas that correspond to every part of the body. Because of that, you can say that functions taking place in the body are mirrored in the brain. In fact, you can say the whole body is known there. That is where sensations go and that's where they're known.

The mind then takes sense data and projects it into an imaginary "feeling-body." The feeling-body is mind-made and mirrors the physical body, being coincident with it. It's essentially a phantom body—a mental construct which simulates the physical body. This mind-made body is what we know through feeling.

If a feeling is located somewhere in the feeling-body, we associate that part of the body with the feeling. For example, when we feel pain, say in the leg, we give the pain a location based on what the feeling-body tells us. But the pain merely appears to be in the leg, when actually it's experienced solely in the phantom feeling-body. That is to say, it's experienced somewhere in the realm of the mind. The pain seems as though it's in the leg because, in our mental construct of the body, we've learned to relate the registering of certain nerve impulses to that particular area of the body.

This is an example of how wisdom can lead a practitioner from the establishment of mindfulness in the domain of the gross physical body to the establishment of mindfulness in the subtle feeling body's domain. In fact, in the realm of experience, the two domains of body and feeling cannot be separated. Both function together as part of a whole, forming one contemplation with two aspects.

At the same moment that body and feeling are co-dependent, citta or states of mind are actively involved with those domains. Thoughts and concepts, and the subtle states of mind that determine them, define our perceptions of the phantom body of feeling. And mental feelings, subtler still, are closely associated with mental states.

Various factors make up the processes of the mind. There are feelings and memories; then the two major factors that make up thought, which are sankhāras and dhammas. By sankhāras, we mean the mental formations that create thoughts and ideas. When sankhāras group together, they form states of mind, which are combinations of many different factors, like anxiety, anger, conceit, compassion, concentration and so on. In the case of establishing mindfulness in the domain of mental states, we see the arising and ceasing of the factors that comprise those states, and the relationship between those states and our experience of body and feeling.

The fourth domain of satipaṭṭhāna, dhammā, refers to the content of the mind. The dhammas are the basic elements that make up mental formations and states of mind, and those elementary factors cannot be reduced any further. They are qualities and faculties that arise in the mind. For instance, pure hatred and pure greed are dhammas. They simply arise on their own, and they cannot be dissected any further.

The content of the mind is very subtle, and thus difficult to investigate. It incorporates principles that are intrinsic to our perceptions of both body and mind. These principles are ruled by a set of immutable laws, like the law of cause and effect and the law of constant change. The content of mind exists in a never-ending flux.

Certain phenomena arise in combination with other phenomena, both in the internal world and the external world. This creates two factors: the phenomena that arise, and the combinations that they create. The phenomena that arise are the elementary things, or dhammas; the combinations are sankhāras. So sankhāras are made up of dhammas. Within the content of the mind, we find the whole nature of the world and everything that is known. Therefore, wise contemplation of phenomena in the mind leads to a clear comprehension of the totality of physical and mental processes as they unfold. In that profound sense, the dhammā contemplation of the Satipaṭṭhāna means knowing the basis of everything within the realm of the mind.

The Four Foundations of Mindfulness deal with the different aspects of experience that exist at any one moment. Because the four factors are all functioning together, in practice, they can't be separated from one another. In one precise moment, all we can say is: This is the way of body, this is the way of feeling, this is the way of citta, and this is the way of dhammā. Each has a specific function, but they're all part of one experience. Contemplation of the Four Foundations of Mindfulness is an analysis of what's essentially one mental process. Because of that, the Four Foundations of Mindfulness are pointing at different aspects of a single state, meaning they don't arise consecutively, one at a time. All of them must be present simultaneously in any moment of experience.

The contemplation of the Four Foundations of Mindfulness progresses not only from the external to the internal, from the coarse to the refined, but it also progresses from basic awareness to more enhanced states of concentration and wisdom. The establishment of mindfulness in each domain leads to calmer and more focused mental faculties and to a clearer and more insightful knowledge and understanding about ourselves. Insight into the truth about ourselves, in turn, fosters a profound sense of detachment. When insights have gone deep enough, when wisdom has done its job, when understanding has come, then attachments are relinquished without our conscious intention.

The purpose of establishing mindfulness in each of the Four Satipaṭṭhāna is to gradually overcome personal attachments in the domains of body and mind. In the domain of the body, we consider how the human body is part of the physical world. It's composed of earthly substances; it's sustained by nutrients from the earth; and it decays and returns to the earth after death. At the same time, we know the body internally in a way that is different from the way we perceive the external world.

From the point of view of our attachment to the body, knowing the internal aspects of the body is more important than knowing the external, material aspects. That's why we are encouraged to establish mindfulness *inside* the body. When we keep our attention inside, we begin to realize that our knowledge of the body comes to us almost exclusively through sensation, through feeling. As the feeling-body gradually supersedes the physical body in our perceptions of what we are, our attachment to the gross, material body drops away while attachment to the more subtle feeling-body takes its place.

When mindfulness is well established in the internal body, the relationship between feelings and the states of mind that define and interpret them becomes apparent. In other words, the way we interpret the feelings that define how we experience the body is determined by our mental state. From that understanding, we realize that the mind is the true basis of feeling. As our contemplation moves deeper into mental states, our attachment to the domain of feeling—an essential aspect of our personal identity—starts to fade into the background. Feelings now appear external, and the primary focus turns inward to our mental states.

With the establishment of mindfulness firmly based in the domain of mental states, the subtle phenomena that make up the content of the mind are more readily perceived. These mental phenomena are far more refined than the states of mind they bring into being, and therefore more "internal" in relation to mental processes. In the final analysis, attachment to these subtle phenomena must be overcome in order to attain the mind's liberation.

The more we contemplate the four domains of satipaṭṭhāna, the more we become aware that everything is internal. Then we ask ourselves: If everything is internal, what is meant by external? In searching for the answer, we reach a point where the whole question of inner and outer ceases to have much meaning. Strictly speaking, making a distinction between outside and inside is the wrong way to look at the issue—it's nearly all inside. Then again, if everything is inside, there can be no outside. Ultimately, this quandary can be resolved only at the highest and subtlest levels of meditation practice.

In order to contemplate the Four Satipaṭṭhāna until we reach the subtlest levels of Dhamma, we must cultivate wisdom to a sharp and incisive degree. We must reach a state of wisdom in which we see the implications of what we are investigating. We may know theoretically what the implications of having a body are, yet still not see them in ourselves. We still think and act very much as though the body is what we are.

When we arrive at a true understanding through wisdom, it's like standing back and viewing the body from a detached perspective.

When we perceive it truly with wisdom, a complete knowing arises that the body is in no way oneself. This wisdom state is different from mere thinking and reflecting. It starts with the external aspects of body contemplation and systematically moves inward, step by step, probing deeply at each successive stage, until all attachments to the body are clearly known and relinquished.

Thinking, on its own, is jumpy; it doesn't stay long on one object. Wisdom, however, remains fixed on the meditation object. The mind goes deep into a meditative state where it ponders the object calmly and clearly without wavering in the least. The mind with wisdom simply knows the object with all its profound implications.

It's not so much that one sees something that one has never seen. It's more like seeing something that one has seen many times before, but seeing it from a completely new perspective. The understanding comes from quite deep inside, so there's no possibility of being deceived. It's seeing something that one has seen before in such a new and different way that the truth of it suddenly becomes very obvious. When that happens, the understanding penetrates straight to the heart. Thinking won't reach the heart. It's as though thinking erects a barrier which prevents wisdom from developing in the heart.

A state of wisdom is more prolonged than a flash of insight. It will arise, last for a period of time as an intense state of knowing where nothing escapes your attention, and then die away. You may look at your own body and intuitively realize its true nature in a profound way. Then you become aware of another person nearby and feel certain that he must be able to see your body in the same way. Of course, the other person cannot perceive your body in that way because his mind is not in a state of wisdom. But when you are in that state, the truth seems so obvious that it feels as though everyone else should be able to perceive it too.

A prolonged and focused state of wisdom is what we're aiming to attain. Wisdom in this sense means penetrative knowing and understanding, not as stored knowledge accumulated from study or research, but as an active function of mind, such as the act of knowing or the act of understanding. Wisdom is the type of profound understanding that arises only through spiritual training. It pulls together a broad spectrum of cause-and-effect relationships and understands intuitively how they interconnect on many different levels.

In the case of the four domains of satipaṭṭhāna, each domain must be thoroughly investigated so as to develop a conceptual understanding of how it functions and how it interacts with the other domains. From that broad understanding, wisdom then singles out certain patterns and principles fundamental to all phenomena and uses them as a means to contemplate the physical and mental phenomena that occur in our own experience. When those phenomena are understood to be subject to change, bound up with suffering and not-self, disenchantment follows naturally. Wisdom's illumination of the true nature of mind and body leads directly to their relinquishment, and ultimately culminates in the mind's purification and freedom from suffering.

GLOSSARY

Ajaan. Teacher, mentor; also used as a term of respect when referring to a senior monk.

Anāgāmī. Non-returner. An Anāgāmī is one who has abandoned the five lower fetters that bind the mind to the cycle of rebirth, and who after death appears in one of the worlds called the Pure Abodes, to eventually attain Nibbāna and thus never return to this world again.

Arahant. One who, by following the Buddha's Path to Freedom, has totally eradicated his mental defilements (kilesas) and thus possesses the certainty that all traces of ignorance and delusion have been destroyed, never to arise in his heart again in the future. Having completely severed the fetters that once bound him to the cycle of repeated birth and death, he is no longer destined for future rebirth. Thus, the Arahant is the individual who has attained Nibbāna.

Āsavas. The āsavas are mental pollutants that "flow out" from the mind to create a "flood" of repetitive birth and death cycles.

Avijjā. Fundamental ignorance. Avijjā is the central factor in the delusion about the true nature of oneself and therefore the essential factor binding living beings to the cycle of rebirth.

Bhikkhu. A Buddhist monk; a male member of the Buddhist Sangha who has gone forth into homelessness and received the higher ordination. In Theravāda countries today, bhikkhus form the nucleus of the Buddhist community. Living entirely off donations of food and other basic requisites, their monastic lifestyle is based on the principles of poverty, celibacy, virtue and meditation.

Citta. The citta is the mind's essential knowing nature, the fundamental quality of knowing that underlies all sentient existence. When associated with a physical body, it is referred to as "mind" or "heart." The true nature of the citta is that it simply "knows." The citta does not arise or pass away; it is never born and never dies. Ultimately, the "knowing nature" of the citta is timeless, boundless and radiant, but this true nature is obscured by the defilements (kilesas) within it.

Deva. Literally, "shining one;" an inhabitant of one of the celestial realms of sensual bliss, which are located immediately above the human realm. With bodies composed entirely of ethereal light, devas exist in a spiritual dimension that lies beyond the range of normal sense faculties.

Kamma. Volitional actions of body speech or mind. Such actions carry with them a specific moral content—good, bad or neutral—and leave in the ongoing continuum of consciousness a potential to engender corresponding results in the future.

Kilesa. Mental defilement. Kilesas are negative psychological and emotional forces existing within the hearts and minds of all living beings. These defilements are of three basic types: greed, hatred and delusion. Their manifestations are many and varied. They include passion, jealousy, envy, conceit, vanity, pride, stinginess, arrogance, anger, resentment and so on; plus other more subtle variations that produce the unwholesome and harmful states of mind which are responsible for so much human misery.

Khandha. Literally, "group" or "aggregate." In the plural, khandhas refer to the five physical and mental components of personality (body, feelings, memory, thoughts and consciousness) and to sensory experience in general (sights, sounds, smells, tastes and tactile sensations). Also known as "aggregates of attachment" because they are the objects of a craving for personal existence, they are, in fact, simply classes of natural phenomena that continuously arise and cease and are devoid of any enduring self-identity.

Kuti. Monk's residence, usually a small hut.

Mettā. Goodwill; friendliness; loving kindness.

Nāga. A special class of nonhuman beings comprising all kinds of serpents. Nāgas include snakes, deities associated with bodies of water, and spirits of the earth and the realm beneath it. Nāgas are a class of beings whose primary role is that of protector and benefactor. In the ancient texts nāgas were known to have great respect for the Buddha and his disciples.

Nimitta. Mental image; vision. A samādhi nimitta is an image that arises spontaneously during the course of meditation. Nimittas may take the form of extrasensory perceptions, visualizations, symbolic representations of reality or prophetic dreams.

Pāli. An ancient variant of Sanskrit, Pāli is the literary language of the early Buddhists and the language in which the texts of the original Buddhist Canon are preserved.

Pāṭimokkha. The Buddhist monastic code of discipline. It comprises 227 rules of conduct and is usually recited rule by rule before an assembly of monks twice a month, on the days of the new-moon and the full-moon.

Sakadāgāmī. The second of the four stages culminating in the attainment of Nibbāna.

Sāmaṇera. A novice monk in Theravāda monasticism. Novices are candidates for bhikkhu ordination who shave their heads, wear the yellow robes and observe the ten basic precepts.

Sotāpanna. Stream-enterer; one who has abandoned the first three fetters that bind the mind to the cycle of rebirth and has thus entered the stream leading to Nibbāna.

Stream-entry. The event of becoming a Sotāpanna, or stream-enterer; the first stage of enlightenment.

Sutta. A discourse spoken by the Buddha. After the Buddha's death, the suttas he delivered to his disciples were passed down in the Pāli language according to a well-established oral tradition. They were finally committed to written form in Sri Lanka around 100 BCE and form the basis for the Buddha's teachings that we have today.

Taṇhā. Craving, for sensuality, for becoming or for not-becoming.

Tipiṭika. The three baskets, meaning the three groups of books making up the Pāli Buddhist Canon.

Upajjhāya. Preceptor; the senior monk who officiates at a bhikkhu's ordination.

Uposatha Hall. The monastic building where, on the new-moon and full-moon uposatha days, monks assemble for a recitation of the Pāṭimokkha rules.

Vihāra. A monastic dwelling place.

Vimutti. The mind's freedom from delusion and defilement.

Vimuttiñāṇadassana. Knowing and seeing the state of freedom.

Vinaya. The Buddhist monastic rules and the books containing them.

AUTHOR

Ajaan Dick Sīlaratano was born as Richard E. Byrd, Jr. at Winchester, Virginia in 1948. He began his life as a Buddhist monastic in 1975 in Bangalore, India, where he ordained as a novice monk with Venerable Buddharakkhita Thera. While still a novice, he moved to Sri Lanka, taking full bhikkhu ordination in June 1976 at Sri Vajiragnana Dharmayatanaya, Maharagama. In early 1977, Bhikkhu Sīlaratano traveled to Thailand, where he was ordained into the Dhammayut Nikāya at Wat Bovornives Vihāra, Bangkok, on April 21, 1977. He soon moved to Baan Taad Forest Monastery in Udon Thani province, where he lived and practiced under the tutelage of Venerable Ajaan Mahā Boowa Ñāṇasampanno and his senior disciples for over thirty years.

Shortly before Ajaan Mahā Boowa passed away in January 2011, Ajaan Dick Sīlaratano decided the time was right to establish a meditation monastery in America in the lineage of the Thai Forest tradition. In 2012, with the generous support of the laity in Thailand, the U.S. and abroad, Forest Dhamma Monastery was established on a tract of woodland in the Allegheny foothills of Rockbridge County, Virginia, where Ajaan Dick Sīlaratano resides today.

Ajaan Dick Sīlaratano's other works and translations include *Ācariya Mun Bhūridatta Thera: A Spiritual Biography, Arahattamagga Arahattaphala: The Path to Arahantship, Mae Chee Kaew: Her Journey to Spiritual Awakening and Enlightenment* and *Samaṇa,* an introduction to the life and teachings of the Venerable Ajaan Mahā Boowa Ñāṇasampanno. All of Ajaan Dick Sīlaratano's works are available for free download at www.forestdhamma.org.

FOREST DHAMMA MONASTERY

Forest Dhamma Monastery is a meditation monastery in the lineage of the Thai Forest tradition. Established by Ajaan Dick Sīlaratano in 2012, Forest Dhamma Monastery is situated on a tract of woodland in the Allegheny foothills of Rockbridge County, Virginia. Our community consists primarily of monks, novices and postulants. Although Forest Dhamma Monastery is not a meditation center, there are facilities for a limited number of male and female guests to stay at the monastery and practice with the resident monastic community. We request that our guests follow the daily routines of the monks as much as possible. In monastic life, qualities such as cooperation, respect and self-sacrifice facilitate communal harmony and individual growth in the practice.

The training at Forest Dhamma Monastery aims to follow the teaching and the code of monastic discipline laid down by the Buddha, both in letter and in spirit. Monastic life encourages the development of simplicity, renunciation and quietude. Our deliberate commitment to this way of life creates a community environment where people of varied backgrounds, personalities and temperaments can cooperate in the effort to practice and realize the Buddha's path to liberation.

More information about life at Forest Dhamma Monastery can be found on the monastery's website, www.forestdhamma.org.